M-COMMERCE

Dr. Shiney Chib

B.Tech., MBA, MIRPM, MCM, M.A. (Pub. Admn.), M.Phil. (IT), LL.B., Ph.D.

Professor,
Datta Meghe Institute of Management Studies,
Nagpur.

First Edition : 2011

Himalaya Publishing House

MUMBAI • NEW DELHI • NAGPUR • BENGALURU • HYDERABAD • CHENNAI • PUNE • LUCKNOW • AHMEDABAD • ERNAKULAM • BHUBANESWAR • INDORE • KOLKATA • GUWAHATI

First Edition : 2011

Edition-2018

Published by : Mrs. Meena Pandey for **Himalaya Publishing House Pvt. Ltd.,**
"Ramdoot", Dr. Bhalerao Marg, Girgaon, **Mumbai - 400 004.**
Phone: 022-23860170/23863863, Fax: 022-23877178
E-mail: himpub@vsnl.com; Website: www.himpub.com

Branch Offices :

New Delhi : "Pooja Apartments", 4-B, Murari Lal Street, Ansari Road, Darya Ganj, New Delhi - 110 002.
Phone: 011-23270392, 23278631; Fax: 011-23256286

Nagpur : Kundanlal Chandak Industrial Estate, Ghat Road, Nagpur - 440 018.
Phone: 0712-2738731, 3296733; Telefax: 0712-2721215

Bengaluru : No. 16/1 (Old 12/1), 1st Floor, Next to Hotel Highlands, Madhava Nagar, Race Course Road, Bengaluru - 560 001. Phone: 080-32919385; Telefax: 080-22286611

Hyderabad : No. 3-4-184, Lingampally, Besides Raghavendra Swamy Matham, Kachiguda, Hyderabad - 500 027. Phone: 040-27560041, 27550139; Mobile: 09848130433

Chennai : No. 85/50, Bazullah Road, T. Nagar, Chennai - 600 017.
Phone: 044-28144004/28144005

Pune : First Floor, "Laksha" Apartment, No. 527, Mehunpura, Shaniwarpeth (Near Prabhat Theatre), Pune - 411 030.
Phone: 020-24496323/24496333

Lucknow : Jai Baba Bhavan, Church Road, Near Manas Complex and Dr. Awasthi Clinic, Aliganj, Lucknow - 226 024.
Phone: 0522-2339329, 4068914;
Mobile: 09305302158, 09415349385, 09389593752

Ahmedabad : 114, "SHAIL", 1st Floor, Opp. Madhu Sudan House, C.G. Road, Navrang Pura, Ahmedabad - 380 009. Phone: 079-26560126;
Mobile: 09327324149, 09314679413

Ernakulam : 39/104 A, Lakshmi Apartment, Karikkamuri Cross Rd., Ernakulam, Cochin - 622011, Kerala. Phone: 0484-2378012, 2378016;
Mobile: 09344199799

Bhubaneswar : 5 Station Square, Bhubaneswar (Odisha) - 751 001. Mobile: 09861046007

Indore : Kesardeep Avenue Extension, 73, Narayan Bagh, Flat No. 302, IIIrd Floor, Near Humpty Dumpty School, Narayan Bagh, Indore - 452 007 (M.P.).
Mobile: 09301386468

Kolkata : 108/4, Beliaghata Main Road, Near ID Hospital, Opp. SBI Bank, Kolkata - 700 010, Phone: 033-32449649, Mobile: 09910440956

Guwahati : House No. 15, Behind Pragjyotish College, Near Sharma Printing Press, P.O. Bharalumukh, Guwahati - 781009. (Assam).
Mobile: 09883055590, 09883055536

DTP by : HPH, Editorial Office, Bhandup (Swapnali, Nalini)

Printed by : **7 Hills Printers,** Hyderabad.

I would like to dedicate this book to the precious assets in my life,

My Family

PAUL'S & CHIB'S

Preface

Commerce application deployment. Countries like Japan, South Korea, Singapore, and Hong Kong are adopting the mobile payment system enthusiastically. In Japan and South Korea, major wireless operators like NTT DoCoMo and SKTelecom have successfully implemented M-commerce. Japan has nearly 65% of mobile penetration and now mobile phones are also doubling up as 'mobile wallets' (cash and credit cards) combined with services such as GPS and location-based targeting, which are opening new market possibilities with new revenue streams.

M-commerce has the potential to provide huge satisfaction to end-users, generate business opportunities, and provide quick access. There are a number of technologies that enable mobile commerce such as infrared, SMS, interactive voice response, mobile scan and contactless chips. These technologies are transforming the mobile phone into a replacement for petty cash, and debit and credit cards; here the payments are charged either through the mobile phone bill or to the bank account.

Despite all the hype, M-commerce has still not gained speed in the country. The overriding hype and expectation has kind of built a wall around M-commerce. The prevalent assumption is that this service is for the elite, which is not the case. Another area which needs to be dealt with is the issue of security and reliability. The Indian user is still not comfortable with the idea of giving away his debit or credit card number over the phone. Also, security is a major concern for M-commerce to flourish. There are a number of payment options for people such as cheque pick-up, cash on delivery, etc., so the number of people actually paying through cards is not very significant. Security is not a concern technologically; it is just a matter of the mindset that needs to be changed. There are ways such as tamper-proof digital certificates to authenticate the identity of users, for example PIN or passwords. Biometrics such as voice recognition is another area, which can be used to offer greater protection.

Although in a nascent stage, a number of players have ventured into the Indian M-commerce segment. Online Mobile provides services such as movie ticket booking through its voice systems. Paymate has tied up with Citibank to provide SMS-based M-commerce services and Jigrahak has launched a payment platform called "NGpay" for online mobile shopping, to name a few. Telecom service providers such as Reliance and Airtel have been providing services such as bill payments, railway and airline ticket booking, etc. To sum it up, it is evident that the opportunity is immense and mobile commerce can be seen as a potential revenue driver for the industry players. The possibilities are innumerable. Once the pace is set, M-commerce will become the way of life on mobile.

This book is an effort to explain the concept of M-commerce, its growing adaptation, the various hurdles due to which its usage has not gained the momentum, in India. This book can be used as elementary reading as far as M-commerce is concerned. Glossary is included in the last part of this book, which gives the idea about the technical jargons used throughout this book.

— Dr. Shiney Chib

Acknowledgement

I am immensely grateful to my family, friends, well-wishers, mentors and fellow professionals who were of great help to me in bringing out this book.

— Dr. Shiney Chib

Brief Contents

CHAPTER — 1

M-COMMERCE — AN OVERVIEW

LEARNING OBJECTIVE

This chapter of the book focuses on the basic concept of M-commerce. The motive is to elucidate the readers the fundamentals of M-commerce concept. The readers go through:

- Introduction
- M-commerce — The Concept
- M-commerce — Customer's View
- M-commerce — Provider's View
- M-commerce — Benefits
- Characteristics of Wireless *vs.* Wired
- M-commerce *vs.* E-commerce
- Summary
- Study Questions

Introduction

M-commerce is defined as 'the ability to purchase goods anywhere through a wireless Internet-enabled device. Primary mobile communication exists through web-enabled wireless phones.

It can also be defined as:

- *"Providing E-commerce in a mobile context."*
- *"Using mobile technology to sell or buy items, access business information, conduct a transaction, perform supply chain or demand chain functions.*

Mobile Commerce refers to wireless electronic commerce used for conducting commerce or business through a handy device like cellular phone or [1]Personal Digital Assistant (PDA). It is also said that it is the next generation wireless E-commerce that needs no wire and plug-in devices. Mobile commerce is usually called as **'M-commerce'** in which user can do any sort of transaction including buying and selling of goods, asking any services, transferring ownership or rights, transacting and transferring money by accessing wireless internet service on the mobile handset itself. The next generation of commerce would most probably be mobile commerce or M-commerce. Presuming its wide potential reach, all major mobile handset manufacturing companies are making [2]WAP (Wireless Application Protocol) enabled smartphones and providing the maximum wireless internet and web facilities covering personal, official and commerce requirement to pave the for way M-commerce that would later be very fruitful for them.

M-commerce has several major advantages over its fixed counterparts because of its specific inbuilt characteristics such as ubiquity, personalization, flexibility and distribution. Mobile commerce promises exceptional business market potential, greater efficiency and higher fruitfulness. Thus it is not surprising that mobile commerce is emerging much faster than its fixed counterpart. M-commerce is more personalized than E-commerce and thus needs a gentle approach to appraise M-commerce applications.

NOTE:* PDA-The PDA has an electronic visual display enabling it to include a web browser, but some newer models also have audio capabilities, enabling them to be used as mobile phones or portable media players.*

[2] *Wireless Application Protocol (WAP) is an open international standard for application-layer network communications in a wireless-communication environment. Most use of WAP involves accessing the mobile web from a mobile phone or from a PDA.A WAP browser provides all of the basic services of a computer-based web browser but simplified to operate within the restrictions of a mobile phone, such as its smaller view screen. Users can connect to WAP sites: websites written in, or dynamically converted to, WML (Wireless Markup Language) and accessed via the WAP browser.*

The difference between E-commerce and M-commerce is that E-commerce is limited to PC users with an Internet Connection. With M-commerce moving to an SMS platform among other things, M-commerce is open to almost the entire mobile population. An important barrier to M-commerce is the state of mobile networks today because there is a risk of transactions not maturing due to poor networks. For M-commerce an ecosystem between application developers, financial institutions, and mobile phone networks is required, for its effective utility. Simplicity is the key to proliferation of M-commerce coupled with the idea of developing trust with audiences.

Now a days the cell phone, on its own or in conjunction with an organizer is used for much more than simply making phone calls. It also acts as a flexible terminal for a huge range of applications. So the availability of information (weather forecasts, economic data, news), e-shopping, e-ticketing, e-banking and e-brokerage is greater than ever before, regardless of time or place. The WAP (Wireless Application Protocol) and [3]WML (Wireless Markup Language) open standards mean the Internet's innovative solution strategies can now be applied to mobile telephony too.

Mobile Commerce (also known as M-commerce, M-commerce or U-commerce, owing to the ubiquitous nature of its services) is the ability to conduct commerce, using a mobile device e.g. a mobile phone (or cell phone), a PDA, a Smartphone while on the move, and other emerging mobile equipment, like dash top mobile devices. In an academic definition it is characterized in the following terms:

M-COMMERCE — THE CONCEPT

"Mobile Commerce is any transaction, involving the transfer of ownership or rights to use goods and services, which is initiated or completed by using mobile access to computer-mediated networks with the help of an electronic device." This definition provides for a differentiation of Mobile Commerce from other related fields such as Electronic Commerce, Electronic Business and Mobile Business. M-commerce is at a very early stage. It's about purchase and sale of goods and services through the mobile with the use of a financial institution. Purchase and sale of [4]VAS content cannot be classified as M-commerce.

---

[3] ***NOTE:*** *WML-Wireless Markup Language, based on XML, is a markup language intended for devices that implement the Wireless Application Protocol (WAP) specification, such as mobile phones, and preceded the use of other markup languages now used with WAP, such as HTML/XHTML..*

[4] ***NOTE:*** *Mobile value-added services (**VAS**) are those services that offer differentiation and the ability for mobile operators to charge a premium price. Mobile VAS include non-voice advanced messaging services such as **SMS**, MMS etc.*

"M-commerce is the use of mobile devices to communicate, inform transact and entertain using text and data via a connection to public and private networks." (Lehman Brothers)

"The core of mobile E-commerce is the use of a terminal (telephone, PDA, PC device or custom terminal) and public mobile network (necessary but not sufficient) to access information and conduct transactions that result in the transfer of value in exchange for information, services or goods." (Ovum)

"Business-to-consumer transactions conducted from a mobile device." (J.P. Morgan)

"E-commerce over mobile devices." (Robinson-Humphreys)

"Mobile Commerce refers to any transaction with monetary value that is conducted via a mobile telecommunications network." (Durlacher)

"The use of mobile handheld devices to communicate, interact via an always-on high-speed connection to the Internet." (Forrester)

"The use of wireless technologies to provide convenient personalized and location-based services to your customers, employees and partners." (Mobilocity)

MobileInfo.com's Definition

MobileInfo.com definition is closer to that of Ovum. It defines M-commerce as "Any electronic transaction or information interaction conducted using a mobile device and mobile networks (wireless or switched public network) that leads to transfer of real or perceived value in exchange for information, services or goods.

Typical Examples of M-commerce are:

- Purchasing airline tickets
- Purchasing movie tickets
- Restaurant booking and reservation
- Hotel booking and reservation

"Mobile Commerce is any transaction, involving the transfer of ownership or rights to use goods and services, which is initiated and/or completed by using mobile access to computer-mediated networks with the help of an electronic device." This definition provides for a differentiation of Mobile Commerce from other related fields such as Electronic Commerce, Electronic Business and Mobile Business.

The Different Areas that Come Under M-commerce

(a) **Travel and Ticketing** – convenience is the key. Mobiles are and will reiterate their time saving devices.

(b) **Movie Ticketing**

(c) **Bill payments** – making payments to utility and service companies.

(d) **Merchant Transactions/Retail Transactions** – Mobile and Internet transactions over the Internet is difficult as of now due to low speed of the Internet.

(e) **Money Transfer** – transfer from person to person through a financial intermediary.

The difference between E-commerce and M-commerce is that, E-commerce is limited to PC users with an internet connection. With M-commerce moving to an SMS platform among other things, M-commerce is open to almost the entire mobile population.

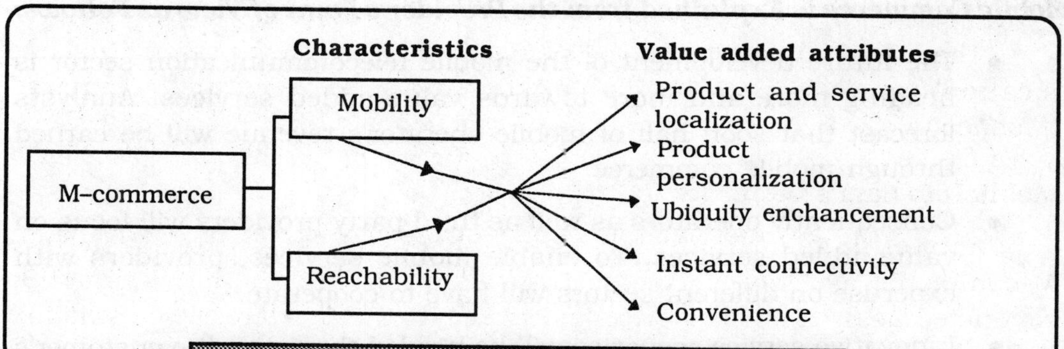

Fig. 1.1: CHARACTERISTICS OF M-COMMERCE

Mobile commerce is generally known as, any E-commerce done in a wireless environment, especially via the Internet

- Can be done via the Internet, private communication lines, smart cards, etc.
- Creates opportunity to deliver new services to existing customers and to attract new ones.

M-commerce — Customer's View

Mobile Commerce is Explained from the Customer's Point of View as Follows:

- The customer wants to access information, goods and services any time and in any place on his mobile device.
- He can use his mobile device to purchase tickets for events or public transport, pay for parking, download content and even order books and CDs.
- He should be offered appropriate payment methods. They can range from secure mobile micropayment to service subscriptions.

M-commerce — Provider's View

Mobile Commerce is Explained from the Provider's Point of View as Follows:

- The future development of the mobile telecommunication sector is heading more and more towards value-added services. Analysts forecast that soon half of mobile operator's revenue will be earned through mobile commerce.
- Consequently operators as well as third party providers will focus on value-added services. To enable mobile services, providers with expertise on different sectors will have to cooperate.
- Innovative service scenarios will be needed that meet the customer's expectations and business models that satisfy all partners involved.

M-commerce — Benefits

The Benefits from Mobile Commerce Includes:

- Internet offerings are easier and more convenient to access.
- It offers considerable flexibility when conducting business.
- It offers intense customer orientation and high customer loyalty, and this is due to innovative service strategies.
- It offers lower transaction and personnel costs, which is due to the widespread automation.

CHARACTERISTICS OF WIRELESS *VS.* WIRED

- **Ubiquity:** The use of wireless device enables the user to receive information and conduct transactions anywhere, at anytime.
- **Accessibility:** Mobile device enables the user to be contacted at virtually any time and place. The user also has the choice to limit their accessibility to particular persons or times.
- **Convenience:** The portability of the wireless device and its functions from storing data to access to information or persons.
- **Localization:** The emergence of location-specific based applications will enable the user to receive relevant information on which to act.
- **Instant Connectivity (2.5G):** Instant connectivity or "always on" is becoming more prevalent with the emergence of 2.5 G networks, GPRS or EDGE. Users of 2.5 G services will benefit from easier and faster access to the Internet.
- **Personalization:** The combination of localization and personalization will create a new channel/business opportunity for reaching and attracting customers. Personalization will take the form of customized information, meeting the users' preferences, followed by payment mechanisms that allow for personal information to be stored, eliminating the need to enter credit card information for each transaction.
- **Time Sensitivity:** Access to real-time information such as a stock quote that can be acted upon immediately or a sale at a local boutique.
- **It reaches the destination server:** And has to cover the same path again in reverse to complete the trip. There are many physical links (hops), wireless and wired line, between the end user's client application software and the information server. There are also several pieces of software involved, many of which featuring queuing (i.e., they are asynchronous).
- "M-commerce in its true form is the ability to charge an amount of currency to a mobile phone either by applications like Mobilcash or Near Field Communications, the amount to be charged is actually taken from the Mobile device's account or preloaded [5]RFID chip"

---

[5] ***NOTE:* RFID:** *Radio-frequency identification (RFID) is the use of an object (typically referred to as an RFID tag) applied to or incorporated into a product, animal, or person for the purpose of identification and tracking using radio waves. Some tags can be read from several meters away and beyond the line of sight of the reader.*

M-COMMERCE *VS.* E-COMMERCE

Separating Mobile Commerce From Electronic Commerce

Table 1.1: Difference between E-commerce and M-commerce

Technology	*E-commerce*	*M-commerce*
Device	PC	Smartphone's, pagers, PDAs,
Operating System	Windows, Unix, Linux	Symbian (EPOC), PalmOS, Pocket PC, proprietary platforms.
Presentation Standards	HTML	HTML,WML,HDML, i-Mode
Browser	Microsoft Explorer, Netscape	Phone.com UP Browser, Nokia browser, MS Mobile Explorer and other micro browsers
Bearer Networks	TCP/IP & Fixed Wire line Internet	GSM, GSM/GPRS, TDMA, CDMA, CDPD, paging networks

Frequently M-commerce is represented as a "subset of all E-commerce" thus implying that any E-commerce site could and should be made available from a wireless device. Such conclusions are misleading. M-commerce should be recognized as a unique business opportunity with its own unique characteristics and functions, not just an extension of an organization's Internet-based E-commerce channel. Of course, there are similarities between E-commerce and M-commerce from being able to purchase a product or service in a "virtual" *vs.* a build and mortar environment.

SUMMARY

In this chapter, you have gone through the concept of M-commerce. After going through the chapter, be sure the following facts are well versed:

- Concept and definition of M-commerce
- Explanation of M-commerce with respect to customer's point of view and provider's point of view.
- Characteristic, benefits and application area of M-commerce.
- Characteristic of Wireless *vs.* Wired
- Differences between M-commerce and E-commerce.

STUDY QUESTIONS

1. Explain the concept of M-commerce.
2. How M-commerce is defined with different perceptives?
3. What are the different characteristics of M-commerce?
4. Explain the concept, benefits and application of M-commerce.
5. List the differences between Wireless and Wired services.
6. Differentiate M-commerce with E-commerce.

CHAPTER – 2

HISTORY OF M-COMMERCE

LEARNING OBJECTIVE

In this chapter you go through evolution of M-commerce. The motive of this chapter is to acquaint the readers to the generation of mobile technology and the emerging mobile commerce services.

- History of M-commerce
- Mobile Commerce Generations
- Evolution Scenarios for Emerging Mobile Commerce Services
- Summary
- Study Questions

History of M-commerce

Despite of the popularity of mobile commerce, it is yet in the initial stage and can be further expanded to all the fields, which affect the human life. The assumption of mobile commerce is not so young as it mushroomed so early from adopting this technology. In the beginning, two-way radios (known as mobile rigs) were used in vehicles such as taxicabs, police cruisers, and ambulances, but were not mobile phones because they were not normally connected to the telephone network. Users could not dial phone numbers from their vehicles. A large community of mobile radio users, known as the mobileers, popularized the technology that would eventually give way to the mobile phone. Originally, mobile two-way radios were permanently installed in vehicles, but later versions such as the so-called transportable or "bag phones" were equipped with a cigarette lighter plug so that they could also be carried, and thus could be used as either mobile or as portable two-way radios. During the early 1940s, Motorola developed a backpacked two-way radio, the Walkie-Talkie and later developed a large hand-held two-way radio for the US military. This battery powered "Handie-Talkie" (HT) was about the size of a man's forearm.

In 1910 Lars Magnus Ericsson installed a telephone in his car, although this was not a radio telephone. While travelling across the country, he would stop at a place where telephone lines were accessible and using a pair of long electric wires he could connect to the national telephone network. In Europe, radio telephony was first used on the first-class passenger trains between Berlin and Hamburg in 1926. At the same time, radio telephony was introduced on passenger airplanes for air traffic security. Later radio telephony was introduced on a large scale in German tanks during the Second World War. After the war German police in the British zone of occupation first used disused tank telephony equipment to run the first radio patrol cars. In all of these cases the service was confined to specialists that were trained to use the equipment. In the early 1950s ships on the Rhine were among the first to use radio telephony with an untrained end customer as a user. In 1946 soviet engineers G. Shapiro and I. Zaharchenko successfully tested their version of a radio mobile phone mounted inside a car. The device could connect to local telephone network with a range of up to 20 kilometers.

The first person to have a mobile phone in the United Kingdom was reputedly Prince Philip, who had a system fitted into the trunk of his Aston Martin in 1957. The Prince could make phone calls to the Queen while driving, which was thought to be quite amazing at the time. The Duke of Gloucester heard about the mobile phone and tried to obtain one, but the Post Office denied his request. They were prepared to indulge the husband of Her Majesty, but nobody else, as the system used an entire dedicated radio frequency. The first fully automatic mobile phone system, called MTA (Mobile Telephone system A), was developed by Ericsson and commercially released in Sweden in 1956. This was the first system that did not require any kind of manual control in base stations, but had the disadvantage of a phone weight of 40 kg (90 lb). MTB, an upgraded version with transistors, weighing 9 kg (20 lb), was introduced in 1965 and used DTMF signaling. It had 150 customers in the beginning and 600 when it shut down in 1983. In 1957 young Soviet radio engineer Leonid Kupriyanovich from Moscow created the portable mobile phone, named after himself as LK-1 or "radiophone". This true mobile phone consisted of a relatively small-sized handset equipped with an antenna and rotary dial, and communicated with a base station. Kupriyanovich's "radiophone" had 3 kilogram of total weight, could operate up to 20 or 30 kilometers, and had 20 or 30 hours of battery lifespan. In 1958, Kupriyanovich resized his "radiophone" to "pocket" version. The weight of improved "light" handset was about 500 grams. In 1958 the USSR also began to deploy the "Altay" national civil mobile phone service specially for motorists. The newly-developed mobile telephone system was based on Soviet MRT-1327 standard. The main developers of the Altay system were the Voronezh Science Research Institute of Communications (VNIIS) and the State Specialized Project Institute (GSPI). In 1963 this service started in Moscow, and in 1970 the Altay service already was deployed in 30 cities of the USSR. The last upgraded versions of the Altay system are still in use in some places of Russia as a trunking system. In 1959 a private telephone company located in Brewster, Kansas, USA, the S&T Telephone Company, (still in Business today) with the use of Motorola Radio Telephone equipment and a private tower facility, offered to the public mobile telephone services in that local area of NW Kansas. This system was a direct dial up service through their local switchboard, and was installed in many private vehicles including grain combines, trucks, and automobiles. For some as yet unknown reason, the system after being placed online and operated for a very brief time period was shut down. The management of the company was immediately changed, and the fully operable system and related equipment was immediately dismantled in early 1960, not to be seen again. In 1966, Bulgaria presented the pocket mobile automatic phone RAT-0,5 combined with a base station RATZ-10 (RATC-10) on Interorgtechnika-66 international exhibition. One base station, connected to one telephone wire line, could serve up to six customers. In 1967, each mobile phone had to stay within the cell area serviced by one base station throughout the phone call. This did not provide continuity of automatic telephone service to mobile phones moving through several cell areas. In 1970 Amos E. Joel, Jr., another Bell Labs engineer, invented an automatic "call handoff" system to allow mobile phones to move through several cell areas during a single conversation without loss of conversation. In December 1971, AT&T submitted a proposal for cellular service to the Federal Communications Commission (FCC). After years of hearings, the FCC approved the proposal in 1982 for Advanced Mobile Phone System (AMPS) and allocated frequencies in the 824–894 MHz band. Analog AMPS was superseded by Digital AMPS in 1990. One of the first successful public commercial mobile phone networks was the ARP network in Finland, launched in 1971. Posthumously, ARP is sometimes viewed as a *zero generation* (0G) cellular network, being slightly above previous proprietary and limited coverage networks.

The history of mobile phones are classified into following generations:

First Generation (1-G) Phones

The very first mobile phones are now referred to as first generation (1G) mobile phones. The first handheld phone to be released on the US market was the Motorola DynaTAC 8000X in 1983. Mobile phones started to gain popularity in the eighties with the introduction of cellphones that were based on cellular networks. Mobile phones were originally much larger than current ones, and they were initially designed for installation in vehicles only, which is why they were called the car phone. These chunky units were later converted for use as transportable phones the size of a small suitcase and the rest is history.

Second Generation (2-G) Phones

Second generation, also called 2-G, mobile telephones were introduced in the nineties. 2-G telephone systems were different because of their use of digital circuit switched transmission and the introduction of advanced and quick telephone to network signals. The introduction of 2-G systems saw telephones move from historic 1-G telephones to small hand held items, which were much more portable. This change was made possible through improvements in technology such as more advanced batteries and energy efficient electronics. In the 1990s, **'second generation'** (2G) mobile phone systems such as GSM, IS-136 ("TDMA"), iDEN and IS-95 ("CDMA") began to be introduced. In 1991 the first GSM network (Radiolinja) opened in Finland. 2-G phone systems were characterized by digital circuit switched transmission and the introduction of advanced and fast phone-to-network signaling. In general the frequencies used by 2-G systems in Europe were higher than those in America, though with some overlap. For example, the 900 MHz frequency range was used for both 1-G and 2-G systems in Europe, so the 1-G systems were rapidly closed down to make space for the 2-G systems. In America the IS-54 standard was deployed in the same band as AMPS and displaced some of the existing analog channels.

Coinciding with the introduction of 2-G systems was a trend away from the larger "brickle" phones toward tiny 100–200g hand-held devices, which soon became the norm. This change was possible through technological improvements such as more advanced batteries and more energy-efficient electronics, but also was largely related to the higher density of cellular sites caused by increasing usage levels. This decreased the demand for high transmission powers to reach distant towers for customers to be satisfied.

The second generation introduced a new variant to communication, as SMS text messaging became possible, initially on GSM networks and eventually on all digital networks. The first machine-generated SMS message was sent in the UK in 1991. The first person-to-person SMS text message was sent in Finland in 1993. Soon SMS became the communication method of preference for the youth. Today in many advanced markets the general public prefers sending text messages to placing voice calls. 2-G also introduced the ability to access media content on mobile phones, when Radiolinja (now Elisa) in Finland introduced the downloadable ring tone as paid content. Finland was also the first country where advertising appeared on the mobile phone when a free daily news headline service on SMS text messaging was launched in 2000, sponsored by advertising. The second generation mobile telephones had several advantages over 1-G items. These included SMS messaging, which initially became possible on GSM networks and eventually on all digital networks. The very first machine-sent message was sent in Great Britain in 1991. The very first person-to-person SMS text message was sent in 1993 in Finland. SMS text messaging soon became the communication method of choice and the general public now prefer sending messages to placing voice calls.

In the world of cell phones, 2.5G wireless technology is a stepping stone that bridged 2-G to 3-G wireless technology. While 2-G and 3-G have been formally defined as wireless standards, 2.5-G has not been and was created only for the purposes of marketing. As an interim step from 2-G to 3-G, 2.5G saw some of the advances inherent in 3-G networks (including packet-switched systems). The evolution from 2-G to 3-G ushered in faster and higher-capacity data transmission. 2.5-G is a stepping stone between 2-G and 3-G cellular wireless technologies. The term "second and a half generation" is used to describe 2G-systems that have implemented a packet switched domain in addition to the circuit switched domain. It does not necessarily provide faster services because bundling of timeslots is used for circuit switched data services as well.

FROM 2.5G TO 2.75G (EDGE)

GPRS networks evolved to EDGE networks with the introduction of 8PSK encoding. Enhanced Data rates for GSM Evolution (EDGE), Enhanced GPRS (EGPRS), or IMT Single Carrier (IMT-SC) is a backward-compatible digital mobile phone technology that allows improved data transmission rates, as an extension on top of standard GSM. EDGE was deployed on GSM networks beginning in 2003 — initially by Cingular (now AT&T) in the United States. EDGE is standardized by 3-GPP as part of the GSM family, and it is an upgrade that provides a potential three-fold increase in capacity of GSM/GPRS networks. The specification achieves higher data-rates (up to 236.8 kbit/s) by switching to more sophisticated methods of coding (8PSK), within existing GSM timeslots. By the end of 2007 there were 295 Million subscribers on 3-G networks worldwide, which reflected 9% of the total worldwide subscriber base. About two thirds of these are on the WCDMA standard and one third on the EV-DO standard. The 3-G telecoms services generated over 120 Billion dollars of revenues during 2007 and at many markets the majority of new phones activated were 3-G phones. In Japan and South Korea the market no longer supplies phones of the second generation. Earlier in the decade there were doubts about whether 3-G might happen, and also whether 3-G might become a commercial success. By the end of 2007 it had become clear that 3-G was a reality and was clearly on the path to become a profitable venture. Live streaming of radio and television to 3-G handsets is one future direction for the industry, with companies such as RealNetworks and Disney recently announcing services.

Third Generation (3-G) Phones

3-G is the third generation of mobile phone standards and technology, which succeeded 2-G mobile technology. The birth of 3-G technologies enabled network operators including orange to give their users a wider range of advanced services. This includes broadband internet, in addition to high-tech video calls. The first pre-commercial 3-G mobile phone network was launched in Japan in May of 2001. 3-G was later commercially released in Japan on October, 1 2001. Despite the success of 3-G, there has also been many complaints about it. These include criticism over the cost of 3-G phones, a lack of network coverage because it's still a new service and the high power usage of 3-G phones. Not long after the introduction of 2-G networks, projects began to develop third generation (3-G) systems. Inevitably there were many different standards with different contenders pushing their own technologies. Quite differently from 2-G systems, however, the meaning of 3-G has been standardized in the IMT-2000 standardization processing. This process did not standardize on a technology, but rather on a set of requirements. At that point, the vision of a single unified worldwide standard broke down and several different standards have been introduced.

The first pre-commercial trial network with 3-G was launched by NTT DoCoMo in Japan in the Tokyo region in May 2001. NTT DoCoMo launched the first commercial 3-G network on October 1, 2001, using the WCDMA technology. In 2002 the first 3-G networks on the rival CDMA2000 1xEV-DO technology were launched by SK Telecom and KTF in South Korea, and Monet in the USA. Monet has since gone bankrupt. By the end of 2002, the second WCDMA network was launched in Japan by Vodafone KK (now Softbank). European launches of 3-G were in Italy and the UK by the Three/Hutchison group, on WCDMA. 2003 saw a further eight commercial launches of 3-G, six more on WCDMA and two more on the EV-DO standard. The first major step in the evolution of GSM networks to 3-G occurred with the introduction of [6]General Packet Radio Service (GPRS). CDMA2000 networks similarly evolved through the introduction of 1xRTT. So the cellular services combined with enhanced data transmission capabilities became known as '***2.5G.***'

GPRS could provide data rates from 56 kbit/s up to 114 kbit/s. It can be used for services such as Wireless Application Protocol (WAP) access, Multimedia Messaging Service (MMS), and for Internet communication services such as email and World Wide Web access. GPRS data transfer is typically charged per megabyte of traffic transferred, while data communication via traditional circuit switching is billed per minute of connection time, independent of whether the user actually is utilizing the capacity or is in an idle state. During the development of 3-G systems, 2.5-G systems such as CDMA2000 1x and GPRS were developed as extensions to existing 2-G networks. These provide some of the features of 3-G without fulfilling the promised high data rates or full range of multimedia services. CDMA2000-1X delivers theoretical maximum data speeds of up to 307 kbit/s. Just beyond these is the EDGE system which in theory covers the requirements for 3-G system, but is so narrowly above these that any practical system would be sure to fall short.

3-G networks offer a greater degree of security than 2-G predecessors. By allowing the UE (User Equipment) to authenticate the network it is attaching to, the user can be sure the network is the intended one and not an

---

[6] ***NOTE:*** *GPRS:* ***General packet radio service (GPRS)*** *is a packet oriented mobile data service available to users of the 2G cellular communication systems global system for mobile communications (GSM), as well as in the 3G systems. In 2G systems, GPRS provides data rates of 56-114 kbit/s. GPRS data transfer is typically charged per megabyte of traffic transferred, while data communication via traditional circuit switching is billed per minute of connection time, independent of whether the user actually is using the capacity or is in an idle state. GPRS is a best-effort packet switched service, as opposed to circuit switching, where a certain quality of service (QoS) is guaranteed during the connection for non-mobile users.*

impersonator. 3-G networks use the KASUMI block crypto instead of the older A5/1 stream cipher. In addition to the 3-G network infrastructure security, end-to-end security is offered when application frameworks such as IMS are accessed, although this is not strictly a 3-G property.

Applications

The bandwidth and location information available to 3-G devices gives rise to applications not previously available to mobile phone users. Some of the applications are:

- **Mobile TV:** A provider redirects a TV channel directly to the subscriber's phone where it can be watched.
- **Video on demand:** A provider sends a movie to the subscriber's phone.
- **Video conferencing:** Subscribers can see as well as talk to each other.
- **Tele-medicine:** A medical provider monitors or provides advice to the potentially isolated subscriber.
- **Location-based services:** A provider sends localized weather or traffic conditions to the phone, or the phone allows the subscriber to find nearby businesses or friends.

About Global 4G Open Mobile Initiative

Ever since the launch of 3-G mobile telephone technology, people have been discussing 4-G. 4-G technology will signify the future of mobile telephones, producing the most advanced handsets and best services to date. At his inauguration, U.S. President Obama stressed the need for bold and swift action in laying foundations for growth. Appreciating the role of technology in improving effective services and efficient delivery, he acknowledges the demands of a new age with infrastructure and digital line investments required. More recently, global leaders at WEF Davos have also highlighted the importance of innovation in forthcoming solutions. Regardless the difficulty of circumstances, or direness of situation, opportunity arises out of crisis. More than ever, relationship-building and technology innovation are crucial. The 4th generation (4-G) mobile technology is becoming the emerging solution to drive the new growth of the industry, and help foster state-of-the-art technology, novel partnership arrangements or transformational business models. Our 4-G events, the world's leading platforms of the 4G industry, are steadfast in supporting the industry and confident in the ability to uncover and advance the opportunities. Future wireless mobile communications will be shifted from today's traditional transmission-specific radio technology to an interface-based technology in order to be more compatible with computer system architecture. The future mobile device will therefore be first and foremost a computer, then an open wireless architecture (OWA) low-power terminal. This OWA technology offers an optimal solution to open up the wireless platform for complete openness and simplicity and would support the service-oriented architecture and infrastructure that is necessary for future mobile phone development and advancement.

Though different regions have diversified approaches towards the next generation mobile communication technology (called 4th generation mobile, or 4G Mobile), the future trend is same: Convergence among fixed, mobile and wireless communications. No single wireless radio transmission technology (RTT) can do both broadband high-speed data-rate and seamless mobility, and therefore we need multiple RTTs to complement each other in any optimal way to ensure the information is delivered to the mobile user in a more cost-effective way and in a more spectrum-efficient way.

4G Mobile Technology — The Mobile Race to Innovate, Includes the following Innovations:

1. The mobile communications comprise two steps: access to the mobile network, and access to the mobile services. Traditionally, these two steps are all controlled by one operator in a closed and proprietary way. In the 4G mobile era, the access to the mobile services will be evolved to an open Mobile Cloud so that it is fully open to any developers and providers. In this way, any non-wireless industries, such as Google, Microsoft, Oracle, SAP, GM, Bank of America can provide services for their mobile users. The access to the mobile network is still controlled by the traditional wireless operators such as AT&T, Verizon, T-Mobile and China Mobile. Of course, the operators are very reluctant to go this trend, but for the mobile users and for the future global movement, it is just a matter of time to do it.

2. The mobile device system architecture will be open in order to converge multiple RTTs (radio transmission technologies) in one same device. Same as laptop computer, the future Smartphone will be based on open wireless architecture (OWA) technology which means, when you change the wireless standards, you do not need to change phone. It is totally different from current multi-standards phone which is in closed system architecture, and users can not remove the unused RTT modules and basically cannot do anything on the mobile phone system. In the OWA system, you can just change RTT card in your Smartphone to switch your wireless standards, or you can integrate multiple wireless standards in one RTT SIM card. Based on this OWA

platform, you can integrate home phone, office phone and mobile phone into one common Personal device - it is more beyond just a phone. In fact, this 4G mobile device is a system to bring the world to your hand, or we call it iHand - the World in Hand, which is more better than calling it an iPhone.

3. Any portable consumer electronics device can be a mobile phone by inserting the OWA-powered mobile RTT(s) card. This approach is truly converging the mobile wireless technology with the computer technology by providing the OWA virtualization layer between the high-layer computer-based OS (operating systems) and applications solutions and the underlying wireless transmission-based different mobile networks access means.

4. More breakthrough technologies are being developed for efficient utilization of wireless spectrum, and the dynamic and open spectrum management. Wireless is totally different from wired communications, and therefore the overall performance relies on both system performance and transmission performance where spectrum is one of the key issues.

5. Power efficiency is another critical issue for mobile device. The system architecture must be open to enable removable of unused modules, and the processing architecture must be optimized to the lowest possible in terms of the whole system performance. Meanwhile, the RF radio modules should be narrowed to the minimal meeting the basic requirements of necessary RTTs.

The world is moving rapidly towards this 4G open mobile movement. In China, the government has in fact, targeted for 4G mobile industry. In European Union, evolution to 4G has been the mission-critical strategy since 2003. Japan and Korea started 4G regulations in 2002. The US mobile market is a pretty different case, because FCC as a law enforcement agency, basically has no power to enforce law. The operators pay huge to the congress, and congress manages the FCC. So eventually, the operator "makes" the law. However, nobody can stop future and it is just a matter of time when this 4G open mobile comes to life.

i-mode

i-mode was launched in Japan on 22 February 1999. NTT DoCoMo's **i-mode** is a mobile internet(as opposed to wireless internet) service popular in Japan. Unlike Wireless Application Protocol or WAP, i-mode encompasses a wider variety of internet standards, including web access, e-mail and the packet-switched network that delivers the data. i-mode users have access to various services such as e-mail, sports results, weather forecast, games, financial services and ticket booking. Content is provided by specialized services, typically from the mobile carrier, which allows them to have tighter control over billing. Like WAP, i-mode delivers only those services that are specifically converted for the service, or are converted through gateways. This has placed both systems at a disadvantage against handsets that use "real" browser software, and generally use a flat pricing structure for data.

i-mode phones have a special i-mode button for the user to access the start menu. There are more than 12,000 official sites and around 100,000 or more unofficial i-mode sites, which are not linked to DoCoMo's i-mode portal page and DoCoMo's billing services. NTT DoCoMo supervises the content and operations of all official i-mode sites, most of which are commercial. These official sites are accessed through DoCoMo's i-mode menu but in many cases official sites can also be accessed from mobile phones by typing the URL or through the use of QR code (a barcode). An i-mode user pays for both sent and received data. There are services to avoid unsolicited e-mails.

The first enabling M-commerce technologies were presented through Wireless Application Protocol (WAP) and i-mode mobile Internet service. WAP builds on digital phone technology and first emerged on 2.5G (2.5th Generation) phone technology that allowed users to browse the Internet. This technology cemented the way of M-commerce, which has strongly developed on 3G (3rd Generation) phone technology. Nokia has first introduced M-commerce application software Nokia toolkit version 4.0. The future of M-commerce seems extremely bright because several experiments are going on to introduce the upgraded version of mobile likely to be emerged with the evolution of 4G (4th Generation) mobile technology.

EVOLUTION SCENARIOS FOR EMERGING MOBILE COMMERCE SERVICES

The Wireless Revolution

Mobile phones have become mobile platforms for delivering digital data, used for recording and downloading photos, video and music, Internet access, and transmitting payments. An array of technologies provides high-speed wireless access to the Internet for PCs and other wireless handheld devices and cell phones. Businesses increasingly use wireless to cut costs, increase flexibility, and create new products and services. Wireless communication helps businesses, easily stay in touch with customers, suppliers, and employees. Wireless networking increases worker productivity and output, as workers take less time to establish contact with people and to access information.

Companies can save on wiring offices, moving, and making network changes by using wireless networks. Wireless technology has also been the source of new products, services, and sales channels in a variety of industries, e.g. OnStar, Starbucks "hot spots". All wireless media rely on various parts of the electromagnetic spectrum. Microwave systems transmit high-frequency radio signals through the atmosphere. Communication satellites are used for geographically dispersed organizations.

Devices for Wireless Transmission:

- Wireless Transmission Media and Devices
- Paging systems

Paging Systems are wireless communication systems that are designed to send brief messages to a subscriber. It's a one-way messaging system in which Base Station send messages to all subscribers. The Paging System transmits the message also known as Page, along with Paging System access number, throughout the service area using Base Station, which broadcast the page on a radio link.

- E-mail handhelds
- Cellular telephones
- Personal Digital Assistants (PDAs)

A **personal digital assistant (PDA),** also known as a **palmtop computer,** is a mobile device which functions as a Personal information manager and connects to the internet. The PDA has an electronic visual display enabling it to include a web browser, but some newer models also have audio capabilities, enabling them to be used as mobile phones or portable media players. Many PDAs can access the internet, intranets or extranets via Wi-Fi, or Wireless Wide Area Networks (WWANs). Many PDAs employ touchscreen technology.

- Smart phones

A [7]**smartphone** is a mobile phone offering advanced capabilities, often with PC-like functionality (PC-mobile handset convergence). There is no industry standard definition of a smartphone. For some, a smartphone is a phone that runs complete operating system software providing a standardized

---

7 ***NOTE:*** *A smartphone is a mobile phone offering advanced capabilities, often with PC-like functionality (PC-mobile handset convergence).*

interface and platform for application developers. For others, a smartphone is simply a phone with features considered advanced at the time of its release - e.g., in the early 2000s this was features such as e-mail and Internet, but now these are commonplace on non-smartphones.

Cellular Network Standards and Generations Standards:

- **Global System for Mobile Communication (GSM)**

GSM (Global System for Mobile Communications: originally from *Groupe Spécial Mobile*) is the most popular standard for mobile telephony systems in the world. The GSM Association, its promoting industry trade organization of mobile phone carriers and manufacturers, estimates that 80% of the global mobile market uses the standard. GSM is used by over 2 billion people across more than 212 countries and territories. Its ubiquity enables international roaming arrangements between mobile phone operators, providing subscribers the use of their phones in many parts of the world. GSM differs from its predecessor technologies in that both signaling and speech channels are digital, and thus GSM is considered a *second generation* (2G) mobile phone system

- **Code Division Multiple Access (CDMA)**

Code Division Multiple Access (CDMA) is a channel access method utilized by various radio communication technologies. One of the basic concepts in data communication is the idea of allowing several transmitters to send information simultaneously over a single communication channel. This allows several users to share a bandwidth of different frequencies. This concept is called multiplexing. CDMA employs spread-spectrum technology and a special coding scheme (where each transmitter is assigned a code) to allow multiple users to be multiplexed over the same physical channel.

The **Institute of Electrical and Electronics Engineers** or **IEEE** is an international non-profit, professional organization for the advancement of technology related to electricity. It has the most members of any technical professional organization in the world, with more than 395,000 members in around 150 countries. The Institute of Electrical and Electronics Engineers (IEEE) established a hierarchy of complementary standards for wireless computer networks.Global Wireless Network Standards

- IEEE 802.15 (Bluetooth) for the Personal Area Network (PAN)

IEEE 802.15 is the **15th** working group of the IEEE 802 and specializes in Wireless PAN (Personal Area Network) standards.

- IEEE 802.11 (Wi-Fi) for the Local Area Network (LAN)

IEEE 802.11 is a set of standards carrying out wireless local area network (WLAN) computer communication in the 2.4, 3.6 and 5 GHz frequency bands. They are created and maintained by the IEEE LAN/MAN Standards Committee (IEEE 802).

- IEEE 802.16 (WiMax) for the Metropolitan Area Network (MAN)

IEEE 802.16 is a series of Wireless Broadband standards authored by the IEEE. The current version is **IEEE 802.16-2009** amended by IEEE 802.16j-2009. IEEE 802.16 is written by a working group established by IEEE Standards Board in 1999 to develop standards for the global deployment of broadband Wireless Metropolitan Area Networks. The Workgroup is a unit of the IEEE 802 LAN/MAN Standards Committee. Although the 802.16 family of standards is officially called WirelessMAN in IEEE, it has been commercialized under the name "WiMAX" (from "Worldwide Interoperability for Microwave Access") by the industry alliance called the WiMAX Forum. The mission of the Forum is to promote and certify compatibility and interoperability of broadband wireless products based on the IEEE 802.16 standards.

- IEEE 802.20 (proposed) standard for the Wide Area Network (WAN)

IEEE 802.20 or Mobile Broadband Wireless Access (MBWA) is an IEEE Standard to enable worldwide deployment of multi-vendor interoperable mobile broadband wireless access networks.

Bluetooth

Bluetooth is the code name for a small, low-cost, short range wireless technology specification. Bluetooth uses a Time-Division Duplex scheme for full duplex transmission. In other words, Bluetooth technology is simply used to connect an electronic device to another without the physical cable. Bluetooth is intended to be a standard that works at two levels:

- It provides agreement at the physical level (radio-frequency standard).
- It also provides agreement at the next level up, where products have to agree on when bits are sent, how many will be sent at a time and how the parties in a conversation can be sure that the message received is the same as the message sent.

It enables users to connect a wide range of computing and telecommunication devices easily and simply, without the need to buy, carry, or connect cables. Bluetooth enables mobile phones, computers and PDAs to connect with each other using short-range radio waves, allowing them to "talk" to each other. It is also cheap. Can link up to 8 devices in 10-m area. Low power requirements.

It is a very nice technology but the security issue has to be taken into serious consideration. Risks are inherent to any wireless technology. And the most significant risk in the wireless technology is that the underlying communication medium is open to everybody, including authentic users as well as the intruders. Bluetooth used short-range radio which is very vulnerable. For instance, if the intruders had the frequency to connect to your PC, they can use their own Bluetooth technology monitor and mouse to get access. So they can have all information in your PC. And if the attackers' headsets connected to your mobile phone by hacking the frequency, you will never know somebody bugged your phone and everything will be unsafe. Therefore we need to put extra efforts in security section to make sure the technology is safe for the users. The Bluetooth technology needs to sort out the following specific threats

- All the vulnerabilities that exist in a conventional wired network apply to wireless technologies.
- Malicious entities may gain unauthorized access to an agency's computer network through wireless connections, bypassing any firewall protections.
- Sensitive information that is not encrypted (or that is encrypted with poor cryptographic techniques) and that is transmitted between two wireless deices may be intercepted and disclosed.
- Malicious entities may steal the identity of legitimate users and masquerade as them on internal or external corporate networks.
- Sensitive data may be corrupted during improper synchronization.
- Malicious entities may be able to violate the privacy of legitimate users and be able to track their movements.
- Malicious entities may deploy unauthorized equipment (e.g., client devices and access points) to surreptitiously gain access to sensitive information.
- Handheld devices are easily stolen and can reveal sensitive information.
- Data may be extracted without detection from improperly configured devices.
- Viruses or other malicious code may corrupt data on a wireless device and subsequently be introduced to a wired network connection.
- Malicious entities may, through wireless connections, connect to other agencies or organizations for the purposes of launching attacks and concealing their activities.

- Interlopers, from inside or out, may be able to gain connectivity to network management controls and thereby disable or disrupt operations.
- Malicious entities may use third-party, untrusted wireless network services to gain access to an agency's or other organization's network resources.
- Internal attacks may be possible via ad hoc transmissions.

Because of these many new risks that a new technology like Bluetooth creates, a good security design is essential for it to be successful. However, since Bluetooth is a relatively recent invention, and we are well aware of the security risks and needs for technologies in today's world (especially having the similar 802.11 wireless technology available to examine), the architecture of Bluetooth security was very well thought out to begin with. Thus, Bluetooth is considered a relatively secure form of communication, especially when considering it uses a wireless medium. The design of secure interaction between devices in Bluetooth consists of the following phases:

An initial phase, called pairing, in order to establish a "link" key, which will then be used for encryption and decryption for secure connections. This is the most dangerous stage of connecting 2 Bluetooth devices together; as if an attacker can spy on this part of the interaction then he may be able to establish what is the link key is. During this pairing, an initialization key is generated based on each device's address, and a PIN which is shared between the devices. Once pairing has occurred, each device considers the other to be "trusted", and thus it grants it access to certain things on itself. Due to the fact that someone spying on this would be able to determine what is the initialization key, and thus the link key, the Bluetooth Special Interests Group (SIG) recommend that this stage is carried out in private, and that PIN should be long and manually input if possible. The PIN should also be random and not common PINs like "0000".

Using this initialization key, the devices then agree on a link key which they will use to establish a secure connection between each other when needed. There are 2 types of link key. The first is a unit key, where a device's individual unit key (which every Bluetooth device has) is chosen as the link key. This method clearly allows other a device to spy on data being transferred between a device it is trusted by and some other device, or even to send false data to another device by impersonating using the unit key. The other method is combination keys, in which an individual link key is generated for each individual link between 2 devices, based on each of their Bluetooth addresses. Whenever a device wishes to access another Bluetooth device, it gets the other to send it a challenge. It then encrypts this challenge using the link key along with other information (using a safer+ algorithm) and returns a partial result to the device he wishes to access. This other device then verifies the partial result and communication can take place using encrypted wireless interaction. This can then be mirrored in reverse to complete a mutual pairing.

When data is then being communicated, the link key is used to help generate a ciphering for an E0 encryption algorithm, which again makes it more secure as the link key is not used directly for encryption or decryption during the communication.

Wi-Fi

Wi-Fi is a trademark of the Wi-Fi Alliance that manufacturers may use to brand certified products that belong to a class of wireless local area network (WLAN) devices based on the IEEE 802.11 standards. Because of the close relationship with its underlying standard, the term *Wi-Fi* is often used as a synonym for IEEE 802.11 technology. The Wi-Fi Alliance, a global association of companies, promotes WLAN technology and certifies products if they conform to certain standards of interoperability.

- **Three standards:** 802.11a, 802.11b, 802.11g.
- **Infrastructure mode:** Devices use access point to communicate with wired network.
- **Ad-hoc mode (peer-to-peer):** Wireless devices communicate directly with each other.

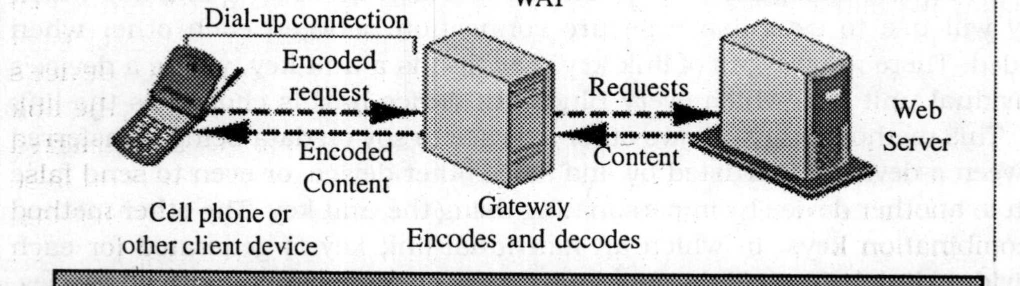

Fig. 2.1: WIRELESS APPLICATION PROTOCOL (WAP) VERSUS I-MODE

Wireless Technologies

Link Layer (examples): **WAN:** Analog/AMPS

The Data Link Layer is the protocol layer which transfers data between adjacent network nodes in a wide area network or between nodes on the same local area network segment. The Data Link Layer provides the functional and procedural means to transfer data between network entities and might provide the means to detect and possibly correct errors that may occur in the Physical Layer. Examples of data link protocols are Ethernet for local area networks (multi-node), the Point-to-Point Protocol (PPP), [8]HDLC and [9]ADCCP for point-to-point (dual-node) connections. The Data Link Layer is concerned with local delivery of frames between devices on the same LAN. Data Link frames, as these protocol data units are called, do not cross the boundaries of a local network. Inter-network routing and global addressing are higher layer functions, allowing Data Link protocols to focus on local delivery, addressing, and media arbitration. In this way, the Data Link layer is analogous to a neighborhood traffic cop; it endeavors to arbitrate between parties contending for access to a medium.

Cellular Digital Packet Data (CDPD) was a wide-area mobile data service which used unused bandwidth normally used by AMPS mobile phones between 800 and 900 MHz to transfer data. Developed in the early 1990s, CDPD was large on the horizon as a future technology. However, it had difficulty competing against existing slower but less expensive Mobitex and DataTac systems, and never quite gained widespread acceptance before newer, faster standards such as GPRS became dominant.

Time Division Multiple Access (TDMA) is a channel access method for shared medium networks. It allows several users to share the same frequency channel by dividing the 'signal into different time slots. The users transmit in rapid succession, one after the other, each using his own time slot. This allows multiple stations to share the same transmission medium (e.g. radio frequency channel) while using only a part of its channel capacity. TDMA is used in the digital 2G cellular systems such as Global System for Mobile Communications Global System for Mobile Communications (GSM), IS-136, Personal Digital Cellular (PDC) and iDEN, and in the Digital Enhanced Cordless

---

[8] ***NOTE: High-Level Data Link Control*** *(HDLC) is a bit-oriented synchronous data link layer protocol developed by the International Organization for Standardization (ISO).*

[9] *ADCCP-In telecommunication,* ***Advanced Data Communication Control Procedures*** *(or* ***Protocol****) (ADCCP) is a bit-oriented data link layer protocol used to provide point-to-point and point-to-multipoint transmission of data frames that contain error control information. It places data on a network and ensures proper delivery to a destination. ADCCP is based on the IBM's SDLC protocol.*

Telecommunications (DECT) standard for portable phones. It is also used extensively in satellite systems, and combat-net radio systems.

Code Division Multiple Access (CDMA) is a channel access method utilized by various radio communication technologies. One of the basic concepts in data communication is the idea of allowing several transmitters to send information simultaneously over a single communication channel. This allows several users to share a bandwidth of different frequencies. This concept is called multiplexing. CDMA employs spread-spectrum technology and a special coding scheme (where each transmitter is assigned a code) to allow multiple users to be multiplexed over the same physical channel.

GSM (Global System for Mobile Communications: originally from ***Groupe Spécial Mobile*****)** is the most popular standard for mobile telephony systems in the world. The GSM Association, its promoting industry trade organization of mobile phone carriers and manufacturers, estimates that 80% of the global mobile market uses the standard. GSM is used by over 2 billion people across more than 212 countries and territories. Its ubiquity enables international roaming arrangements between mobile phone operators, providing subscribers the use of their phones in many parts of the world. GSM differs from its predecessor technologies in that both signaling and speech channels are digital, and thus GSM is considered a *second generation* (2G) mobile phone system.

Messaging

Short Message Service (SMS): Technology that allows for sending of short text messages on some cell phones.

Enhanced Messaging Service (EMS): An extension of SMS capable of simple animation, tiny pictures, and short tunes.

Multimedia Messaging Service (MMS): The next generation of wireless messaging; will be able to deliver rich media.

SUMMARY

In this chapter you have gone through evolution of M-commerce. After going through the chapter, be sure that the following facts are well versed.

- History of M-commerce
- Mobile Commerce Generations
- 1G, 2G, 2.5G, 3G, 4G.
- PDA, SMS, EMS, MMS, Smartphone.
- The Wireless Revolution

Devices for Wireless Transmission

GSM,CDMA

Global Wireless Network Standards

Application layer Technologies.

Evolution Scenarios for Emerging Mobile Commerce Services.

STUDY QUESTIONS

1. Write note on the history of M-commerce.
2. Explain the concept of Wireless Revolution. Mention its advantages.
3. Write short notes on:
   (a) Blue tooth
   (b) Wi-Fi
   (c) WiMax
   (d) GSM
   (e) CDMA
   (f) PDA
   (g) Smartphone

CHAPTER — 3

DRIVERS OF M-COMMERCE

LEARNING OBJECTIVE

In this chapter you go through the Drivers of M-commerce. The motive of this chapter is to tell the emergence of M-commerce as emerging media of commerce.

- Fundamental Attributes of Mobile Customer
- Technologies in Use
- What is Driving M-Commerce?
- Evolution Scenarios for Emerging Mobile Commerce Services
- Mobile Commerce: Attributes and Benefits
- Summary
- Study Questions

The Indian mobile subscriber base has crossed the 113 mn mark. And every month approximately 5 mn plus subscribers are added to this huge user base. Another interesting aspect is that though volumes in the Indian telecom segment are high, the margins are low, so the key for success here is innovation. The mobile market is maturing and competition between service providers is intensifying. The operators cannot realize substantial margins only with mobile voice services. So, as they work towards creating new business models, mobile commerce is emerging as a service which has great potential to help service providers to make substantial profit. It is being considered as the next big thing. M-commerce is emerging as an exclusive channel of distribution leveraging on the fact that mobiles are quickly becoming more than just communication devices.

FUNDAMENTAL ATTRIBUTES OF MOBILE CUSTOMER

- **Expectations:** Web *vs.* Wireless experience Education (M-commerce study disappointed in their M-commerce experience)
- **Education.**
- **Don't Set/Sell Unrealistic Expectations:** Limit Hyped-Up possibilities, such as, Wireless Web – misleading – one can not push a Web service onto the cell phone
- Newness of the Wireless Internet attracting media and marketing hype, promoting unrealistic expectations among consumers.
- Offering customers something new that could not do without a wireless device.
- **General characteristics:** empowered consumer, educated, computer savvy, and seeking customer service.
- Voice is still the Killer application.
- Most customers use wireless phones for voice phone calls. Wireless data features are much less popular than wireless voice
- **Personalization:** Began with the personalized services/customized information and services via the Internet. Act on only relevant information *vs.* Information overload.
- Wireless devices as a personal companion.
- Expect companies to offer information relevant to their needs and interests and presented in a simplified manner.

- Seeking an easy and simplified M-commerce experience.
- Advertising relevant (authorized).
- Personalized billing/payment functionality.
- Dependency on location and Time
- Understand the customer's activity schedule, for instance, services accessed during working hours will differ from those on during the evening or on weekends.
- Device used will determine mode of access.
- Consumer Behavior.
- Patience will be demanded of players, as consumer behavior requires both time and effort to change.
- Evolution of the industry from networks to handsets will require players to educate their customers.

The criteria for M-commerce services or products

- Limited but precise choice.
- Predictable availability.
- Does not require lengthy and in-depth decision making (appeal to impulsive buying behavior).
- Convenience.

Examples:

- The New York Times bestseller list meets all three criteria. It would be easy to purchase any of the listed books via a wireless device.
- Tickets to popular entertainment events, such as concerts, live theatre, movies, sports events, trade shows, public forums.
- Mircro-transactions: purchasing a fast food item, such as a soda pop from a vending machine.
- Payment of bills, banking, restaurant bill.

According to Ovum's research, there is a lot of uncertainty about which mobile commerce applications will be successful and make money. The research/consulting firm classified M-commerce applications into three categories.

The Take-off

The idea of M-commerce took shape a long time back, yet it has only been an overly ambitious goal of the industry. One of the main reasons being that cellular networks capable of securely routing transactions to a payment gateway are new to India. The other reason: lack of appropriate technology and the issues pertaining to security and reliability of networks.

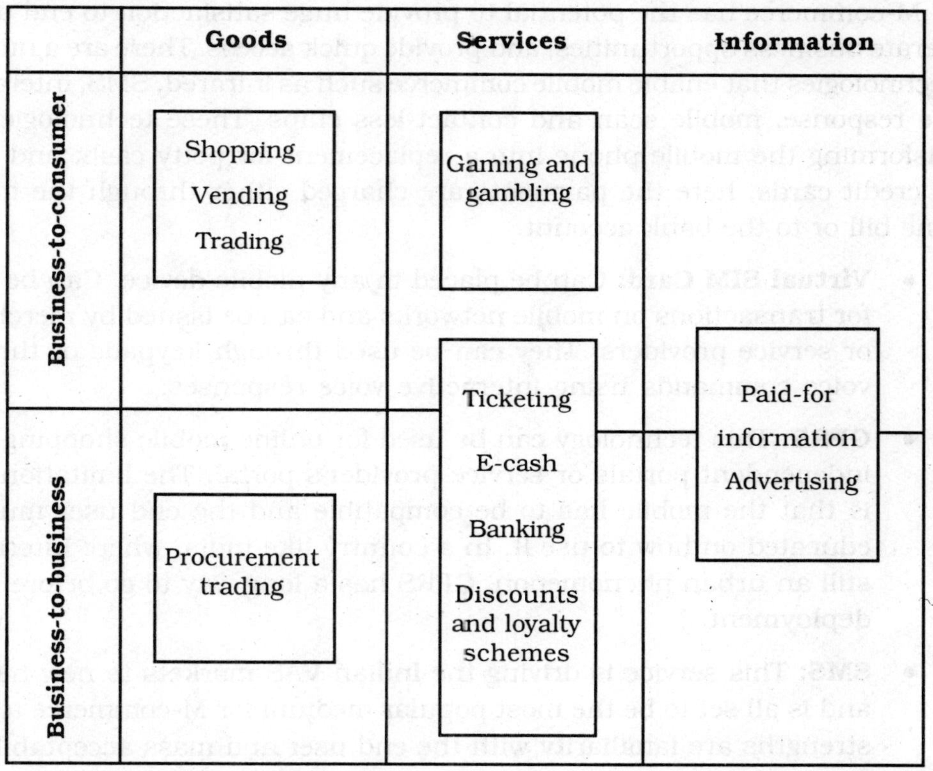

Source: Ovum (MEC/A)

Fig. 3.1: M-COMMERCE PROCESS

However, the Asia Pacific region has emerged as the leader in M-commerce application deployment. Countries like Japan, South Korea, Singapore, and Hong Kong are adopting the mobile payment system enthusiastically. In Japan and South Korea, major wireless operators like NTT DoCoMo and SK Telecom have successfully implemented M-commerce. Japan has nearly 65% of mobile penetration and now mobile phones are also doubling up as 'mobile wallets' (cash and credit cards) combined with services such as GPS and location-based targeting, which are opening new market possibilities with new revenues streams. Between the two types of transactions-low end (downloads and alerts) and high end (credit and debit card transactions)-the latter is more prevalent in India. Movie ticket booking, railway ticket booking, impulse shopping etc are the areas that are gaining considerable traction.

TECHNOLOGIES IN USE

M-commerce has the potential to provide huge satisfaction to end users, generate business opportunities, and provide quick access. There are a number of technologies that enable mobile commerce such as infrared, SMS, interactive voice response, mobile scan and contact-less chips. These technologies are transforming the mobile phone into a replacement for petty cash, and debit and credit cards; here the payments are charged either through the mobile phone bill or to the bank account.

- **Virtual SIM Card:** Can be placed in any mobile device. Can be used for transactions on mobile networks and can be issued by merchants or service providers. They can be used through keypads or through voice commands using interactive voice responses.
- **GPRS:** This technology can be used for online mobile shopping from independent portals or service provider's portal. The limitation here is that the mobile has to be compatible and the end user must be educated on how to use it. In a country like India, where Internet is still an urban phenomenon, GPRS has a long way to go before mass deployment.
- **SMS:** This service is driving the Indian VAS markets to new heights and is all set to be the most popular medium for M-commerce too. Its strengths are familiarity with the end user and mass acceptability.
- **Voice:** Voice being a convenient medium for those who are not very tech savvy will take M-commerce to a larger user base including the rural areas of the country.

Although in a nascent stage, a number of players have ventured into the Indian M-commerce segment. On Mobile provides services such as movie ticket booking through its voice systems. Paymate has tied up with Citibank to provide SMS-based M-commerce services and Jigrahak has launched a payment platform called "NGpay" for online mobile shopping, to name a few. Telecom service providers such as Reliance and Airtel have been providing services such as bill payments, railway and airline ticket booking etc. To sum it up, it is evident that the opportunity is immense and mobile commerce can be seen as a potential revenue driver for the industry players. On the retail section, M-commerce provides new sales channels; and financial institutions can gain real competitive advantage by offering services such as m-banking. The possibilities are innumerable. Once the pace is set, M-commerce will become the way of life on mobile.

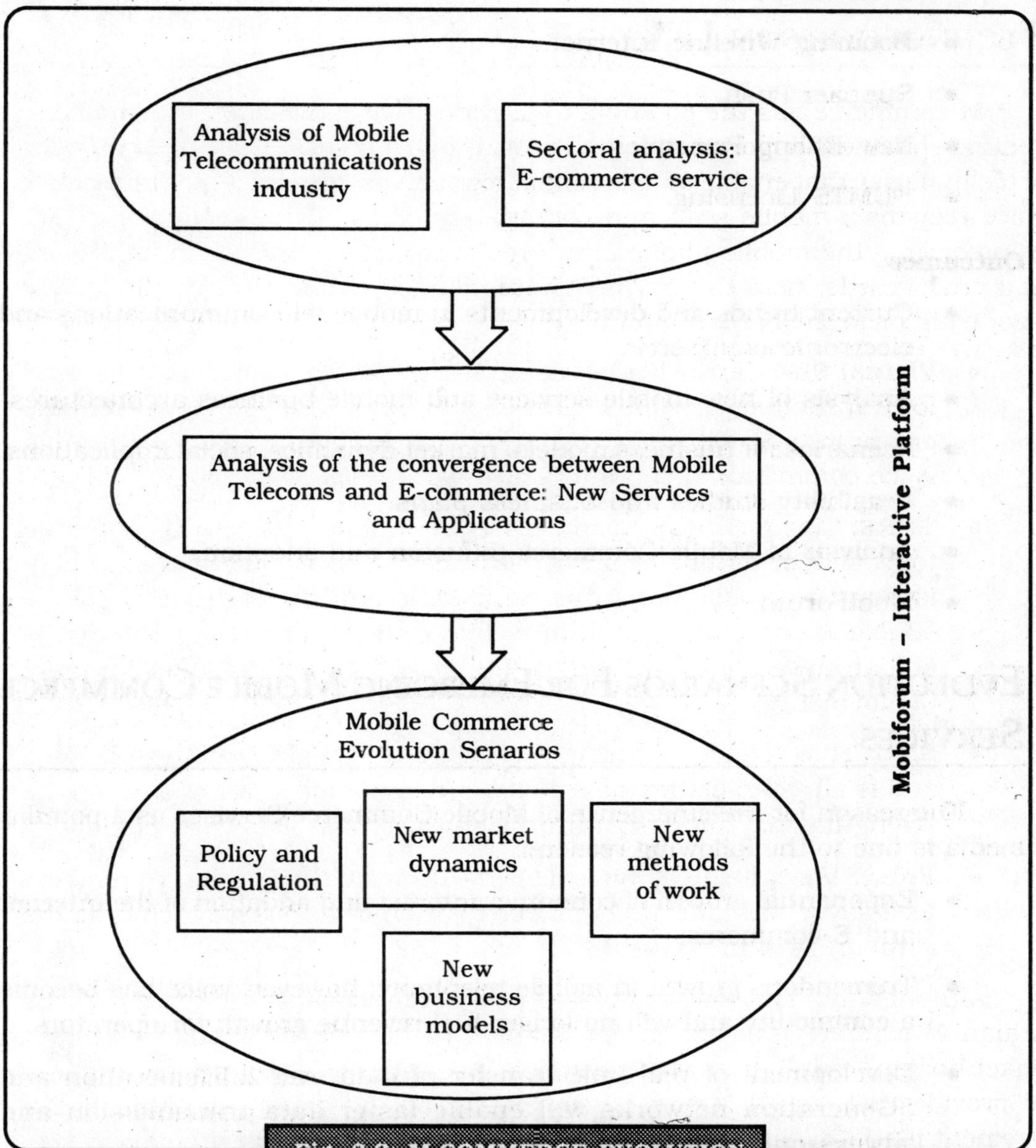

Fig. 3.2: M-COMMERCE EVOLUTION

WHAT IS DRIVING M-COMMERCE?

M-commerce Market Drivers

- Mass Adoption.
- Booming Wireline Internet.
- Supplier Push.
- New Billing Principles.
- [10]UMTS Licensing.

Outcomes

- Current trends and developments in mobile telecommunications and electronic commerce.
- Analysis of new mobile services and mobile business architectures.
- Scenarios for business models, market dynamics, social implications.
- Feasibility studies and business plans.
- Analysis of Mobile Commerce diffusion and adoption.
- MobiForum.

EVOLUTION SCENARIOS FOR EMERGING MOBILE COMMERCE SERVICES

The reason for the emergence of Mobile Commerce Services as a popular media is due to the following reasons:

- Exponential growth of consumer interest and adoption of the Internet and E-commerce.
- Tremendous growth in mobile telephony; however, voice has become a commodity and will no longer fuel revenue growth for operators.
- Development of real-time transfer of data over 2.5Generation and 3Generation networks will enable faster data transmission and 'always-on' connectivity.

---

[10] *Universal Mobile Telecommunications System (UMTS) is one of the third-generation (3G) mobile telecommunications technologies, which is also being developed into a 4G technology. Being a complete network system, UMTS also covers the radio access network (UMTS Terrestrial Radio Access Network, or UTRAN), the core network (Mobile Application Part, or MAP), as well as authentication of users via USIM cards (Subscriber Identity Module).*

- The evolution of the handheld devices incorporating WAP and now GPRS.
- Mobile E-commerce market is worth $3.5 billion in 2000 and will grow to over $200 billion by 2005 (Ovum).
- Cost of entry into mobile E-commerce is low for most entrants, for example, a bank can implement a sophisticated m-banking solution in under six months for around $1 million.
- The unique features of the mobile device, such as its compactness for convenience and personalized functions; subsequently, people have become quite attached to their devices.

Attracting players from all economic sectors from technology, finance, retail, media, anticipating that M-commerce will increase customer acquisition and retention and generate new revenue opportunities.

Mobile Commerce: Attributes and Benefits

Specific Attributes of M-commerce

- Mobility
- Broad reach

Benefits of Value-added Attributes

- Ubiquity
- Convenience
- Instant connectivity
- Personalization
- Localization of products and services

Attributes of M-commerce and its Economic Advantages

- Mobility — users carry cell phones or other mobile devices
- Broad reach — people can be reached at any time
- Ubiquity — easier information access in real-time
- Convenience — devices that store data and have Internet, intranet, extranet connections

- Instant connectivity — easy and quick connection to Internet, intranets, other mobile devices, databases
- Personalization — preparation of information for individual consumers
- Localization of products and services — knowing where the user is located at any given time and match service to them.

SUMMARY

In this chapter you have gone through, drivers of M-commerce. After going through the chapter, be sure that the following facts are:

- Fundamental attributes of Mobile Users.
- M-commerce process.
- Technologies used in M-commerce.
- Driving force of M-commerce.
- Evolution scenarios for emerging mobile commerce services.
- Benefits and attributes of M-commerce.

STUDY QUESTIONS

1. Explain the reason why M-commerce is emerging as a popular media of commerce?
2. Enlist the various attributes which is common to all mobile users.
3. Explain M-commerce process with its block diagram.
4. Describe the various technologies used by M-commerce.
5. Explain the drivers of M-commerce and its outcome.
6. The future of M-commerce in India is very bright. Why?
7. Elucidate the attributes and benefits of M-commerce.

CHAPTER – 4

SUPPORTING TECHNOLOGIES

LEARNING OBJECTIVE

In this chapter you go through the Supporting Technology of M-commerce. The objective of this chapter is to acquaint the readers about the technological requirement of M-commerce.

- Hardware
- Software
- Network
- Technical Design Issues
- Mobile Computing Networks
- Mobile Computing Infrastructure
- Summary
- Study Questions

The following components comprise a complete end-to-end solution for mobile computing applications:

HARDWARE

- Mobile computing device be it, a notebook, handheld computer, pen computer, PDA, PalmOS compatible PDA, Symbian EPOC handheld device, Windows CE/Pocket PC device, or a modern smartphone with Wireless Internet connectivity
- A suitably-configured wireline or wireless WAN modem, wireless LAN adapter, or a flash card either as a distinctly separate accessory or embedded on the device as is the trend now.
- A Web Server with wireless support, WAP gateway, a Communications Server and/or [13]MCSS (Mobile Communications Server Switch) or a wireless gateway embedded in wireless carrier's network this server provides communications functionality to allow the handheld device to communicate with the Internet or Intranet infrastructure.
- An application or database server (the hardware piece) with application logic and business application database - tier 2 server.
- Optionally, a large enterprise application server (tier 3) in the form of a Unix super server, IBM's AS/400 server or IBM's OS/390 mainframe.

SOFTWARE

Mobile client OS-type software that resides in the mobile device it may be Windows98/2000/NT, PalmOS, Win CE (or Pocket PC), EPOC, a specialized OS like Blackberry, or a Web browser:

- Mobile application user interface with application logic in a handheld PDA, Smartphone, Palm or a Wintel notebook. In the Internet world, it is often under the control of a browser or microbrowser.
- Application server and/or database server software
- Back-end legacy application software on large Unix servers (from vendors such as Sun, IBM, and HP), IBM AS/400 or IBM S/390 mainframes.

---

[13] **NOTE: MSCS**-*The* ***mobile switching centre server*** *is a soft-switch variant of the mobile switching centre, which provides circuit-switched calling, mobility management, and GSM services to the mobile phones* roaming *within the area that it serves.*

- Application middleware (a piece of software that communicates with back end legacy systems and web-based application servers). IBM's WebSphere, BEA's WebLogic or Oracle's 9i are typical examples in this category.
- Wireless middleware that links multiple wireless networks to application servers.
- Data synchronization software that synchronizes data in the mobile device with the network server or the backend server.
- Mobile Device management software like XcelleNet's Afaria, Synchrologic Mobile suite or Mobile Automation's MA2000.
- Finally, the most useful software - end user application like messaging, sales force automation, public query, data collection, etc.

Network

A wireless network this may be either a private network that police agencies and emergency health services use or a public shared network that is provided by network providers, such as Cingular (formerly Bell South Wireless Data), Verizon, Sprint PCS, Nextel, Bell Mobility (Canada), Roger's AT&T (Canada), Vodafone in Europe, BT inUK, NTT DoCoMo (Japan), etc.

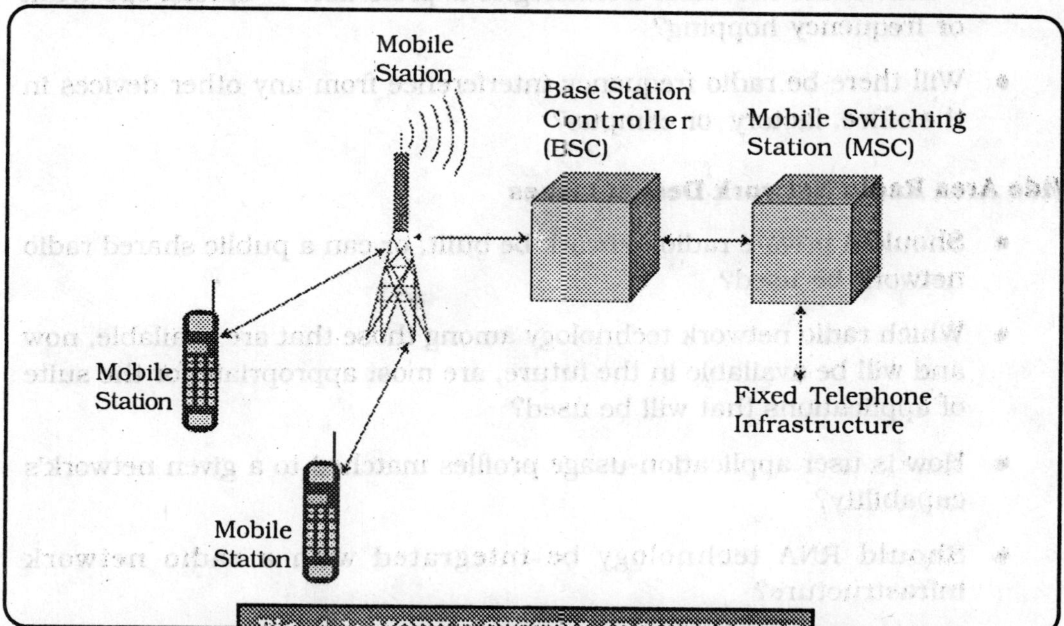

Fig. 4.1: MOBILE SYSTEM ARCHITECTURE

Technical Design Issues

Wireless LAN Design Issues

- How many mobile users in total will use the wireless LAN? How many will be active during the peak period?
- Which LAN applications will they be accessing? Remember that wireless LANs operate at much slower speeds than wired LANs. Will the slower speed be acceptable to the intended users?
- Is a notebook with a wireless NIC going to be the primary end user device? The use of notebooks as primary computers is being increasingly mandated even in fixed-location offices.
- In which areas of a building or campus will users be roaming?
- How many access points will be needed?
- Where should access points be located?
- What is the access point range?
- What impact will construction materials like steel frames used in walls and ceilings have on signal penetration?
- Which of the two main technologies is preferable — spread spectrum or frequency hopping?
- Will there be radio frequency interference from any other devices in the office, factory or campus?

Wide Area Radio Network Design Issues

- Should a private radio network be built, or can a public shared radio network be used?
- Which radio network technology among those that are available, now and will be available in the future, are most appropriate for the suite of applications that will be used?
- How is user application-usage profiles matched to a given network's capability?
- Should RNA technology be integrated with a radio network infrastructure?
- How is good coverage and a minimum number of dead spots ensured?

- Should a distributed wireless network design with several MCSS be used?
- Which MCSS should be selected?
- Should agent-based application development tools like Oracle Mobile Agents be used?
- How do various network design options influence the way logical networks will be managed?
- Is network outsourcing a realistic business option to pursue? If it is, does the proposed Network Service Provider (NSP) have the necessary capacity and capability?

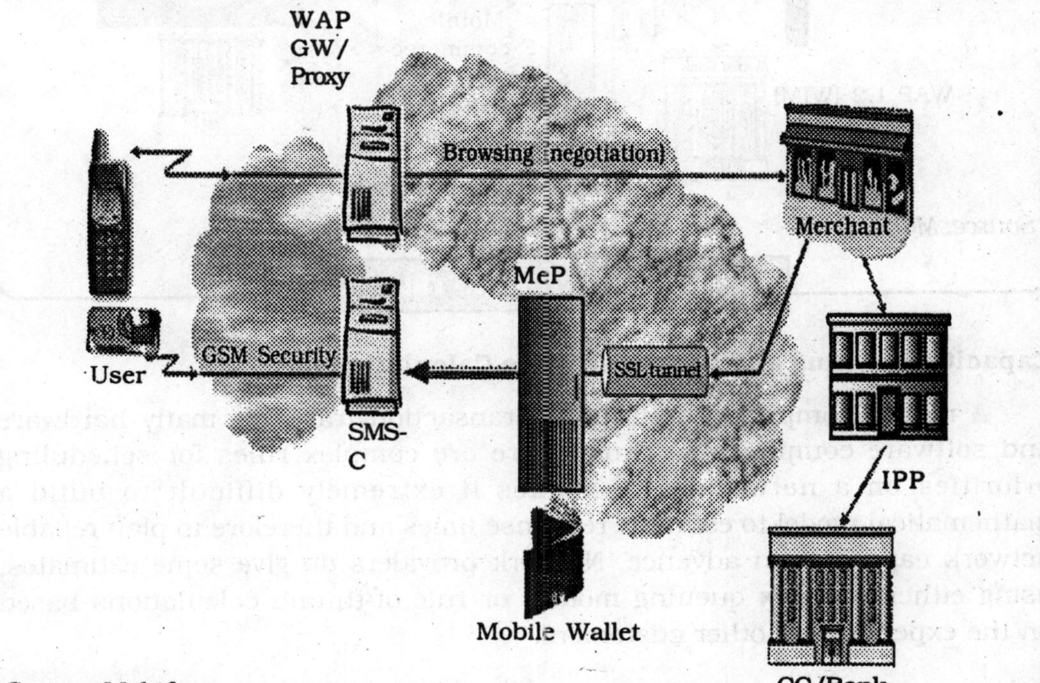

Source: Mobiform

Fig. 4.2: M-COMMERCE WORKING

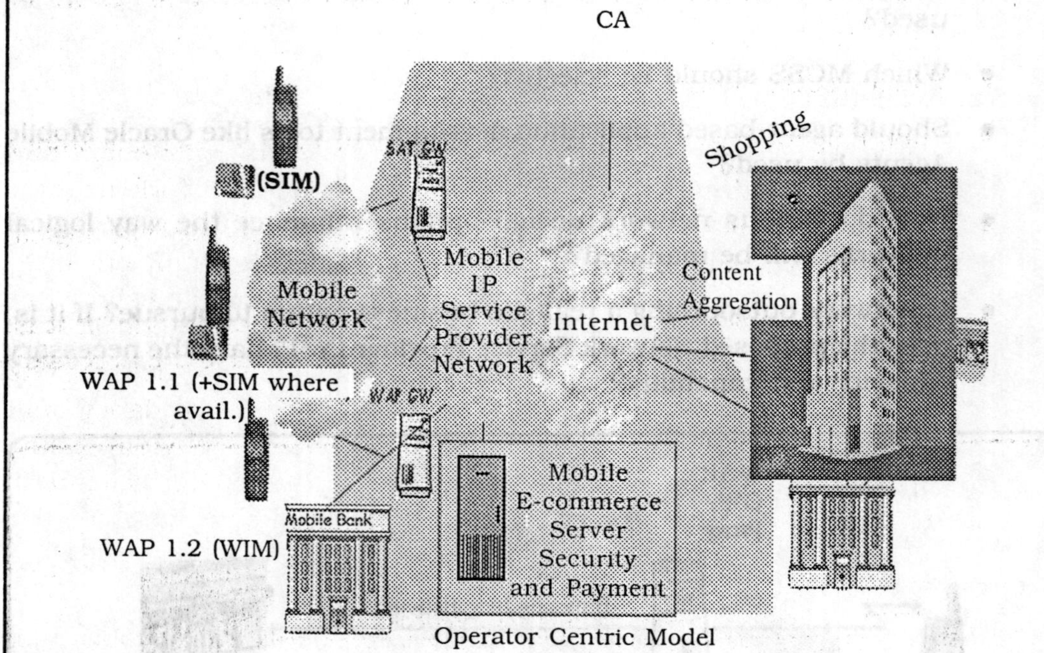

Source: Mobiform

Fig. 4.3: OPERATOR CENTRIC MODEL

Capacity Planning and Response Time Calculations

A mobile computing application transaction traverses many hardware and software components. Thus, there are complex rules for scheduling priorities on a network. This makes it extremely difficult to build a mathematical model to estimate response times and therefore to plan reliable network capacities in advance. Network providers do give some estimates, using either complex queuing models or rule-of-thumb calculations based on the experience of other customers.

Data Compression Considerations

Wireless network bandwidth is scarce and expensive. Every possible technique should be used to get the utmost service out of this bandwidth. Compression of data is one such technique. The most common place to compress data is in the modem. But it is a good idea to go beyond modem hardware in reducing the amount of traffic on wireless networks. Intelligence can be built into client application programs so that short message codes can be used to indicate common data occurrences. Forms and screens should be stored on the mobile computer.

System Availability Design

Typically, wireless networks have redundancies built into them and network service providers guarantee an extremely high network up-time percentage. Generally, base-station hardware and network controllers have hardware redundancy and message switches are typically built on fault-tolerant platforms such as Tandem and Stratus. However, nothing should be taken for granted and public shared network providers should be asked for details of their redundancies. Similar redundancies should also be built into private networks. Another vital component that must have redundancy built into it is the MCSS. Find out if the method of switch-over from failing components to standby components is automatic or manual. If it is manual, is the station staffed, and how long does a switch-over take?

Security Issues

Securing information from unauthorized access is a major problem for any network, especially for wireless networks, since radio signals travel through the open atmosphere where they can be intercepted by individuals who are constantly on the move and therefore difficult to track down.

Here are some examples of common security breaches:

- Networks by criminal elements.
- Interception of credit card authorizations over wireless networks.
- Physical breach of security at unmanned base stations or other communications centers.

Ergonomic And Logistics Design

The designer should evaluate the following factors:

- Form factor of end-user devices
- Battery life
- Input method: keyboard, pen, touch or voice
- Ruggedness

- Health and safety issues
- Portable or fixed

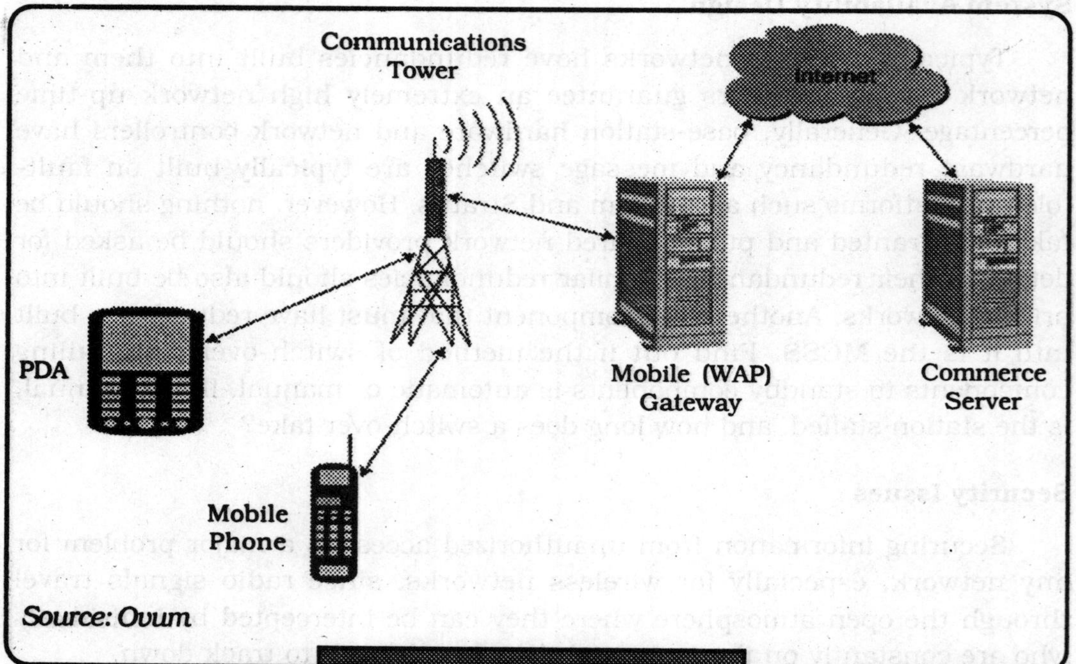

Fig. 4.4: WAP ARCHITECTURE

While wireless network provides true mobility, you may utilize a wireline network for those mobile users who need occasional connection from hotels, motels or airport lounges of airline's regular patrons. Some of these airports are now offering wireless LAN connectivity to wireline back end networks.

MOBILE COMPUTING NETWORKS

There are a number of ways of providing connectivity to mobile workers, telecommuters and remote workers. Following types of networks are the most common methods of mobile connectivity:

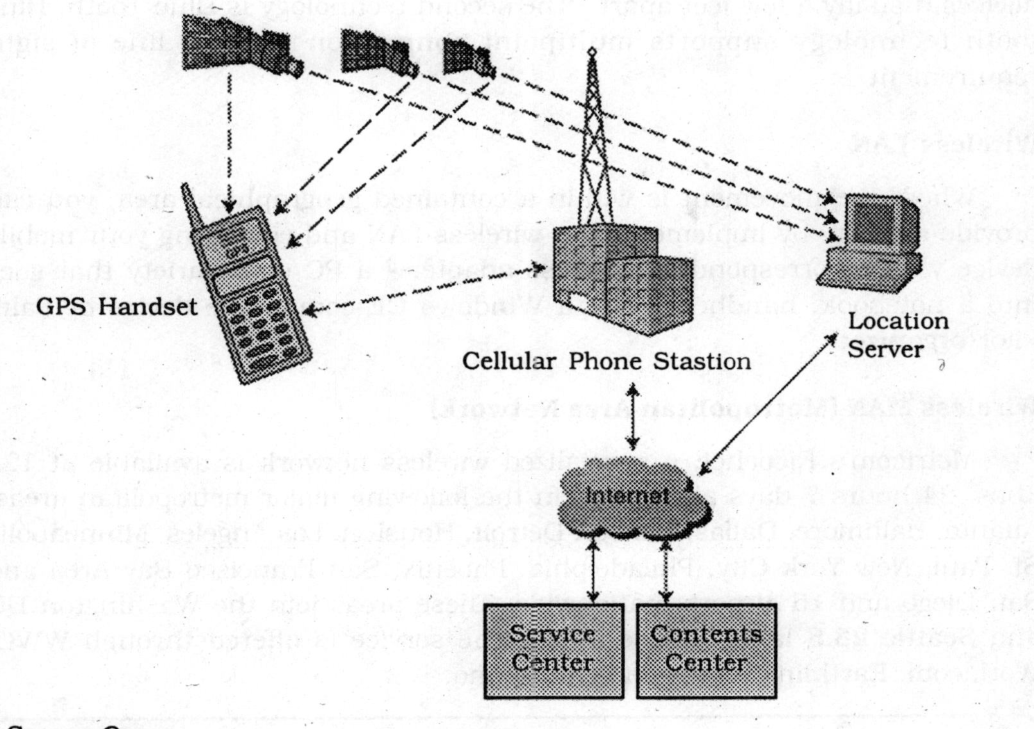

Source: Ovum

Fig. 4.5: GPS SYSTEM

Temporary or Switched Connection via Wire line WAN

Permanent connection between a mobile user and information source is not only expensive but is not always practical because mobile users are constantly on the move. Therefore, the most popular (though not most ubiquitous or pervasive or persistent using the new lingo) method of providing connectivity to mobile workers continues to be one of a temporary wire line connection for a specific use and a required period of time. This can be achieved by using a dial-up connection on a traditional public telephone or cellular network. You call it switched because you switch a circuit from one user to another user for the duration of the call. You may have a switched wire line connection directly between a remote location where the user is at a given moment and the information server or indirectly through the Internet. In either case, you still need to locate a telephone jack of one kind or another.

Wireless PANs (Personal Area Networks)

These are wireless networks that can be installed in a small office or home within 5-15 meter distances. Two technologies being used for this purpose are IrDA which is based on line of sight requirement within two devices, usually a few feet apart. The second technology is Blue Tooth. Blue tooth technology supports multipoint connection without line of sight requirement.

Wireless LAN

Where the movement is within a contained geographical area, you can provide mobility by implementing a wireless LAN and equipping your mobile device with a corresponding wireless adapter - a PC card variety that goes into a notebook, handheld PDA, a Windows CE-compatible device or Palm Pilot organizer.

Wireless MAN (Metropolitan Area Network)

Metricom's Ricochet, a specialized wireless network is available at 128 kbps, 24 hours 7 days always on, in the following major metropolitan areas: Atlanta, Baltimore, Dallas, Denver, Detroit, Houston, Los Angeles, Minneapolis St. Paul, New York City, Philadelphia, Phoenix, San Francisco Bay Area and San Diego and 15 airports nationwide. These areas join the Washington DC and Seattle 28.8 kbps service areas. The service is offered through WWC, Worldcom, Earthlink, GoAmerica and Juno.

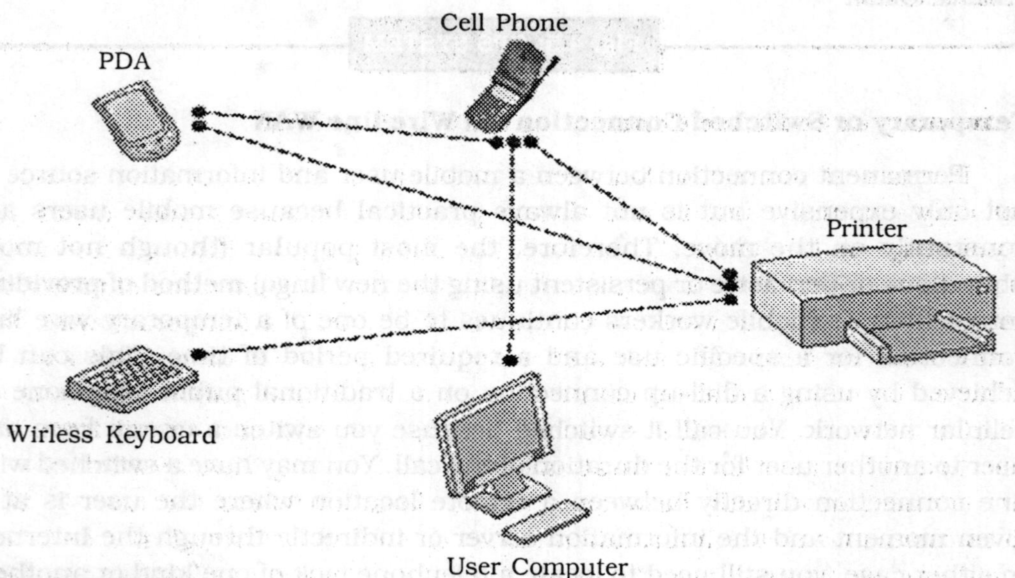

Source: Mobiform

Fig. 4.6: WIRELESS LAN

Wireless WAN - Private or Public

Once we move out of the limited geography of a wireless LAN in a campus or factory setting, we have to utilize wide area wireless network. These networks may be private or public. Large organizations, such as Fedex or public safety agencies, have implemented private CDPD or SMR networks to give wireless connectivity to courier drivers and police officers. However, the current trend is to move towards shared public networks, such as Motient or BellSouth (ex RAM Mobile Data - called Mobitex in Europe and Canada).

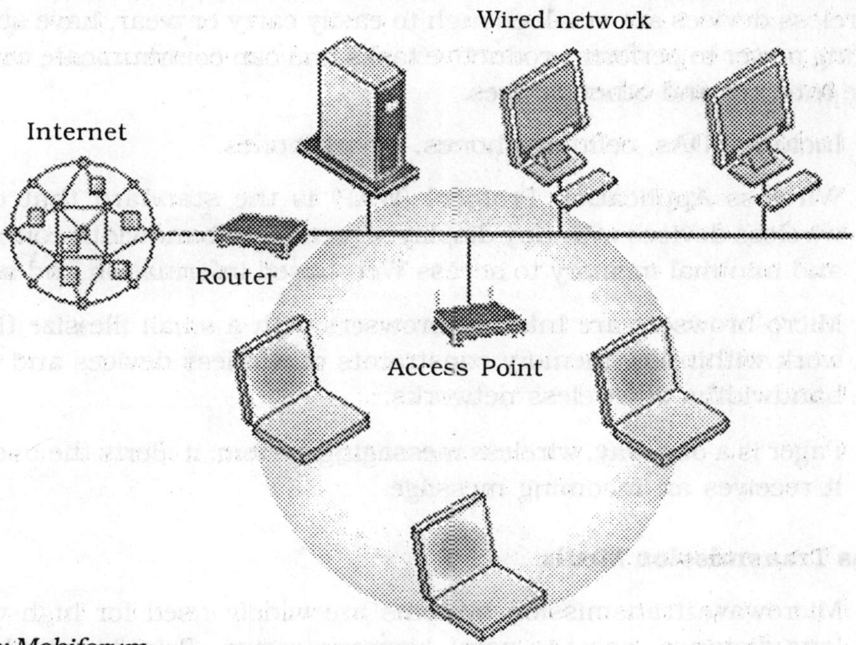

Source: Mobiforum

Fig. 4.7: SATELLITE NETWORKS

Satellite Networks

Even wireless wide area networks may not provide coverage in extremely remote areas, because networks cannot justify the economics of installing a base station everywhere. True universal coverage for these types of mobile users is possible only through wireless networks based on satellites. There are several GEOS, LEOS, and MEOS satellite-based networks that transmit from different heights from the surface of the earth.

The Last Mile Problem for Wireless Networks

One thing worth noting is that it is only the last mile where we need wireless or radio-frequency-based connection. Once we reach a terrestrial network, we can utilize the bandwidth of traditional wire line permanent connections. By the same token, once we reach the Internet Service Provider through a wireless hub or concentrator, we can be home free for riding high-speed connection to the universal information highway.

Wireless Technologies

Wireless devices are small enough to easily carry or wear, have sufficient computing power to perform productive tasks and can communicate wirelessly with the Internet and other devices.

- Include PDAs, cellular phones, smartphones.
- Wireless Application Protocol (WAP) is the standard that enables wireless devices with tiny display screens, low bandwidth connections and minimal memory to access Web-based information and services.
- Micro browsers are Internet browsers with a small file size that can work within low-memory constraints of wireless devices and the low bandwidths of wireless networks.
- Pager is a one-way, wireless messaging system; it alerts the user when it receives an incoming message.

Wireless Transmission Media

- Microwave transmission systems are widely used for high-volume, long-distance, point-to-point communication. *Point-to-point* has two characteristics: first, the transmitter and receiver must be in view of each other (called *line-of-sight*); and second, the transmission itself must be tightly directed from transmitter to receiver.
- Satellite transmission systems make use of communication satellites; three types of satellites, each in a different orbit:
  - ❖ Geostationary (GEO)
  - ❖ Medium-earth-orbit (MEO)
  - ❖ Low-earth-orbit (LEO)
- Footprint is the area of earth's surface reached by a satellite's transmission – overcomes the limitations of microwave data relay stations.

- Broadcast transmission allows satellites to send signals to many receivers at one time.
- Propagation delay is a brief pause in transmissions from GEO satellites which make two-way telephone conversations difficult.

Types of Orbits

- *Geostationary earth orbit (GEO)* orbits 22,300 miles directly above the equator and maintains a fixed position; excellent for TV signals.
- *Medium earth orbit (MEO)* are located 6,000 miles above the earth's surface and move; used for GPS and are less expensive.
- *Low earth orbit (LEO)* are 400 to 700 miles above the surface and move much quicker so they require many to have adequate coverage; use for telephone.

Global Positioning Systems (GPS)

- GPS is a wireless system that uses satellites to enable users to determine their position anywhere on the earth; supported by 24 shared satellites worldwide.

Internet Over Satellite (IOS)

- IOS allows users to access the Internet via GEO satellites from a dish mounted on the side of their homes.
    - ❖ Only option available in some areas.
    - ❖ Can have a propagation delay or be disrupted by environmental conditions.

Radio

- Radio transmission uses radio-wave frequencies to send data directly between transmitters and receivers.
- Satellite radio (digital radio) offers uninterrupted, near CD-quality music that is beamed to your radio from space. (XM satellite radio uses GEO; Sirius uses MEO)
- Infrared light is red light that is not commonly visible to human eyes; common uses in remote control units for TVs, VCRs, DVDs, CD players.

Wireless Computer Networks and Internet Access

- IEEE standards for wireless computer networks include:
  - IEEE 802.15 (Bluetooth) for wireless personal area networks (PANs) and 802.15.4 (Zigbee).
  - IEEE 802.11 (Wi-Fi) for wireless local area networks (WLANs)
  - IEEE 802.16 (Wi-Max) for wireless metropolitan area networks (WMANs)
  - IEEE 802.20 (proposed) for wireless wide area networks (WWANs).

Bluetooth

- Bluetooth is used to create small PANs:
  - can link up to 8 devices within a 10-metre area;
  - uses low-power, radio-based communications;
  - can transmit up to 1 Mbps.
- Personal area network (PAN) is a computer network used for communication among computer devices (example- telephones, PDAs, smart phones) close to one person.

Zigbee

- Zigbee targets applications that need low data transmission rates and low power consumption:
  - Moves data only one-fourth as fast as Bluetooth;
  - Can handle hundreds of devices at once;
  - Most promising application is meter reading.
- Current focus is to wirelessly link sensors that are embedded into industrial controls, medical devices, smoke and intruder alarms and building and home automaton.

Wireless Local Area Networks (WLANs)

- WLAN requires a transmitter with an antenna, called a wireless access point, that connects to a wired LAN or to satellite dishes that provide an Internet connection.
  - Wireless network interface card (NIC) is needed to communicate wirelessly and has a built-in radio and antenna.

   - ❖ Hotspot a wireless access point that provides service to a number of users within a small geographical perimeter (up to a couple hundred feet).
   - ❖ IEEE standard for WLANs is the 802.11 family, known as Wi-Fi, for Wireless Fidelity.
   - ❖ 802.11a can transmit up to 54 Mbps within 30 meters; 802.11b can transmit up to 11 Mbps within 30-50 meter; 802.11g – 54 Mbps, 50 meter.
   - ❖ Benefits are low cost and simple Internet access.

- Problems with Wi-Fi
   - ❖ Roaming – users cannot roam from hotspot to hotspot if the hotspots use different Wi-Fi network services.
   - ❖ Security – because Wi-Fi uses radio waves, it is difficult to protect.
   - ❖ Cost – commercial Wi-Fi services are low cost but not free and each service has its own fees and separate accounts for users to log on.

WiMax

- Worldwide Interoperability for Microwave Access, popularly known as WiMax, is the name for IEEE standard 802.16.
   - ❖ Wireless access range of up to 31 miles;
   - ❖ Data transfer rate of 75 Mbps;
   - ❖ Secure system that offers voice and video.

Wireless Technology and Devices

Wireless Development

- First-generation wireless technology was the cellular phone.
- Second generation wireless technology, which includes digital cellular phones, is currently in use worldwide.
- Third generation, or *3G* technology will enable wireless devices to send and receive data as much as seven times faster than a standard 56K modem.

Wireless Devices

- Personal Digital assistants (PDAs), Palm OS.
- Digital cellular phones (WAP Phones).
- Two-way pagers (RIM)
- MS Windows CE/Pocket PC
- RFID

Wireless Internet Access

- *Code Division Multiple Access* (CDMA)
  - — Each transmission is assigned a specific channel, giving the transmission the benefit of the entire bandwidth within that channel and reducing the possibility that a connection will be broken.
  - — Able to assign each transmission on the network a unique code to ensure security.

Global System for Mobile Communications (GSM)

- Uses Time Division Multiple Access (TDMA) which takes multiple calls and assigns each call to a different time slot on the same radio frequency, eg. Short Message Service (SMS)

Wireless Application Protocol (WAP)

- Developed by Nokia, Ericsson, Motorola, etc.
- A set of communication protocols designed to enable different kinds of wireless devices to communicate and access the Internet.
- Designed to standardize development across different wireless technologies worldwide.
- Intended primarily for Internet-enabled digital phones, pagers and other handheld devices.
- Uses websites specifically designed for wireless handheld devices that have small screens and low-bandwidth constraints.

Wireless Markup Language (WML)

- The scripting language used to create Web content to be delivered to wireless handheld devices, based on XML.

- Removes "unnecessary" content from Web pages.
- WML tags are used to "mark up" a Web page to specify how the page should be formatted on a wireless device.
- WML works with the WAP to deliver the content.
- Similar to HTML, but it does not require input devices.

Microbrowsers

- Designed with limited bandwidth and limited memory requirements.
- Access the Web via the wireless Internet.

WAP and WML Integration

- A WAP gateway, which acts as a proxy server, receives the request, translates it and sends it to the appropriate Internet server.
- Server responds by sending the requested WML document.
- The WAP gateway parses this document's WML (i.e., it analyzes the WML document, checking it for correctness) and sends the proper text to the digital phone.

MOBILE COMPUTING INFRASTRUCTURE

- M-Commerce hardware.
- Cellular (mobile) phones.
- Attachable keyboard.
- PDAs.
- Interactive pagers.
- Screen phones.

A telephone equipped with a color screen, possibly a keyboard, e-mail, and Internet capabilities

- E-mail handhelds.
- Required infrastructure hardware.
- Suitably configured wireline or wireless WAN modem, wireless LAN adapter, or wireless MAN (metro-area network) adapter.

- A Web server with wireless support, a WAP gateway, a communications server, and/or a mobile communications server switch (MCSS).

An application or database server with application logic and a business application database providing E-commerce functionality.

- A GPS locator that is used to determine the location of the person carrying the mobile computing device.
- Software.
- Microbrowsers.

Wireless software designed with limited bandwidth and limited memory requirements.

- Mobile-client operating system.
- Bluetooth.

Chip technology that enables voice and data communications between many wireless devices through low-power, short-range, digital two-way radio frequencies

- Mobile application user interface.
- Back-end legacy application software.
- Application middleware.
- Wireless middleware.
- Wireless Application Protocol.

A set of communications protocols designed to enable different kinds of wireless devices to talk to a server installed on a mobile network so users can access the Internet.

- Wireless Markup Language.

Scripting language used for creating content in the wireless Web environment; based on XML, minus unnecessary content to increase speed.

- Voice XML.

An extension of XML designed to accommodate voice.

- Mobile networks.

Subscriber Identification Module (SIM) card: An extractable storage card used for identification, transaction processing, and the like.

SUMMARY

In this chapter you have gone through Supporting Technologies. After going through the chapter, be sure that the following facts are well versed.

Hardware, Network and software requirement of M-commerce.

Technical Design Issues-Wireless LAN Design issue, Wide Area Radio Network Design Issues, Capacity Planning and Response Time Calculations, Data Compression Consideration, System Availability Design, Security Issues, Ergonomics & Logistics Design.

Mobile Computing Networks, Temporary or Switched Connection via Wireline WAN, Wireless PAN, Wireless LAN, Wireless MAN, Wireless WAN, Satellite Networks, Wireless Technologies, Wireless Transmission Media, Types of Orbits, Global Positioning Systems, Internet Over Satellite, Bluetooth, Zigbee, WLAN, WiMAX, WAP, WML and Mobile Computing Infrastructure.

STUDY QUESTIONS

1. Explain the hardware, software & network specification required for M-commerce.
2. Describe the technological issues in M-commerce.
3. Explain types of computing networks involved in M-commerce.
4. Write a note on the Mobile Computing Infrastructure.
5. Write short notes on:
   (a) WAP Architecture
   (b) WAN
   (c) Wireless PAN, Wireless LAN, Wireless MAN, Wireless WAN
   (d) Satellite Networks
   (e) Wireless Technologies
   (f) Wireless Transmission Media
   (g) GPS
   (h) Zigbee
   (i) WLAN
   (j) WiMAX
   (k) WAP
   (l) WML

CHAPTER – 5

MOBILE SECURITY

LEARNING OBJECTIVE

This chapter explains about the following concepts:

- Introduction
- What is Public Key Infrastructure (PKI)?
- Strategies in Wireless Internet Security
- Security Issues in WTLS
- WTLS Fixes
- WAP Versus SIM Toolkit
- Components of Wireless PKI
- Challenges to Wireless Internet PKI
- Summary
- Study Questions

*In the world of security, we never talk about absolute security, but rather acceptable risk. In the physical world, the entire insurance industry has been built around estimating levels of risk and providing financial protection. Likewise, in the wireless world, we cannot guarantee 100 percent security, but we can make the security so strong that if it is compromised, the data is no longer useful. Thus, it is always important, in any security evaluation, to determine the length of time a piece of data needs to be protected. For example, a product design specification for a company may need to be protected only until the product is retired; however, national defense secrets may need to be protected years after a particular threat has expired.

Currently, carriers of mobile device services do provide some security through the use of encryption protocols. However, without a solution to provide end-to-end security, M-commerce cannot grow to the lofty levels described by so many analyst reports. End-to-end security can be defined as maintaining authentication, confidentially, and integrity of a communication from sender to recipient. In M-commerce, the sender may be a person with a mobile phone executing a financial transaction, for example, with the recipient being the sender's bank's E-commerce server. Implemented properly, even the data carrier has no visibility into the data being carried over its networks. The network/wireless professional will note that there are, in fact, various security provisions built into various mobile standards. However, those standards perform only some level of authentication of the mobile device and encryption, to and from the mobile device to the carrier. In the world of M-commerce, the transaction goes beyond the wire and into the wired world, so our solution to mitigate these security concerns must protect a transaction from its origin at the mobile device through when it reaches the M-commerce destination server.

There are many issues related to security for a mobile device and M-commerce. We can concisely describe these issues as follows:

- **Physical security:** Given that mobile devices are generally small, theft of the device, and thus access to valuable data and digital credentials, can easily compromise any M-commerce network.
- **Carrier bearer:** Since many mobile devices receive service from a public carrier, traditional wireless issues related to interception of mid-air communication and replay-type attacks can hinder M-commerce (this is an increasingly alarming issue for certain wireless communications such as 802. 11b, which is the latest wireless LAN standard).

---

* ***M-commerce Security:*** *A Beginner's Guide-Kapil Raina, Anurag Harsh-Tata McGraw-Hill Publishing Company Limited, P-66-87*

- **Transactional:** Since many M-commerce transactions eventually get routed over a public network, such as the Internet. It is important that security be maintained not only to the carrier but all the way through to the M-commerce server.
- **Post-transaction:** Given that there is a need to provide digital receipts or some type of proof for problem resolution after a transaction has occurred, a system must be maintained to prove, securely, that a particular transaction occurred.

The ideal solution encompasses all of the aforementioned issues. Practically, a mix of technology and solutions are needed to achieve those goals. The most complete solution to securing M-commerce applications has been the implementation of public key infrastructure (PKI) for the wireless world. PKI is perhaps the only technology that provides the key elements of authentication, confidentiality, data integrity, and non-repudiation. Physical security is not addressed directly through PKI (although well-defined policy statements and insurance protection can help mitigate loss), but additional components, such as biometric devices and personal identification number (PIN) locking techniques, can minimize damage done when a mobile device is not physically secure.

WHAT IS PUBLIC KEY INFRASTRUCTURE (PKI)?

Every business and individual has the need for a certain element of confidence that business conducted electronically is safely completed with the expected parties. In the physical world, this is achieved through physical identification with identification cards, voice recognition, facial recognition, legal documents, and so on. However, in the electronic world, we cannot be certain who we are dealing with or who else may be privy to a conversation, and we may even be unsure whether the communication was altered in transit. Furthermore, in physical commerce, contracts or signatures bind a party to a legal transaction. Likewise, electronic transactions also need to be bound to particular parties. Imagine if someone were to purchase an automobile online, prompting a factory to produce that machine to specifications, and then the buyer refuted ever conducting that transaction. Financial losses from these types of events could wipe out businesses A simple, common way of protecting data is by using either proprietary methods or encryption using symmetric keys. Symmetric keys are a mathematical equivalent to physical locks and keys. For example, a single key (like a symmetric key) may unlock a house's door, and that same key may be used to lock that door. The strength of these symmetric keys is measured in the size of the key, or number of bits. Generally, the greater the number of bits used in a key, the more secure the transaction.

The problem with such a method is that to conduct business over the Internet, not knowing or having physical access to the parties involved, how do we ensure that everyone has the keys required to communicate securely? Although we could e-mail such information, we run the risk of those keys' being intercepted and copied so that someone else could then also have the keys to unlock the secret communication. To resolve this problem, the concept of public key technology was developed in the 1970s to provide a method of exchanging these secret keys securely, This approach is somewhat analogous to the situation in which a postal carrier delivers your house key through a mail slot in an office. Only you, the intended recipient, can open the door to the office to access the contents of the mailbox and retrieve the key, but anyone can drop a key through the slot. Once you have retrieved the key, then you can enter your house. This example describes the core aspects of public key technology.

However simply using this public key technology is insufficient for all security needs. After all, since anyone can drop a key into the mail slot, how do you know whether the key is the correct one for your house, whether someone else's key was substituted for your key, or even the identity of the person who mailed the key? For a complete solution, we turn to PKI. One of the generally accepted methods for creating a secure connection on an open system, like the Internet or the wireless world is PKI. A PKI is composed of a number of systems that include policies, legal practices, and technology to deliver a solution for providing essential features for secure M-commerce or E-commerce (also known as M-commerce).

One of the fundamental components of PKI is the concept of public and private keys. In basic terms, the public key (like the mail slot described earlier) is freely available to anyone to send a message securely. The corresponding private key (like the key to the office that accesses the mailbox) is used to decode the message. A characteristic of this mathematical relationship also allows the sender to provide his or her identity by digitally signing, or encoding, a message with the private key rather than the public key. Then, the corresponding public key is used to verify that message. In the mailbox analogy, using digital signatures is akin to someone's being able to describe the secret location of your house key, writing this on a piece of paper, and slipping the paper into your mail slot at the office. In this manner, you can be sure of the identity of the author of the note since only that person could have known the location of the secret house key. To bundle or protect these public keys, digital certificates (often simply called certificates) are used. A certificate is simply a package with some unique data about an entity. This data is in the form of a predefined set of standards, known as X.509 (the latest version widely being used is version 3). To protect this bundle of information from being altered, an issuing authority (called the certificate authority, or CA), uses its private key to digitally sign this bundle, or certificate. This is similar to governments' use of special paper or holograms on paper currency to ensure that the currency has not been forged or altered in any way. In this manner, when the recipient receives the certificate, the recipient can verify that the certificate was not altered by using the CA's public key. Because the public and private keys are mathematically related in a unique way, the CA's signature can be verified with a high degree of confidence. To ensure that the CA's public key, which is used to detect tampering, is delivered without being tampered itself, the key is delivered through some type of secure mechanism. Usually the public key is installed in an application, such as a browser, at the time of the software's creation (otherwise, we may doubt that the CA's public key itself has not been faked). The concept of verifying certificates is described through the use of a certificate hierarchy. This is similar to, for example, the hierarchy of some large non-profit groups, which have an international organization, with various national chapters, each having its own state chapters, and each of those state chapters having local or city chapters. Membership in a local charity allows the member to gain some of the benefits and recognition from all of the other member chapters through the international organization. Each digital certificate, to have successful verification, must contain the highest-level authority (or root key) in the recipient's verifying device (for example, in the PDA, mobile phone, or PC).

How PKI Eases Consumers' Fears

According to a Data monitor/Impact 2001 survey, the majority of Internet users say security is a major concern. To a large extent, this is justified, with a significant portion of all Internet-based transactions being claimed as false. Currently, in the United States, the most popular method of transaction is by credit card. Because the liability for credit card misuse lies with the merchant (that is, the merchant must prove that a transaction is valid), the merchant bears the cost of any forged or improperly used credit cards employed in transactions on the Internet.

Authentication Through PKI

Authentication is the ability to verify an individual or device's identity. Most PKI systems accomplish this by allowing the entity to be verified to sign something and then send that signed text or snippet for verification. The receiver then verifies that the signature of the sent information is still valid. The assumption is that only the sender knows the private key and that it has not been compromised. In most mobile devices, risk from loss of the device that may contain the private key can be mitigated by methods such as PIN-protecting access to the device or terminating mobile service.

Confidentiality and Integrity Through PKI

Almost all valuable transactions require some level of ability to ensure that only the intended parties are privy to the details of the transactions. Furthermore, for sensitive applications, it is imperative that the recipient be aware of whether the message or data was altered. In a PKI-enabled transaction, only the recipient can decode the data; thus, there is a high degree of confidence that the message was not decoded in transit. Integrity is verified through the use of mathematically defined hashing algorithms both before the data is sent and when it is received. If the integrity parameters match, then the data can be said to have maintained integrity.

Non-repudiation Through PKI

Because the assumption in PKI is that the private key is owned by and under the control of only the owner, then all transactions with this key, especially signing functions, prove that the owner has intended and conducted a transaction. This prevents the owner from later refuting that a transaction, for example, a bank withdrawal, has occurred. This level of non-repudiation can be further enhanced through the use of devices such as fingerprint readers, which link the use of the private key to some physical attribute, such as the fingerprint of a person. Mobile devices, due to their form factor (in other words, the shape and size), generally do not take advantage of such technology.

Strategies in Wireless Internet Security

The challenge in the mobile space centers on the fact that the use of PKI requires heavy (relatively) computational ability. Since most mobile devices are optimized for space and battery consumption, the use of standard PKI certificates, as found in the wired world, is not practical. For this reason, the concept of Wireless Transport Layer Security (WTLS) was developed. In addition, the use of the Wireless Application Protocol (WAP) to better address the small display size on a mobile device raises another set of security issues.

WAP Specifications and Security

WAP has become a global standard for presentation and delivery of information and telephony services to mobile devices. Its origin was the WAP Forum, the joint development effort of Ericsson, Nokia, Motorola, and (then) Phone.com. WAP addressed the issue of limited resources, especially the limited size of the display screen, in mobile devices. Web sites have become more and more sophisticated, and it is not possible to display many sites on a mobile device without some type of modification. Wireless Markup Language

(WML), a language based on extensible Markup Language (XML), was developed to enable creation of WAP-compliant web sites. Much like HTML is used in the world of TCP/IP, WML is used in the world of WAP. The initial specifications from the WAP Forum, the main body developing the WAP standard, did not include much security consideration. Later revisions (WAP 1.2) incorporated guidelines on how to address security concerns.

The most important protocol specification for security that the WAP Forum developed is WTLS. WTLS bears some similarity to Transport Layer Security (TLS), the wired world's security protocol specification that provides privacy between two communicating applications using the industry-standard TCP/IP networking protocol.

Wireless Transport Layer Security (WTLS)

WTLS is the security layer in the WAP protocol, similar to the TLS protocol in TCP/IP; however, WTLS has been modified to account for:

- Ability to support connection and datagram protocols.
- Long round-trip times in message communication (up to 10 seconds).
- Dynamic key refreshing
- Low bandwidth (as low as 100 bits per second), processing power, and storage space.

WTLS server certificates were originally defined in WAP 1.1 and are primarily used to validate the identity of a server and provide an encrypted tunnel for subsequent communication. Encrypted tunnels are point-to-point streams of encrypted data. Encrypted tunnels are formed through the use of the public key to encrypt a randomly generated session (symmetric) key that can be exchanged securely and then used for subsequent secure communication. This is something like writing a secret password in a code system, transmitting that coded password, and then having the receiving party decode that phrase to get the password, From that point on, the two parties can use the common password to access the same data. Public-private key technology is more computationally intensive than symmetric encryption. WTLS client certificates, as defined in WAP 1.2, are designed for the client to authenticate itself to the server.

Wireless Markup Language (WML) Script Sign Text

The mobile-world equivalent of HTML in the wired world is WML. To support digital signatures in the wireless worked. The WAP WML Script Sign Text function was developed. This function is part of the WAP Forum-defined cryptographic library. The function defines how a certificate is managed and used.

Wireless Gateways

Wireless gateways (WAP gateways) function as a method of translating HTML to WML so that a feature-rich web site can be simplified for a small display and footprint on a mobile phone. By using a WAP gateway, content providers can write original content using HTTP without worrying about who might access the data. The WAP gateway is then installed to ensure proper, dynamic conversion of that HTTP traffic into WAP traffic.

A wireless gateway is hosted by the network provider or, for high-end content, perhaps the merchant directly (as in some M-commerce enabled bank sites). The choice of who hosts the gateway can influence security policy and controls. This whole concept has given rise to the Wireless Application Service Provider (WASP) market. WASPs provide M-commerce application solutions through a service model, maintaining security and updating software. Some WASPs can host a gateway as well.

The main difference between a wired device and a portable, mobile device lies in the processing and storage capacity of the mobile device. The main functions that are handled differently between wired and wireless systems include generation of keys, storage of keys, and revocation checking of certificates. Another major difference is that most mobile devices do not function with [11]SSL and have to use WTLS (with the exception of the I-mode mobile telephone standard). This requires a PKI gateway to convert a transaction from WTLS to SSL and *vice versa.*

Security Issues in WTLS

As with most protocols, WTLS does have a number of security issues. It is important to note that protocols are simply a roadmap for code developers to follow, and security flaws can occur in the implementation of a protocol. This occurred, for example, in Netscape's implementation of an earlier version of the SSL protocol. Netscape's initial attempts created an implementation flaw that made the Netscape web browser vulnerable to attacks. In later releases, the company fixed the implementation problem. Likewise, the flaws of a protocol may tie mitigated or exacerbated depending on the quality of the

[11] ***NOTE:*** *Transport Layer Security (TLS) and its predecessor, Secure Socket Layer (SSL), are cryptographic protocols that provide security for communications over networks such as the Internet. TLS and SSL encrypt the segments of network connections at the Transport Layer end-to-end. Several versions of the protocols are in widespread use in applications like web browsing, electronic mail, Internet faxing, instant messaging and voice-over-IP (VoIP)*

implementation, We will not discuss all of the possible flaws in this book due to the technical nature and length of discussion; however, we will look at some of the best-known security issues in WTLS, including:

- Weak crypto ciphers
- Null cipher acceptance
- Sequence number weaknesses
- False alert messages

Weak Crypto Ciphers

Earlier versions of WTLS used a 40-bit cipher, which we know today to be very easily broken, thus invalidating any security provided against eavesdropping or sniffing. Later versions of WTLS specifications warn against the use of such a weak cipher; however, due to the need for backward compatibility.

Null Cipher Acceptance

If the implementation of the WTLS protocol accepts null cipher requests (that is, requests without any encryption) without having specifically asked for such requests, the transmission runs the risk of a man-in-the-middle attack. In this type of attack, the attacker poses as both the recipient and sender, without either party knowing. Both sender and recipient then believe that they are sending an encrypted message, yet all traffic is being deciphered and perhaps changed in transit. Later WTLS specifications warned against null cipher acceptance.

Sequence Number Weaknesses

The WTLS protocol uses sequence numbers to identify all data packets associated with a particular session. However, the protocol allows this number not to be used, If the implementation uses this option, then the transmission is subject to playback attacks. Playback attacks are attacks in which a sequence of events is recorded and played back to repeat the original result (for example, logging into a password-protected system). Although higher layers, such as application-level layers, may help mitigate this vulnerability, it is dangerous in a bandwidth- and CPU-constrained environment to rely on any other layer to perform this task.

False Alert Messages

System alert messages under WTLS can be divided into two types: critical and fatal. Whenever a process flags one of these types of errors, the connection between the mobile device and server is broken immediately. Fatal errors force a new session identification and renegotiation of a session. Critical errors may allow future sessions to continue using the same setup parameters. These alerts are meant to give feedback to running applications on the current status.

These alert messages are vulnerable to a denial-of-service attack, where the mobile device and server would not be able to communicate (thus preventing the execution of an M-commerce transaction). A denial-of-service attack is simply a barrage of fake or improper requests directed at the same server, thus tying up the server's resources and preventing legitimate queries from being serviced. An attacker could create false alert messages and, for unencrypted sessions, send alert messages to terminate connections.

WTLS Fixes

The recent version of the WTLS standard does offer a number of fixes over previous versions. However, as is the case with any emerging technology, flaws will be discovered and then addressed later.

Some of the major issues that WTLS addressed in the April 2001 WAP proposal include:

- Increased awareness, through warnings, of various types of attacks to which the protocol is susceptible
- The removal of a particular weak algorithm (SHA_XOR_40)
- Better support for X.509 standards
- Inclusion of more features of elliptical curve cryptographic (ECC), a popular encryption algorithm for mobile devices
- Ability to support stronger RSA algorithms

WAP Versus SIM Toolkit

The subscriber identity module (SIM) toolkit (STK), used in GSM (Global System for Mobile Communications) networks, dominates in Europe and Asia. STK, using SIM, supports communication services, control of the human-machine interface, menu management and application control, and accessory management, among other features. SIM cards through STK, enable the use of personalized menus that provide services offered by the carrier. At present, there is not extensive interoperability between SIM cards from carrier to carrier. Key security advantages of STK for M-commerce applications include the ability to handle public key technology.

Building on the popularity of WAP, WAP 1.2 defines a method for the WAP identity module (WIM). WIM allows authentication of a mobile client. WIM, combined with WTLS, provides strong authentication using WAP. WIM is a tamper-resistant electronic computer chip that can reside in the WAP device or in smartcards. Many devices have slots for such devices. WIM can store critical information such as private and public keys used in initiating and authenticating secure connections.

The use of WIM depends on the penetration of WAP-enabled handsets and mobile devices. Because STKs are available today, they are still popular. Going forward, there will be room for both SIM and WIM (also known as S/WIM) platforms for mobile applications. However, WAP-based technologies will become increasingly used since WAP describes a standard that works across different types of network standards.

Components of Wireless PKI

A traditional PKI system has components to determine the roles of various parties. The basic elements of a wireless PKI system, are slightly modified from those of a wired PKI system. They include:

- A registration authority (RA) that defines who gets a certificate
- A certification authority (CA) that actually generates and issues the digital certificate
- An end entity application (EA), which is the PKI-enabled application that runs in the WAP device on a WIM card
- A directory to store certificates so they can be accessed on demand
- PKI portal that typically acts as the RA and translates requests made by the WAP client to the RA portion and interacts with the CA over the wired network.

The function of a registration authority (RA) is to provide a mechanism for validating an entity's credentials and approving or rejecting the request to receive a digital certificate. The traditional PKI system relies on ASN.1 standards to service requests. These standards are too computationally intensive for mobile devices. Thus, mobile devices use WML and the WML Script Sign Text function.

The modem trend is to use the elliptical curve cryptographic (ECC) function, which can perform encryption and decryption with a smaller bit size (that is, using less computational power) without compromising security strength. Typically, 1,024 bits is considered strong security in the traditional PKI world, whereas equivalent security in ECC is accomplished using only

163 bits. To further increase mobile device efficiencies, wireless PKI (WPKI) certificates are a subset of X.509, with some reduced-length fields in the certificate to conserve resources.

Challenges to Wireless Internet PKI

Although PKI can provide a range of security benefits, limitations of mobile devices force some changes to the standard implementation. We will first discuss how to determine the validity of a certificate and then some of the issues related to the management of WPKI certificates over the Internet.

Control of Revocation of Certificates

One of the fundamental requirements of a well-designed PKI solution is the use of revocation and revocation checking. Imagine if the immigration office revoked a criminal's passport, but never bothered to seize the passport or update computers indicating denial of exit or admission into a particular country. Such lack of enforcement would not limit the movement of the criminal. Likewise, if certificates are issued without the ability to check for revoked certificates, a major security problem occurs. The traditional way to manage this checking in PKI is to use certificate revocation lists (CRLs). [12]CRLs must list all of the revoked certificates for the period of time during which the certificates were originally valid (in most cases, this is up to one year). Obviously, these lists could become quite large, and in the context of mobile devices, even unusable. To address this issue in the world of mobile PKI, WTLS introduced the concept of short-lived certificates. This strategy avoids the use of CRLs.

These short-lived certificates work like this: A master certificate is issued that is valid for, say, a year. Then, based on verification at a wired server, a shorter - term certificate is issued that is valid for, say, a day. Thus, when the master certificate is revoked no short-lived certificates could be issued, thus preventing the use of the certificate. So by limiting exposure to the use of a certificate for a day, we can avoid having to check the validity of the certificate on the mobile device. The validity of the master certificate, however, can be checked because it resides on a fixed or more powerful computer.

Hand-off Between SSL and WTLS

Except for the I-mode mobile phone standard, used in Japan, most wireless PKI solutions must include the use of some type of gateway to translate the

[12] ***NOTE:*** *Certificate Revocation List (CRL) is one of two common methods when using a public key infrastructure for maintaining access to servers in a network. When a potential user attempts to access a server, the server allows or denies access based on the CRL entry for that particular user.*

Internet communication to the wireless portion. The gateway then contains an SSL certificate to identify itself to the rest of the E-commerce servers on the Internet. The gateway also has the ability to issue the WTLS certificate, which is basically a short-term SSL certificate to accommodate mobile devices' various constraints.

The key concern in this architecture is that the gateway is vulnerable (this is sometimes referred to as "the gap in WAP"). In terms of uptime availability, the gateway must be available for the M-commerce service to function. In terms of security, the hand-off by the gateway from SSL to WTLS must be implemented correctly.

We know that the encryption from one side of the WAP gateway must be decrypted, only to be re-encrypted for forwarding onto the Internet, and the opposite situation occurs for communication in the opposite direction. Why is this issue? The gateway is simply a software program. This piece of software may write memory fragments to disk. Should the data being transmitted be written to disk, a hacker may try to obtain this fragment of memory from disk and read its contents. Ideally, such information should never be written to disk, and most gateway solutions take care to avoid such poor security implementations; however, that risk is still there.

To further add to potential risk, unless the M-commerce vendor hosts the gateway directly (as opposed to the mobile service carrier), WAP gateways are usually in an unprotected area of the (carrier's) network called the demilitarized zone, or DMZ. As the costs of gateways drop, more and more M-commerce vendors will host their own gateways in improved security networks. Selection of a gateway should be based on not only feature set, but also the quality of implementation. No one knows when you have good security, but everyone knows when you do not.

The ability to extend confidence through security for mobile devices can be accomplished through the use of public key infrastructure (PKI) technology such as certificates. With mobile versions of these certificates, an adequate solution can be presented to enable authentication, confidentiality, integration, and non-repudiation. The use of PKI technology on mobile devices can enable users to conduct transactions with confidence. This allows application such as financial or other confidential transactions to extend outside a typical enterprise. Furthermore, given that there is legal support for digital signatures in most parts of the world, mobile transactions can be legally binding.

Implementation Issues

Implementation of a PKI infrastructure, especially as a security solution for the M-commerce world, must be approached with careful planning. The key elements in planning include:

- Certificate use (vendor and contents of certificates)
- PKI gateway/portal for translation between the wired and wireless worlds
- Ensuring that the mobile device has the required embedded root certificates
- Ensuring that the mobile device is compatible with the chosen gateway solution and certificate vendor
- Costs, which are typically on a subscription basis for the certificates, but license fees may apply for the gateway and custom development
- Management of certificates for WPKI, which can be easy for low numbers, but will require a separate PKI management system for large numbers.

Security Issues

The use of WAP and WTLS does bring up a number of security issues We will take a look at some of the major issues and highlight some strategies to minimize this risk.

- **Risk:** WAP gateways do pose a small security risk that may be increased or decreased depending on the network architecture and who hosts the gateway.

  Mitigation: Perform rigorous testing of the chosen gateway and understand from the vendor the architecture and method of dealing with the SSL/WTLS translation. Hardening (that is, removing as many known security holes as possible) the machine (UNIX or NT) on which the gateway resides should also mitigate risks.
- **Risk:** Physical security of the gateway and other components.

  Mitigation: Host the WAP gateway onsite, and house the gateway with the same level of security as other data processing systems.
- **Risk:** Physical security of the mobile device.

  Mitigation: Use policy and procedures to ensure whatever protection the mobile device offers (PIN, password, physical locks, and so on). Ensure that backup is performed regularly, and that the user of the mobile device understands the importance of protecting the physical device.

SUMMARY

In this chapter you have gone through:

M-commerce security overview, PKI, Wireless Internet Security strategies, Security issues in WTLS and Challenges to Wireless Internet.

STUDY QUESTIONS

1. Explain the concept of PKI.
2. How PKI technology ensures internet security?
3. Explain the security issues in WTLS.
4. Make a comparative study between WAP and SIM Tool kit.
5. Explain the components of Wireless PKI.

CHAPTER – 6

M-COMMERCE APPLICATIONS

LEARNING OBJECTIVE

In this chapter, we have gone through various application areas of M-commerce. The objective is to introduce the readers to wide applications of M-commerce as an emerging media of commerce:

- M-commerce Application — Overview
- Mobile Application: Financial Tool
- Mobile Applications: Marketing, Advertising, and Customer Service
- Mobile Portals
- Mobile Intra Business and Enterprise Applications
- Mobile B2B and Supply Chain Applications
- Applications of Mobile Devices for Consumers/Industries
- Telecommunication Sectors
- M-commerce Services and Applications
- Horizontal Application Index
- Vertical Application Index
- Mobile Marketing and Advertising
- Service/Retail Sectors
- Information Sector
- Mobile Ticketing
- Content Purchase and Delivery
- Location Based Services
- Playing Games? Wireless Telemedicine
- New and Novel Application Opportunities
- Telemetry Applications
- Twelve Applications of M-commerce? Support for Mobile Employees
- Mobile Entertainment
- Summary
- Study Questions

M-COMMERCE APPLICATION — OVERVIEW

In the current commerce industry, mobile commerce or M-commerce has been entered in finance, services, retails, tele-communication and information technology services. In these sectors, M-commerce is not only being widely accepted but also it is being more used as a popular way of business and commerce. Mobile has a wide application in today's competitive scenario. The applications are mentioned as follows, sector wise.

Vehicles:

- Transmission of news, road condition, etc.
- Adhoc network with near vehicles to prevent accidents.

Emergencies:

- Early transmission of patient data to the hospital.
- Adhoc network in case of earthquakes, cyclones.
- Military.

Travelling Salesmen:

- Direct access to central customer files.
- Consistent databases for all agents.
- Mobile office.

Web Access:

- Outdoor Internet access.
- Intelligent travel guide with up to date location dependent information.

Location Aware Services

- Find services in the local environment, example printer.

Information Services

- Push: example, stock quotes.
- Pull: example, nearest cash ATM.

Disconnected Operations

- Mobile agents, example, shopping.
- Wireless access.

- Alerting services.
- Location services.
- Intranet applications.
- Banking services.
- Web access.

Entertainment

- Adhoc networks for multi user games.
- Mobile Applications in Industry.

Mobile Application: Financial Tool

Mobile Commerce works vastly in finance sector including all big and major financial institutes, banks, stock market and share brokers. Whenever any user needs money or wants any sort of banking and finance related services, he/she can access the services or register services via voice calling or via Short Message Services (SMS) services. WAP based mobile handsets allow the user to access the official website of the institute. User can transact money or transfer money, or pay the bill from its bank account using mobile commerce facilities. Banks also provide round the clock customer care services, which can be used any time through voice calling. Some customer care services, also provide non-voice services on mobile that is known as insta-alert facility. While in the stock market, the user can access the stock market quotes and get in live touch with current trading status on mobile in two forms either voice (customer assistance) or non-voice (SMS alerts) or both. The share broker sends market trends and tips of trading on their clients' mobile. Also broker can suggest the appropriate stock for intra-day trading to their users.

Mobile Banking

A large percentage of banks offer mobile access to financial and account information. The uptake of mobile banking has been minimal. Surveys indicate there is strong latent demand for these offerings that is waiting for the technology and transmission speeds to improve.

- **Wireless Electronic Payment Systems:** Wireless payment systems transform mobile phones into secure, self-contained purchasing tools capable of instantly authorizing payments over the cellular network for goods and services.

- **M-wallet (mobile wallet):** A wireless wallet that enables cardholders to make purchases with a single click from their wireless device.

Mobile Vouchers/Coupons/Loyalty Cards

In combination with POS terminals this technique can be used for distributing vouchers for top up of mobile phone accounts. Advantage of this system is to reduce cost for distribution, main disadvantage is that you need a widely spread network of POS terminals. There are two models present in the market: voucher distribution (PIN based), where hidden recharge number (PIN) is printed on terminal and direct top up, where subscribers number is entered on terminal and recharged automatically.

Source: Courtesy of Nokia, nokia.com.

Fig. 6.1: BILL PAYMENT BY CELLPHONE

As mobile devices become more secure, the main payment methods used to enable mobile commerce are:

- Mobile banking.
- Bill payment services.
- M-brokerage services.
- Mobile money transfers.
- Mobile micropayments.
- Replace ATM's and credit cards.

- Wireless Electronic Payment Systems.
- Mobile phones acts as secure, self-contained purchasing tools capable of instantly authorizing payments.

Types:

- Micropayments
- Wireless wallets (m-Wallet)
- Bill payments

Examples:

- Swedish Postal Bank
  - Check Balances/Make Payments and Conduct some transactions.
- Dagens Industri
  - Receive Financial Data and Trade on Stockholm Exchange.
- Citibank
  - Access balances, pay bills and transfer funds using SMS.

MOBILE APPLICATIONS: MARKETING, ADVERTISING AND CUSTOMER SERVICE

Wireless Advertising

There is no doubt that advertising industry is extremely excited about the prospect of reaching high-income earners anywhere and everywhere in order to promote the products and services of its sponsors. As soon as the word got out of market research companies like ARC, Strategy Analytics, Gartner and Forrester that there will be billion plus cellular phones in the hands of consumers soon, they have been thinking aloud as to how wonderful it would be to send promotional message to these phones. Wireless internet makes this technically feasible. Mobile Info thinks that there are more perils and dangers in wishful thinking of the wireless advertising executives than the potential benefits to consumers and businesses. In our view, in the first phase of evolution of our industry, primary use of cellular phones was for critical communication with business and personal contacts. Now, cellular mode of communication has become more pervasive and has gone beyond purely critical and urgent mode. It is a matter of convenience and routine communication. From consumer and business professionals' perspective, cellular communication should be personal and private with full control left between the caller and called party with the network only providing an infrastructure to conduct this communication. We cannot use the analogy of fixed wire line networks where telemarketing personnel use an essentially-free service to promote their products and services. When people are mobile and away from their fixed place of work or residence, they are less prepared to receive unsolicited calls much less advertising messages. By well-established notions of our society and business conduct, use of wireless advertising would be intrusion into personal and business privacy, unless the recipient has agreed to receive this message. Mobile marketing is an emerging concept, but the speed with which it's growing its roots is remarkable. Mobile marketing is highly responsive sort of marketing campaign, especially from brands' experience point of view. And almost all brands are getting higher campaign response rates. Corporations are now using M-commerce to expand everything from services to marketing and advertisement. Although there are currently very few regulations on the use and abuses of mobile commerce, this will change in the next few years. With the increased use of M-commerce comes increased security. Cell phone companies are now spending more money to protect their customers and their information from online intrusions and hackers.

Advertisements can also be location sensitive, informing a user about various ongoing special sales in shops, malls. SMS messages or short paging messages can be used to deliver these ads to cell phones and pagers, respectively. For example, in Singapore, thousands of people subscribe to the free minutes in exchange, for listening to the ads. Future of wireless advertising Wireless advertising initiatives to date have all been "trials". Wireless ads will be incorporated with other advertising media.

Mobile Portals

Mobile Banking

Banks and other financial institutions are exploring the use of M-commerce to allow their customers to not only access account information, but also make transactions, example, purchasing stocks, remitting money, via mobile phones and other mobile equipment. This service is often referred to as Mobile Banking or m-Banking. More negative issues like ID theft, phishing and pharming are lurking when it comes to mobile banking, particularly done on the mobile web. Net security technology free from redundancy and paradigm shifts away from mobile web-based banking will be an optimal solution to mobile banking in the near future.

Mobile Brokerage

Stock market services offered via mobile devices have also become more popular and are known as Mobile Brokerage. They allow the subscriber to react to market developments in a timely fashion and irrespective of their physical location.

Auctions

Over the past three years mobile reverse auction solutions have grown in popularity. Unlike traditional auctions, the reverse auction (or low-bid auction) bills the consumer's phone each time they place a bid. Many mobile PSMS commerce solutions rely on a one-time purchase or one-time subscription; however, reverse auctions are high return applications as they allow the consumer to transact over a long period of time.

Mobile Purchase

Mobile purchase allows customers to shop online at any time in any location. Customers can browse and order products while using a cheap, secure payment method. Instead of using paper catalogues, retailers can send customers a list of products that the customer would be interested in, directly to their mobile device or consumers can visit a mobile version of a retailer's E-commerce site. Additionally, retailers will also be able to track customers at all times and notify them of discounts at local stores that the customer would be interested in. New technology from companies like Shop Text allow consumers to purchase products from their cell phones using text messaging and technology from companies like mshopper and mPoria allow retailers to launch their own mobile commerce shopping sites.

- "A customer interaction channel that aggregates content and services for mobile users." Charge per time for service or subscription based.

  Example: I-Mode in Japan

MOBILE INTRA BUSINESS AND ENTERPRISE APPLICATIONS

Support of Mobile Employees by 2005, 25% of all workers could be mobile employees sales people in the field, traveling executives, telecommuters, consultants working on-site, repair or installation employees need same corporate data as those working inside company's offices.

- **Solution:** wireless devices.
- **Wearable devices:** cameras, screen, keyboard, touch-panel display.

Mobile B2B and Supply Chain Applications

Mobile computing solutions enable organizations to respond faster to supply chain disruptions by proactively adjusting plans or shifting resources related to critical supply chain events as they occur.

- Accurate and timely information.
- Opportunity to collaborate along supply chain.
- Must integrate mobile devices into information exchanges.

Example: "telemetry" integration of wireless communications, vehicle monitoring systems, and vehicle location devices lead to reduced overhead and faster service responsiveness (vending machines).

Supply Chain Applications

Mobile computing solutions enable organizations to:

- Respond faster to supply chain disruptions.
- Proactive adjustment of plans or shifting resources related to critical supply chain events as they occur.
- Wireless telemetry is an integrated messaging system that combines.
- Wireless communications.
- Vehicle monitoring systems.
- Vehicle location devices.
- Technology enables.
- Large-scale automation of data capture.
- Improved billing timeliness and accuracy.
- Reduced overhead associated with the manual alternative.
- Increased customer satisfaction through service responsiveness.

Applications of Mobile Devices for Consumers/Industries

- Personal Service Applications.
  - ❖ Example Airport
- Mobile Gaming and Gambling.
- Mobile Entertainment.
  - ❖ Music and Video

- Hotels.
- Intelligent Homes and Appliances.
- Wireless Telemedicine.
- Other Services for Consumers.

TELECOMMUNICATION SECTORS

Mobile has played a giant role in communication technology through its versatility and superiority. The ubiquity and easy usage has further made it extremely popular across the globe. It has already surpassed the fixed phone in the world. Software platform is essential for operating any mobile and this tool has revolutionized the communication world because of its functioning as a small computer. The booming popularity has forced the corporate world to develop a new commerce platform that can reach to the masses. Mobile commerce has attracted massive traffic because of its unique characteristics. The user can change the service of any financial institute or banks if, he gets a better product and service or user is unsatisfied with the service of the subscribing company. Besides this, several bills can be paid using mobile and user can also check the available balance, the status of cheques, the status of requested processing and customer care support. Several dealings can be handled through mobile phones.

Mobile Payment for M-commerce

- Mobile payment can be offered as a stand-alone service.
- Mobile payment could also be an important enabling service for other M-commerce services (example mobile ticketing, shopping, gambling).
- It could improve user acceptance by making the services more secure and user-friendly.
- In many cases offering mobile payment methods is the only chance the service providers have to gain revenue from an M-commerce service.
- The consumer must be informed of:
  - ❖ What is being bought?
  - ❖ How much to pay? And
  - ❖ Options to pay:

The payment must be made, payments must be traceable.

- Customer requirements:
  - ❖ A larger selection of merchants with whom they can trade.
- A more consistent payment interface when making the purchase with multiple payment schemes, like:
  - ❖ Credit Card payment.
  - ❖ Bank Account/Debit Card payment.
- Merchant benefits:
  - ❖ Brands to offer a wider variety of payment.
  - ❖ Easy-to-use payment interface development.
- Bank and financial institution benefits
  - ❖ To offer a consistent payment interface to consumers and merchants.

M-COMMERCE SERVICES AND APPLICATIONS

- Information-based services: Instant messaging, e-mail, searching for a movie or restaurant using a cell phone or handheld PDA.
- Transaction-based services: Purchasing stocks, concert tickets, music, or games; searching for the best price for an item using a cell phone and buying it in a physical store or on the Web.
- Personalized services: Services that anticipate what a customer wants based on that person's location or data profile, such as updated airline flight information or beaming coupons for nearby restaurants.

While most of the success with mobile computing has, so far, been in the vertical industries, there are now a number of horizontal mobile computing applications that have become very popular among end-users, and within all enterprises, large and small, across various vertical industries. Proliferation of the Internet and increasing reliance on the e-mail as the preferred method of communication has made wireless e-mail as a killer application. In fact, there is more activity in the internet-based horizontal application market now than ever before.

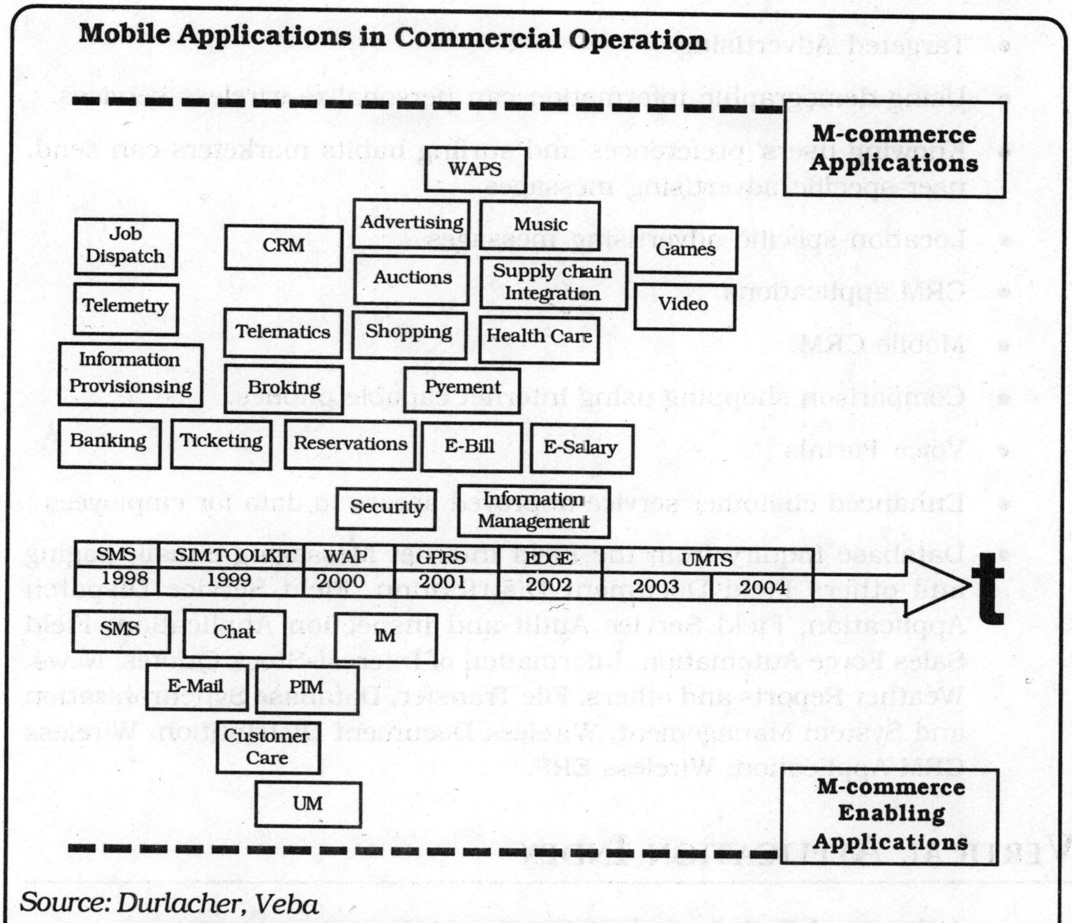

Fig. 6.2: MOBILE APPLICATION IN COMMERCIAL OPERATION

HORIZONTAL APPLICATION INDEX

- Shopping from Wireless Devices.
- Have access to services similar to those of wire line shoppers.
- Shopping carts.
- Price comparisons.
- Order status.
- Future.
- Will be able to view and purchase products using handheld mobile devices.

- Targeted Advertising.
- Using demographic information can personalize wireless services.
- Knowing users' preferences and surfing habits marketers can send, user-specific advertising messages.
- Location-specific advertising messages.
- CRM applications.
- Mobile CRM.
- Comparison shopping using Internet capable phones.
- Voice Portals
- Enhanced customer service improved access to data for employees
- Database inquiry from the Field Internet Messaging-e-mail, paging and others Field Document Distribution, Field Service Dispatch Application, Field Service Audit and Inspection Application, Field Sales Force Automation, Information of Interest-Stock Quotes, News, Weather Reports and others, File Transfer, Database Synchronization and System Management, Wireless Document Distribution, Wireless CRM Application, Wireless ERP.

Vertical Application Index

- Airline and Railway Industries.
- Airline Applications.
- Railway Applications.
- Construction Industry.
- Crew Card Data Collection.
- Site Inspection and Project Status Reporting.
- Distribution Industry.
- Warehouse Inventory Applications.
- Electronic News Communication.
- Electronic News Applications.
- Financial Industry.
- Banking and Financial Institutions.

- Healthcare Industry.
- Hospitality Industry.
- Hospitality Industry Applications.
- Manufacturing and Mining Industries.
- Manufacturing and Mining Applications.
- Miscellaneous Industry Applications.
- Automated Toll Collection.
- Public Sector.
- Emergency Services.
- Retail Industry.
- Transportation Industry.

SERVICE/RETAIL SECTORS

Service and Retail sectors are also among the leading sectors, which have nurtured most from mobile commerce. M-commerce has proved a major boon for these sectors. Several business dealings no matter how big or small are being finalized on the mobile phone. A Customer would be able to book the order, can hire carrier/courier services and above all, could also pay the dues related to it through mobile.

INFORMATION SECTOR

After the bursting of dotcom bubble, E-commerce has gone downwards to hell. But the evolution of M-commerce has again worked as ambrosia for them. A separate sector has been evolved to exercise on this field for the IT experts. The webmasters have skillfully exploited this new area of IT-enabled commerce. In the IT field, mobile commerce has been used massively to deliver financial news, stock updates, sports figures and traffic updates and many more on to a single handheld device 'mobile'.

Information Services

Accessing Information

Mobile Portal aggregates and provides content and services for mobile users that include news, sports, e-mail, entertainment, travel and restaurant information, community services and stock trading. Voice Portal is a Web site with an audio interface and can also be accessed through a standard or cell phone. A wide variety of information services can be delivered to mobile phone users in much the same way as it is delivered to PCs. These services include:

- News services.
- Stock data.
- Sports results.
- Financial records.
- Traffic data and information.

Particularly, more customized traffic information, based on Users' travel patterns, will be multicast on a differentiated basis, instead of broadcasting the same news and data to all Users. This type of multicasting will be suited for more bandwidth-intensive mobile equipment.

MOBILE TICKETING

Tickets can be sent to mobile phones using a variety of technologies including [14]bCODE and NFC. Users are then able to use their tickets immediately by presenting their phones at the venue. Recently, WiMAX-enabled dash top mobile payment platforms made a debut, ID on kiosk keypads at the entrance of ballparks, airports, train stations instead of physical tickets, but this dash top mobile equipment will take some years to get commercially implemented. The travel industry is realizing the potential benefits of M-commerce, and is working on technologies that will eventually equal the ratio of bCode and [15]NFC, update customers on flight status, notify them when this information changes and will offer to make new arrangements based on preset user preferences requiring no input from the user. Therefore, a customer's entire trip can be scheduled and maintained using a mobile device. Mobile ticketing for airports, ballparks, and train stations, for example, will not only streamline unexpected metropolitan traffic surges, but also help users remotely secure parking spots (even while in their vehicles) and greatly facilitate mass surveillance at transport hubs.

Mobile delivery enables:

- Economy of scale.

---

[14] *NOTE: A bCODE is an identifier that can be sent to a mobile phone/device and used as a ticket/ voucher/identification or other type of token. The bCODE is an SMS message that can be read electronically from the screen of a mobile device.*

[15] *NFC-Near Field Communication or NFC, is a short-range high frequency wireless communication technology which enables the exchange of data between devices over about a 10 centimetre (around 4 inches) distance.*

- Quicker and easier delivery.
- Effective target marketing.
- Privacy-friendly data mining on consumer behavior.
- Environment-friendly and resources-saving efficiency.

Content Purchase and Delivery

Currently, mobile content purchase and delivery mainly consists of the sale of ring-tones, wallpapers and games for mobile phones. The convergence of mobile phones, mp3 players and video players into a single device will result in an increase in the purchase and delivery of full-length music tracks and video. Download speeds, if increased to 4G levels, will make it possible to buy a movie on a mobile device in a couple of seconds, while on the go. A new online shopping trend of "booking on the web for pickup later in stores" is evolving into a new concept: Just In Time (JIT) pickup for mobile shopping behind the wheel. This JIT pickup for mobile shopping indicates a "real-time bridge between virtual world and real world".

Location Based Services

Unlike a home PC, the location of the mobile phone user is an important piece of information used during mobile commerce transactions. Knowing the location of the user allows for location based services such as:

Local maps.

Local offers.

Local weather.

People tracking and monitoring.

Location-based Applications

- Shopping from Wireless Devices - online vendors allow customers to shop from wireless devices.
- Location-based Advertising is when marketers know the current locations and preferences of mobile users; they can send user-specific advertising messages to wireless devices about nearby shops, malls and restaurants.
- Location-based Services provide information to customers about local services and conditions via cell phones.

Playing Games

Cellular carriers, card companies, and transaction processors need to provide consumers with a more compelling reason to embrace M-commerce. Contrary to popular belief, that does not necessarily mean expanding the base of merchants through which consumers can buy goods or services using their mobile phones. Instead, it means persuading U.S. consumers to view their mobile phones as a technology platform that can deliver content, allow them to surf the Internet, communicate with others using text messaging, and make purchases, rather than merely as telephones. With more than 1 billion cell phones in use today the potential audience for mobile games is substantially larger than the market for other platforms. Games can be programmed directly into the phone's chipset and shipped with the phone. WAP games are played by accessing the game provider's mobile or Web portal.

Wireless Telemedicine

Telemedicine is the use of modern telecommunications and information technologies for the provision of clinical care to individuals located at a distance and for the transmission of information to provide that care.

Storing and transferring digital images from one location to another.

Allowing a patient in one location to consult with a medical specialist in another in real time through videoconferencing.

Using robots to perform remote surgery, in most cases, the patient is in a rural area and the specialist is in an urban area.

Wireless technology has advanced the ways in which prescriptions are filled.

Mobile communications has provided a valuable telemedicine application for emergency situations that arise during airplane flights.

The storage and forwarding of digital images from one location to another. Videoconferencing used for real-time consultation with a patient in one location and a medical specialist in another.

New and novel application opportunities:

- On wearable heart monitors linked to cell phones
- Portable devices that transmit the vital signs of avalanche victims

- Mobile communications used to attend to medical emergencies occurring on planes
- Mobile [16]telesurgery applications that enable surgeons in one location to remotely control robotic arms for surgery in another location

TELEMETRY APPLICATIONS

Telemetry is the wireless transmission and receipt of data gathered from remote sensors.

- Technicians can use telemetry to identify maintenance problems in equipment;
- Doctors can monitor patients and control medical equipment from a distance;
- Car manufacturers use telemetry for remote vehicle diagnosis and preventive maintenance.

Current applications.

- Conduct online transactions.
- Make purchases.
- Trade stocks.
- Send e-mail.

Future applications

- A wireless office, where computers, phones and other office equipment are all networked without cables.

TWELVE APPLICATIONS OF M-COMMERCE

- Mobile financial applications (B2C, B2B).
- Mobile advertising (B2C).
- Mobile inventory management (B2C, B2B).
- Proactiveservice management (B2C, B2B).
- Product locating and shopping (B2C, B2B).

---

[16] ***NOTE:*** *Telesurgery is a new approach to surgical care in which a surgeon performs operations using a surgical robot and advanced computer technology on a patient located miles away.*

- Wireless re-engineering (B2C, B2B).
- Mobile auction or reverse auction (B2C).
- Mobile entertainment services (B2C).
- Mobile office (B2C).
- Mobile distance education (B2C).
- Wireless data center (B2C, B2B).
- Mobile music/music-on-demand (B2C).

Support for Mobile Employees

Mobile employees need the same corporate data available to employees working inside the company's offices.

Wearable devices: Mobile wireless computing devices for employees who work on buildings and other difficult-to-climb places.

Examples of wearable devices

- Cameras
- Screen
- Keyboard
- Touch-panel display

Job Dispatch

No Voice mobile services can be used to assign jobs to mobile employees, along with detailed information about the task.

- Target areas
- Transportation
- Taxis
- Utilities
- Field services
- Health care
- Security

Class of Applications	Example
Mobile financial applications (B2C, B2B)	Banking, brokerage and payments for mobile users
Mobile advertising (B2C)	Sending user-specific and location-sensitive advertisements to users
Mobile inventory management (B2C, B2B)	Location tracking of goods, boxes, troops, and People
Proactive service management (B2C, B2B)	Transmission of information related to distributing components to vendors
Product locating and shopping (B2C, B2B)	Locating/ordering certain items from a mobile device
Wireless reengineering (B2C, B2B)	Improvement of business services
Mobile auction or reverse auction (B2C)	Services for customers to buy or sell certain items
Mobile entertainment Services (B2C)	Video-on-demand and other services to a mobile user
Mobile office (B2C)	Working from traffic jams, airport, and conferences
Mobile distance education (B2C) Wireless data center (B2C, B2B)	Taking a class using streaming audio and video Information can be downloaded by mobile users/vendors
Mobile music/music-on-demand (B2C)	Downloading and playing music using a mobile device

Source: U. Varshney and R. Vetter, "Recent Advances in Wireless Networking," IEEE Computer, June 2000.@ 2000 IEEE.

Mobile Entertainment

The availability of portable MP3 players has lead to the development of music devices integrated with mobile phones. With higher bandwidth, music vendors can offer instant delivery of songs from their music libraries for online purchase. Handset vendors have cell phones that enable users to send pictures from one device to another. As the 3G handsets hit the market, mobile devices will begin to support the downloading and real-time playback of audio and video clips.

SUMMARY

In this chapter, you have gone through different application area of M-commerce. After going through this chapter, be sure that the following facts are well versed.

- M-commerce Application-Overview.
- Mobile Application: Financial Tool

- Mobile Applications: Marketing, Advertising and Customer Service Mobile Portals.
- Mobile Intra business and Enterprise Applications.
  Mobile B2B and Supply Chain Applications.
- Applications of Mobile Devices for Consumers/Industries.
- Telecommunication Sectors Applications.
- M-commerce Services and Applications.
- Horizontal Application Index.
- Vertical Application Index.
- Information Sector Applications.
- Location Based Services.
- Wireless Telemedicine.
- New and Novel application opportunities.
- Telemetry Applications.
- Twelve applications of M-commerce.
- Mobile Entertainment Applications.

STUDY QUESTIONS

1. Discuss the different application areas of M-commerce.
2. Focus on the application of M-commerce in area of Finance.
3. Explain the application of M-commerce in field of Marketing.
4. Enlist the different Mobile portals.
5. Describe the commercial operation of M-commerce.
6. Enlist the Horizontal Application Index of M-commerce.
7. Enlist the Vertical Application Index of M-commerce.
8. Explain the twelve application area of M-commerce.
9. Explain in brief the following:
   (a) Blue tooth
   (a) M-commerce application in entertainment & games
   (b) Telecommunication sector application of M-commerce.
   (c) Information Sector Applications.
   (d) Wireless Telemedicine Applications.
   (e) Telemetry Applications.

CHAPTER – 7

L-COMMERCE

LEARNING OBJECTIVE

In this chapter, we go through the advancement in M-commerce, that is L-commerce. The objective is to introduce the readers the concept of L-commerce and its application in business.

- Introduction
- Necessary Location-Based and Network Technologies
- Barriers to L-commerce
- L-commerce Technologies
- Objective
- Origin and Evolution
- Technology and Infrastructure
- Impact on the Business World
- Pros and Cons
- Summary
- Study Questions

INTRODUCTION

Location-based commerce (L-commerce): M-commerce transactions targeted to individuals in specific locations, at specific times

L-commerce Offers:

- Convenience.
- Safety.
- Productivity.

L-commerce basic services revolve around five key areas:

1. Location.
2. Navigation.
3. Tracking.
4. Mapping.
5. Timing.

NECESSARY LOCATION-BASED AND NETWORK TECHNOLOGIES

- Position Determining Equipment (PDE).
- Mobile Positioning Center (MPC).
- Location-based technology.
- Geographic content.

Location-specific Content

Global positioning system (GPS): A wireless system that uses satellites to enable users to determine their position anywhere on the earth.

GPS handsets can be:

- Stand-alone units.
- Plugged into a mobile device or completely embedded in one.

Geographical information system (GIS): System that integrates GPS data onto digitized map displays.

Wireless 911 (e-911): Calls from cellular phones to providers of emergency services.

[17]Automatic crash notification (ACN): Device that automatically sends the police the location of a vehicle that has been involved in a crash.

Telematics: The integration of computers and wireless communications to improve information flow using the principles of telemetry.

BARRIERS TO L-COMMERCE

- Accuracy.
- The cost-benefit justification.
- The bandwidth of GSM network.
- Invasion of privacy.

Accuracy: Less expensive but less accurate technologies can be used instead to find an approximate location.

The cost-benefit justification: The benefits of L-commerce do not justify the price of the hardware or the inconvenience and time required to utilize the service.

The bandwidth of GSM network: will be improved as 3G technology spreads.

Providing Location Based Services Involves Several Technologies:

Position Determining Equipment (PDE) identifies location of mobile device, Mobile Positioning Center (MPC), a server that manages the location info from PDE. Geographic Information System (GIS) geographic contents consists of streets, road maps, addresses, and points of interest. Location-specific content used in conjunction with geographic content to provide the location of particular services.

---

17. ***NOTE:*** Telecommunications, automotive and location definition technologies are now converging to make instant and automatic notification of serious vehicle collisions to emergency call centers possible. ACN systems employ wireless telecommunication technologies to immediately alert an emergency call center when a crash victim presses the car's Mayday button or the car's air bag deploys.

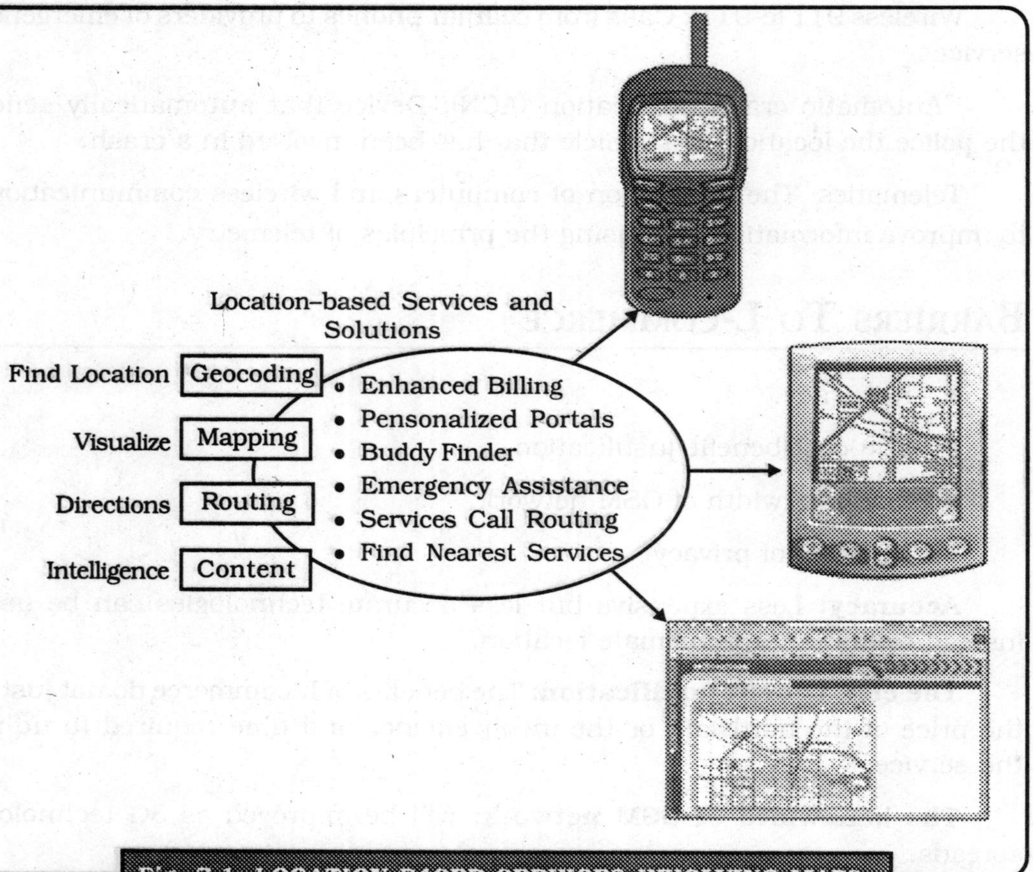

Fig. 7.1: LOCATION BASED SERVICES INVOLVING MAPS

Pervasive computing: Invisible, everywhere computing that is embedded in the objects around us. Also know as:

- ***Ubiquitous Computing***

Ubiquitous computing (ubicomp) is a post-desktop model of human-computer interaction in which information processing has been thoroughly integrated into everyday objects and activities. In the course of ordinary activities, someone "using" ubiquitous computing engages many computational devices and systems simultaneously, and may not necessarily even be aware that they are doing so. This model is usually considered an advancement from the desktop paradigm.

- ***Embedded Computing***

An embedded system is a computer system designed to perform one or a few dedicated functions often with real-time computing constraints. It is embedded as part of a complete device often including hardware and mechanical parts. By contrast, a general-purpose computer, such as a personal computer (PC), is designed to be flexible and to meet a wide range of end-user needs. Embedded systems control many devices in common use today. Embedded systems are controlled by one or more main processing cores that are typically either microcontrollers or digital signal processors (DSP). The key characteristic, however, is being dedicated to handle a particular task, which may require very powerful processors. For example, air traffic control systems may usefully be viewed as embedded, even though they involve mainframe computers and dedicated regional and national networks between airports and radar sites.(Each radar probably includes one or more embedded systems of its own) Since the embedded system is dedicated to specific tasks, design engineers can optimize it to reduce the size and cost of the product and increase the reliability and performance. Some embedded systems are mass-produced, benefiting from economies of scale.

- ***Augmented Computing***

Augmented computing is a term for a live direct or indirect view of a physical real-world environment whose elements are *augmented* by virtual computer-generated imagery. It is related to a more general concept called mediated reality in which a view of reality is modified (possibly even diminished rather than augmented) by a computer.

Radio frequency identification (RFID): Generic term for technologies that use radio waves to automatically identify individual items.

- Properties of pervasive computing.
- Invisible device.
- Embedded microchips.
- Always on.
- Ubiquitous network.
- Life-enhancing applications.
- Consumer-centric solutions.
- Increasing productivity.
- Long-term vision.
- Technical foundation of pervasive computing.
- Everyday objects have to contain embedded microprocessors.
- A ubiquitous network is needed to connect these microprocessors.

- The microprocessors must be able to communicate with the ubiquitous network.
- Pervasive Computing: Applications.

Smart homes — home automation systems support:

- Lighting.
- Energy management.
- Water control.
- Home security and communications.
- Home theater.
- Smart appliances.

The recent developments of mobile, ubiquitous and pervasive technologies have generated a wide range of opportunities for enhancing physical marketplaces and for pushing traditional commerce beyond physical locations of stores, restaurants, and shopping malls. Wireless and mobile peer-to-peer technology is becoming the facilitator for new ambient location-based commerce, also frequently referred to as L-commerce. L-commerce is a fusion of mobile commerce and context aware computing. It exploits consumers' proximity to marketplaces by electronically extending the stores' physical area to cover potential customers before they walk into stores. The virtual expansion of the marketplace has the potential of being a powerful tool for consumers by providing information and services relevant to their current location. Once a customer is inside the store, ambient services can further enhance consumers' shopping experiences by providing consumers with recommendations and other helpful product information. Ambient commerce services allow personalization and custom context-sensitive filtering to consumers.

L-commerce (Location Commerce) is a type of M-commerce. It is based on the location of customers or sellers. L-commerce includes those applications in which a customer can access products, services, advertisements, etc., from his Internet enabled mobile device. Sellers can use these applications to locate the areas where they can market their products or services. L-commerce is the practice of using technologies which provide location information, such as GPS, for business purposes. An example of L-commerce would be to allow cell phone users to find the nearest restaurant to their current location. The term is related to business based on internet technology (E-commerce), based on mobile technology (M-commerce), or based on voice recognition technology (v-commerce). Although this concept reflects the current trend towards individualized and flexible consumerism, privacy concerns have been raised about using a consumer's location in marketing and sales. L-commerce (or Location Commerce) is an evolving marketing and commercial technology that is a mix of mobile commerce and context aware computing. The L-commerce is based on the exploitation of the potential customer's proximity to the marketplaces by first identifying their presence by some identification mechanism electronically and sending a message to their mobile phones thereby in a way extending the shops' physical area even before they enter the buying areas. Technically, the L-commerce is feasible by use of the wireless and mobile peer-to-peer technology along with some recognized technology for enabling LBS (Location Based Service) such as the GPS (Global Positioning System). Beside the GPS, other technologies could be the network based positioning and typically depending upon the various means of triangulation of the signal from cell sites serving a mobile phone. business applications such as location-sensitive billing, traffic updates, fleet management and asset and people tracking. Since the technology to track location is a strategic asset of wireless carriers therefore, this can be leveraged for L-commerce as a VAS (Value-added Service) and also can provide the mobile network operator with a business model based on the differentiation adding to his profitability.

Furthermore, the serving cell site can be used to fix the location of the user to access for messaging or communication. In addition, the GIS (Geographic Information System) can be used to manage point-of-interest data such as location of gas stations, restaurants, repair centers, nightclubs, etc. Since, generally the GIS information also includes information about the radio frequency characteristics of the mobile network, it can facilitate identifying the serving cell site of the user.

Often the potential customers, who are mobile, require personalized information services that are location based. For example there can be a user of the WAP (Wireless Application Protocol) based phone who is in search of an auto repair workshop in the vicinity of his current location, the LBS application using a GIS database and GPS system can track the user's location and provide with a list of auto repair workshops within the proximity to the mobile user. As an extension to L-commerce, the Location Based Services (LBS) can be used for the emergency purposes as well as the enhanced. Location Based Commerce (L-commerce) is M-commerce transactions targeted to individuals in specific locations, at specific times. L-commerce offers the following to consumers and businesses: Safety, Convenience, and Productivity.

L-COMMERCE TECHNOLOGIES

- **Position Determining Equipment** (PDE). This equipment identifies the location of the mobile device.
- **Mobile Positioning Center** (MPC). The MPC is a server that manages the location information sent from the PDE.
- **Location Based Technology** could present a list of addresses of nearby restaurants based on the position of the caller, local street maps, and an electronic database of businesses listed by location.
- **Geographic Content** consists of streets, road maps, addresses, routes, landmarks, and the like.
- **Location Specific Content** is used in conjunction with the geographic content to provide the location of particular services.

Global positioning system (GPS) is a wireless system that uses satellites to enable users to determine their position anywhere on the earth. GPS handsets can be stand-along units for applications such as tracking buses, tracking trucks on the roads, or finding a location in the outdoors."Location-Based Commerce" (L-commerce) refers to the localization of products and services through mobile commerce and context aware computing technologies. L-commerce revolves around 5 key service areas:

Location: determining the basic position of a person or a thing.

Navigation: plotting a route from one location to another.

Tracking: monitoring the movement of a person or a thing.

Mapping: creating maps of specific geographical locations.

Timing: determining the precise time at a specific location.

OBJECTIVE

As the technology improves, our day-to-day life has been affected dramatically; it changed the way we used to work, to shop, to do business and many more. This results on the introduction of a new type of business, L-commerce, which emphasizes the idea of tracking where the end user is, and find the most suitable information for the user's request. The report will describe L-commerce by look at the origin and evolution on the Location-based service, the technology and infrastructure behind it, the potential impact it brings upon the business world, and the pros and cons of this new technology. The examples of the impact on the business world will be focused on B2G and B2B categories of business.

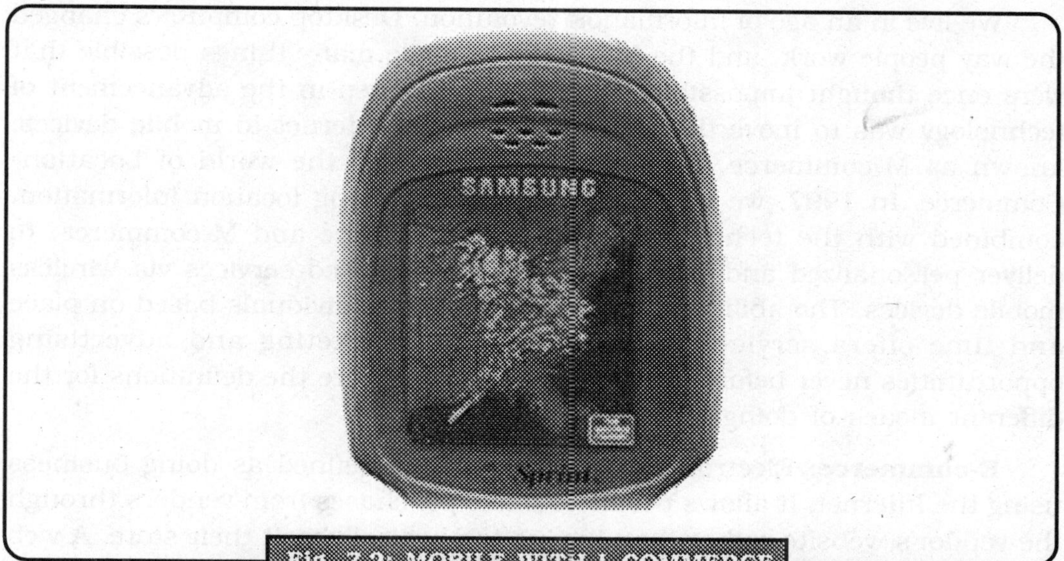

Fig. 7.2: MOBILE WITH L-COMMERCE

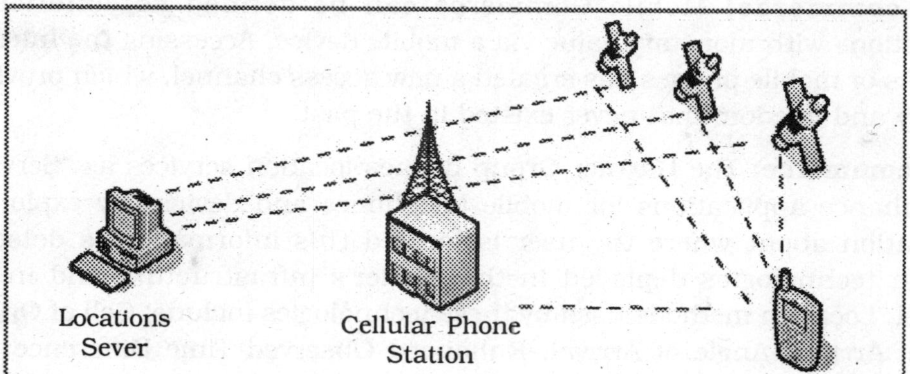

Fig. 7.3: GPS SYSTEM

Origin and Evolution

We live in an age of information revolution. Desktop computers changed the way people work, and the Internet has made many things possible that were once thought impossible. The next logical step in the advancement of technology was to move the convenience of the Internet to mobile devices, known as M-commerce. From there, we move to the world of Location-Commerce. In 1997, we introduced the idea of using location information, combined with the technology used by E-commerce and M-commerce, to deliver personalized and time-sensitive Internet-based services via wireless mobile devices. The ability to specifically contact individuals based on place and time offers service providers targeted marketing and advertising opportunities never before available. The following are the definitions for the different modes of doing business electronically.

E-commerce: Electronic Commerce can be defined as doing business using the Internet. It allows people to make purchases from vendors through the vendor's website rather than having to physically visit their store. A web page displays the goods and offers the user a means of payment for them. Credit cards are the standard means of payment online.

M-commerce: Mobile Commerce can be defined as conducting transactions with monetary value via a mobile device. Accessing the Internet via PDAs or mobile phones has created a new access channel, which provides mobility and freedom that never existed in the past.

L-commerce: The Gartner Group defines location services as "Services that enhance applications for mobile telephones and devices by exploiting information about where the user is located.This information is detected through technologies deployed in the carrier's infrastructure and in the handset. Location methods used by these technologies include; Cell of Origin, Time of Arrival, Angle of Arrival, Enhanced Observed Time Difference and Global Positioning System."

Technology and Infrastructure

There are 3 major technical components involved in L-commerce; mobile phones, the Internet and GIS (Geographical Information System). Each one holds part of the key to the functioning of location-based services (LBS). A Geographical Information System has two essential parts; it has positions and information specific to these positions. Knowing a customer's position is at the heart of L-commerce and this is the information that GIS technologies can provide. Ideally a GIS needs to be able to receive a position and return any data related to that position. In the case of L-commerce, a customer looks for a specific type of service and along with his request he sends his position. The GIS takes both pieces of information into consideration when performing its' search and return details specific to both the user's request and position with the aid of the GPS (Global Positioning System). The global positioning system is essentially a constellation of 24 satellites in geosynchronous orbit. This system was developed, and is run, by the US Department of Defense.

The idea behind the system is that each satellite transmits its own position exactly, along with an approximation of the positions of each of the other satellites in the system. Another option involves the service provider finding the position of the phone through means other than GPS. One such way to do this is Cell of Origin (COO). This method simply involves using the home location of the cell phone as recorded in the service provider's database as the approximate position of the phone. Since COO is not very precise, Time of Arrival (TOA) can be used instead. For TOA, at least three towers get a signal from a cell phone, and due to their different positions they get this signal at slightly different times. With this information, the system can calculate the approximate location of the handset.

So by converting a web-enabled mobile phone into a GPS receiver it is possible for the phone to "know" its location in the world. It can then append this position to any requests it makes of the GIS and receive results pertinent to its position rather than all results that match the request. The following diagram shows the transactions in detail. From the above architecture of the LBS, we can see after the request has been generated from the mobile phones, it passes through the gateway and reaches to the LCS (Location Commerce Service) block where the request and the mobile user's location is converted to MLP (Mobile Location Protocol) messages. The MLP message is then transferred to the LBS (Location-Based Service) system.The LBS then handles the retrieving of related information for the request from the different data sources show on the right most side of the diagram. The information then sent back to the LCS block. After the LCS organized the information, they'll be displayed as small HTML pages on the end user's mobile phone.

Impact on the Business World

Obviously, being mobile and able of accessing the information easily at any time, L-commerce had brought significant impact on the business world. Let's look at a B2G example that occurs in our current business environment – Location Based Service Provider with the US Government Department. The Federal Communication Commission (FCC) in the USA had granted and urged to deploy the Enhanced 911 (E911) rules to improve the effectiveness and reliability of wireless 911 services by providing 911 dispatchers with additional information on wireless 911 calls. Traditionally, when 911 is dialed, it does not have an efficient communication between the 911 call center and the hospitals, police or fire departments. This causes a significant threat towards the emergency service system, since they are dealing with human lives every day. E911 provides the connection between the call center and the LBSP, once 911 is dialed, the call center can easily trace the position of the call, where are the nearest hospitals, police or fire departments, and automatically contacts them. "The wireless E911 program is divided into two parts - Phase I and Phase II. Phase I requires carriers, upon appropriate request by a local Public Safety Answering Point (PSAP), to report the telephone number of a wireless 911 caller and the location of the antenna that received the call. Phase II requires wireless carriers to provide far more precise location information, within 50 to 100 meters in most cases."

In order to deploy E911, an upgrade of the local 911 PSAPs is required, and also the coordination among public safety agencies, wireless carriers, technology vendors, equipment manufacturers, and local wire-line carriers needed to be adjusted. The FCC established a four-year rollout and expects to be completed by December 31, 2005. Once it is completed, the police or any legal departments such as the FBI and/or CIA will have a much greater capability to track down a crime or accident quickly and accurately. Despite all the conveniences the LBS can bring, there are also drawbacks; one of the biggest drawbacks is the threat on privacy. With the GPS receiver implanted into the cell phones, companies or other user's are now able to track down others at any moment, this made our privacy completely vulnerable. They are able to find out what are people's daily habits, with the records, they can tell what exactly we are doing at anytime anywhere since our daily activities usually occur in a routine. In the B2B business world, a sales representative may want his manager to know where he is, but not his other customers. To resolve this privacy issue, different wireless vendors such as InfoMove or GeoCities have developed the technology for the end users to choose "opt-in" or "opt-out" from the tracking mode. This way, the end users can have the authority to participate in the service at anytime they want, and protect their privacy whenever they feel necessary.

Pros and Cons

Advocates for L-commerce believe it will help connect businesses with their most qualified customers, direct individuals to the services/information they want, effective marketing and advertising, and last but not the least, increase the efficiency of emergency services (through being able to quickly and accurately locate callers to 911 emergency services. Following the tragedy of September 11(terrorist attack at WTO in US), attitudes has changed drastically regarding the need to know where people are. Wireless subscriber numbers grew to over 120 million. In the 2 Location information, is no longer just needed for emergency services; it is paramount of many spouses, parents, children, and co-workers wanting to know where their loved ones are. This desire will encourage people to carry location-enabled cell phones. As we have mentioned above, privacy protection is the biggest hurdle that the LBS need to face with; therefore, over exposure of our location information is the greatest "con".

Furthermore, the cost of implementation is currently a concern for the LBS providers. The problem they have now is, since the GIS collects the information globally, the LBS is suppose to provide information in a global perspective as well, which means you are able to request and receive any information regarding to your position anytime anywhere in the world.However, different wireless carriers from different countries are currently functioning under different infrastructures, such as difference between circuit switching and packet switching. No standardization is established for this kind of services, this creates extra cost and difficulty in implementing the service globally since there are not many protocols established and shared between different countries.

Despite the privacy and the cost issues, L-commerce does appear to offer a significant potential to the business community and great conveniences to our daily activities. The potential cost savings for marketing and advertising, the effectiveness and accuracy for emergency services, and last but not the least, the effortlessness of receiving needed information with no physical or time limitation, all makes our lives so much faster and easier. With the speed of technological improvements, the location-based commerce will sooner or later be better controlled and manipulated to enhance its power and flexibility. The vision of L-commerce is not limited to the "traditional" business-to-consumer commerce. It also encapsulates mobile peer-to-peer commerce where mobile peers trade and exchange information, services, and other digital goods. L-commerce also includes business-to-business opportunities by allowing small shops to join and form virtual partnerships therefore increasing their presence in the local marketplace. **Geographical information System** (GIS) is system that integrates GPS data onto digitized map displays. An interesting application of GPS/GIS is now available from several car manufacturers and car rental companies. The GPS knows where the car is at any time, so the application can map the route for the driver to a particular destination.

Telematics and Telemetry Application

Telematics refers to the integration of computers and wireless communications to improve information flow using the principles of telemetry.

Location Based Advertising

Once a wireless device is detected in a location, advertising is directed to the device. A dynamic billboard ad will be personalized specifically for the viewer. Ads on vehicles such as taxicabs will change based on its location. L-commerce can also provide the following benefits: Enhanced Billing, Personalized Portals, Buddy Finder, Emergency Assistance Service, Call Routing, Find Nearest Services.

SUMMARY

In this chapter, you have gone through different application area of M-commerce. After going through this chapter, be sure that the following facts are well versed.

Concept of L-commerce.

Necessary Location-Based and Network Technologies

Barriers to L-commerce

L-commerce Technologies

Origin and Evolution of L-commerce.

Impact of L-commerce On The Business World.

Pros and Cons of L-commerce.

STUDY QUESTIONS

1. Describe the concept of L-commerce. How does it differ from M-commerce?
2. Explain the working of L-commerce.
3. Enlist the L-commerce technologies.
4. Write about the evolution of L-commerce. How it differs from E-commerce and M-commerce?
5. Mention the impact of L-commerce to business world.

CHAPTER – 8

M-COMMERCE — INDIAN SCENARIO

LEARNING OBJECTIVE

In this chapter, we have gone through the concept of M-commerce emerging as a media of commerce. In order impart the usage of M-commerce, few cases are discussed in this chapter.

- Introduction
- Indian scenario
- Cases

INTRODUCTION

Nowadays the cellphone - on its own or in conjunction with an organizer is used for much more than simply making phone calls. It also acts as a flexible terminal for a large range of applications. So the availability of information (weather forecasts, economic data, news), e-shopping, e-ticketing, e-banking and e-brokerage is greater than ever before, regardless of time or place. The WAP (Wireless Application Protocol) and WML (Wireless Markup Language) open standards mean the Internet's innovative solution strategies can now be applied to mobile telephony too.

Benefits from Mobile Commerce

Mobile commerce solutions mean mobile terminals such as cellphones and organizers can now be used to access the Internet. The benefits for your company include the following:

- Internet offerings are easier and more convenient to access.
- Considerable flexibility when conducting business.
- Intense customer orientation and high customer loyalty thanks to innovative service strategies.
- Lower transaction and personal costs, thanks to widespread automation.
- Differentiation from competitors thanks to innovative solution strategies.
- Field staffs are more effective because they have flexible access to internal corporate data.
- Investment security and independence from platforms (terminals, servers) and network operators through the use of open standards.
- The benefits of the Internet are transferred to mobile telephony applications thanks to the systematic use of WAP (Wireless Application Protocol) and SMS (Short Message System).

INDIAN SCENARIO

With the Reserve Bank of India (RBI) doubling the cap on mobile transactions, mobile payment companies are bullish on the prospects for M-commerce — especially in the rural unbanked space. The RBI recently increased the daily transaction limit for cash transactions from ₹ 2,500 to

₹ 5,000 and the daily transaction limit for goods and services from ₹ 5,000 to ₹ 10,000. Companies reason that as the metropolitan users are equipped with card-based payments and the Internet, rural deployment becomes more significant for them. Over 30 per cent of the new mobile subscriptions every month come from villages.

Companies tapping the rural segment are also experimenting with mobile banking through retail points. For instance, Sanjay Swamy, CEO, mChek, says: "mChek is launching a pilot with Grameen Koota, a primarily rural microfinance institution serving over 160,000 members throughout Karnataka." Through the model, mChek will enable Grameen Koota microfinance borrowers to receive loans, make loan repayments, and also make merchant and bill payments in the local villages. The pilot projects will eventually be expanded to other microfinance institutions as well as other institutions working with rural customers. "We believe the rural sector in India is more likely to go cashless than the urban sector," adds Swamy. Pramod Saxena, Chairman and MD, Oxigen Services India, says: "Around 15 per cent of our deployment will happen in semi-urban and rural areas. We are basically evaluating our banking correspondent model through retail points." Oxigen has tie ups with ITC e-choupal, Drishti and Hughes. And a month back it tied up with e-Mitra (an integrated e-governance project) in Rajasthan and is in the process to roll out services with Haryali Kisaan Bazaar. "We are in talks with MicroSave (a financial services programme) to roll out our microfinance related services," Saxena adds.

Besides this, Oxigen is in talks with Railways to bring unreserved (small value, daily tickets) ticket booking services into its offerings. A pilot on this will be worked out in the suburbs of Mumbai once Railways approves it. However, not all are gung-ho over the rural shift. Ajay Adiseshann, MD and Founder, PayMate India, says: "Typically services start urban and then move rural depending on the nature of the service and the markets ability to consume such services. Using the mobile to make payments or for remittances might be a likely scenario in rural areas." Dewang Neralla, Director, Atom Technologies, says: "We are focusing first on financial inclusion as m-payments will take time in rural areas. We have tied up with National Bulk Handling Corporation for that and are in process of tying up with Kisan Vikas Kendra and other institutions which have rural retail kind presence." Atom worked on a pilot project for m-payments in Mumbai with Axis Bank. The pilot was done with 30-odd merchants on the list, wherein payments were done with 1,500 credit and debit cards embedded onto mobiles. Naralla says it had a success rate of 95 per cent.

Mobile telephony is redefining the world of commerce and impacting the way in which consumers pay for goods and services and carry out financial and banking transactions. Bharti Telesoft fully supports the growth of M-commerce, and is already working with leading operators and financial institutions to bring mobile commerce to subscribers worldwide. Its mobiquity™ platform provides a reliable, secure, and highly scalable base from which to offer a range of Bharti Telesoft or third party M-commerce applications, whilst its Monet Hub transforms the ease with which international remittances can be made.

CASES

1. E-Zest Offers Solution Following Proposed Scenarios and Components

E-Zest develops solutions for mobile commerce that are tailored to your specific corporate objectives and are integrated into your company's electronic commerce and IT infrastructure.

Mobile Shopping:

Ordering, checking availability and prices, delivery information with acknowledgment and confirmation.

Mobile Banking:

Statements of account, sales and payment instructions premises.

Mobile Brokerage:

Checking and monitoring prices using watch lists, securities inquiries and orders.

Mobile Access to Corporate Intranets:

Use of intranet applications such as telephone directories and newsboards for mobile access.

Mobile Travel information and booking:

Total Internet solution with WAP enhancement.

2. Star India is Betting Big on Mobile Commerce

Having recently launched a platform to provide a one-point gateway to a bouquet of mobile services, Star India has now tied up with handset maker Sony Ericsson to bring its mobile content services to users of the brand. Under the partnership, the mobile service launched by Star's mobile entertainment division will be exclusively pre-embedded on a range of Sony Ericsson phones in India. The first batch of the new phones is expected to arrive in India from Sony Ericsson's factory next week. "The service will be embedded across some 15 models of Sony Ericsson. We expect this development to significantly broaden our mobile services customer base," Mr Viren Popli, Senior Vice-President (Mobile Entertainment) of Star India, told Business Line.

The mobile service, named Plus, will give easy access to Sony Ericsson users to over 200 videos of TV, music and Bollywood genres every month. It also provides TV show info, unlimited access to sports scores and updates, movie reviews, music downloads, news, mobile banking services through HDFC Bank, travel booking and information on lifestyle products. It was earlier this year that Star launched the Plus service that was designed for consumers to catch up on TV, search for information, shop and bank while on the move through their GPRS mobile phones. Now the company plans to develop this service into a full-fledged M-commerce solution.

"The potential in the M-commerce space is tremendous. We plan to add new services like auction, E-commerce, insurance services and mobile ticketing in the future. And later, it can be used for user-generated networking," Mr. Popli said. India is estimated to have 250 lakhs mobile phone users, out of which at least 10 per cent are mobile Internet users. And it is this group that Star is targeting for its mobile services. Star has tied up with several brands to develop Plus. For example, it is partnering with HDFC for banking and related services, MakeMyTrip, TravelGuru and Yatra for travel and ticketing, Infomedia Group for Yellow Pages information, Universal Music for music content, Overdrive for information on cars, AVMAX for audiophiles and Chip for computing information. At present, Star has 40,000 mobile phone users as its customers for Plus, which is provided for a fee of ₹ 30 per month. While this fee is at present the only revenue stream from Plus, the company intends to use the service to create a new medium for advertisement. The waiting period during downloads into the mobile set could be used for advertisement, which will provide another revenue stream from Plus. "We plan to introduce advertisement at a later date when we would have significantly expanded our customer base," Mr. Popli said. Star is also planning a second round of advertisement campaign for Plus, which will include a TV campaign featuring an animation clipping.

3. About Reliance Mobile World:

Mumbai, February 5, 2008: Reliance Communications today announced its tie-up with Sadhna TV, a renowned social religious channel to beam all the programs online on Reliance Mobile handsets. Reliance Mobile World (R World), the multimedia suite of applications of Reliance Mobile, offers unique experience of viewing Sadhna TV's popular social-religious discourse and various other interesting programs in its 'Mobile TV' portfolio. As the streaming is live 24×7, Reliance Mobile customers can watch their favourite religious content conveniently from anywhere even while on the move within the state or traveling across the country. Reliance Mobile World has gained popularity as a virtual one-stop-shop for entertainment, communication, gaming and M-commerce. Thanks to the wide range of applications, it has endeared itself to users from all walks of life. Reliance Mobile World has over 2500 useful applications and over 2,00,000 content titles which include mobile TV, videos, cricket updates, music, ringtones, phonebook transfer and back-up service, M-commerce services like Mobile Banking, bill payments, mobile e-mail and instant messenger, city and TV guides, booking gas cylinders, tracking Speed Post, Airlines and Railway reservations,

Mr. Mahesh Prasad, President, Applications, Solutions and Content Group, Reliance Communications: "Mobile TV is a natural progression in mobile entertainment that combines the best of TV with the mobility and functionality of a wireless device. Reliance Communications has pioneered video based content on mobile phones in India since its inception. With this major initiative, we are addressing the needs of a market segment which is spiritually inclined." Speaking on this occasion, **Mr. Rakesh Gupta, Managing Director, Sadhna TV,** said, "In a major survey of thousands of people across the country, we have found that apart from news, people are more interested in discourses of religious gurus, astrology, and bhajans. With Reliance's strong presence in the Mobile TV space, this will reach millions of Reliance subscribers throughout the country."

Reliance Communications is at the forefront of providing a variety of applications and content spanning infotainment, sports, music, games, messaging, and M-commerce. Video content on Reliance Mobile World is a very popular service with the genre of content such as movie clips, TV news and shows, music, videos, cricket and sports fashion, glamour and animation, providing thousands of latest entertainment, and information based rich media content. They are available to several millions of subscribers with Reliance Mobile World (R World) enabled handsets supporting video. To avail the above service, Reliance Mobile customers are charged ₹ 15 for 5 minutes.

4. Airtel

To make Airtel an intrinsic part of the consumer's lifestyle and providing them the ability to transact using their respective mobile devices and payment instruments, it introduced M-commerce service, the first of its kind 'mChek on Airtel'. This promises simplicity, convenience, ease of use and safety. This provided the user, a secure and convenient channel to link their existing credit cards, debit cards or bank accounts and carry out commerce transactions, including paying postpaid bills, recharging prepaid, paying

Fixedline and Broadband bills, buying Movie or Air tickets, paying Insurance Premiums and much more.

Postpaid Bill Payment: Pay your outstanding Airtel mobile bills.

Click Here or SMS Pay Airtel <Amount> <Mobile No> to 543219 - Toll Free

Prepaid Recharge: Recharge your Airtel prepaid. Click Here or SMS Pay Airtel <Amount> to 543219-Toll Free

Pay Home Phones & Broadband Bills: Pay your Airtel Fixedline and Broadband bills. Click Here or SMS Pay Airtel <Amount> <STD Code + Fixedline No> to 543219-Toll Free

Flight Tickets: Book through Make My Trip - Click Here. SMS "Fly Source city Destination Date" to 543219-Toll Free

Movie Tickets: Book through Book My Show - Click Here. SMS "Movie Language Date no of tickets" to 543219 -Toll free

Delhi Gurgaon Toll Tag Recharge: No hassles, no queues, recharge your Toll Tag from Anywhere, Anytime.

Simply SMS Pay for DGToll <11 Digit Tag No> <Amount> to '543219',In addition 'mChek on Airtel' is also available as a payment instrument on a variety of E-commerce shopping sites.

India times

Sify Mall

Future Baazar

Yatra.com

Just choose payment option as mChek and enter your mobile no. You will get a payment authorization on the mobile. Enter your mChek pin to confirm payment. Welcome to Airtel's mobile payments option. To transact, all you need to do is enter your credit card details and make your mChek PIN once. For all future transactions just remember your mChek PIN. What's more you can also pay bills and recharge prepaid anywhere, anytime from your mobile phone, without coming online.

- Enter your card details only once. It's Safe, Simple and Secure.
- Just remember your mChek PIN for all future payments.
- Pay bills and recharge on-line and also from your mobile just SMS 'Pay Airtel Amount <Mobile/Landline (with std code) Number>.' to 543219.

- Pay Airtel bills or recharge prepaid of your friends and family too
- VISA and MasterCard accepted.

SUMMARY

In this chapter, we have gone through the concept of M-commerce emerging as a media of commerce. In order to make the reader sensitize about the usage of M-commerce in Indian context, few Indian cases like AIRTEL, Reliance Mobile, star India were discussed.

STUDY QUESTIONS

1. M-commerce is emerging as a very popular media of commerce in India. Explain.
2. Analyze the cases given in this chapter and explain how it is going to benefit the Indian Business Scenario?

CHAPTER – 9

LIMITATIONS OF M-COMMERCE

Learning Objective

This chapter, explains the various challenges M-commerce has to face. In order to acquaint the readers with the various threats M-commerce is subjected to, all most all areas of M-commerce are discussed.

- M-commerce Weaknesses
- Obstacles for M-business Adoption
- Usability Problem
- Technical Limitations
- WAP Limitations
- Potential Health Hazards
- Limitations of the Wireless Network
- Limitations Imposed by Mobility
- Limitations of the Mobile Computer
- WAP Risks
- WML Script
- Bluetooth
- New Security Risks in M-commerce
- Summary
- Study Questions

M-commerce Weaknesses

History tells us tech companies are far too eager to proclaim a revolution. However, history shows that a large new market does not just show up overnight. It takes years for consumers to catch on to a new technological development. Tech companies entering into the market have no idea what kind of business model they should follow. Is a consumer really going to pick up their cell phone and want to hear a commercial, advertising Pepsi?

Wireless Application Protocol (WAP) is required with all web-enabled wireless devices but it has several significant limitations. Adoption of M-commerce cannot justify the costs that go into producing web-enabled wireless devices.

Obstacles for M-business Adoption

Perhaps the main reason why mobile security and wired security take slightly different approaches is because of the constraints of the client-the mobile device. Mobile devices, whether they are mobile phones, PDAs, palm top computers, or whatever, have certain limitations, including:

- Memory
- Computational Processing
- Form factor
- Bandwidth

Memory

While it is common for PCs to have 128 MB or more of memory and many gigabytes of hard drive storage, such capacity on a mobile device, within a reasonable price and form factor, is nearly impossible. New and inventive ways of managing memory on mobile devices have had to be created. Certain devices, such as Pocket PC, have scaled-down versions of applications that are more common for these mobile devices to have flash memory or smartcard storage capability.

Smartcards are quite common in Europe for mobile phones. Smartcards provide features that solve two problems; a place for storage of data such as digital certificates or subscriber identity and the ability to take data from phone to phone. Although smartcard technology can be used for wired devices such

• *M-commerce Security: A Beginner's Guide-Kapil Raina, Anurag Harsh, Tata McGraw-Hill Publishing Company Limited-P-90-125*

as traditional PCs, because the need for portability and extra storage is not so great, smartcard readers (required for smartcards to operate) are not prevalent in PCs.

Computational Processing

Another area in which mobile devices have constraints is in the ability to process large amounts of mathematical functions. Although devices such as PDAs have increased computational abilities that rival those of some older PCs, in general for cheaper devices and for mobile phones, there is a great gap between PCs and mobile devices.

One method that has become a standard for reducing computational need for encryption, while still maintaining strong security, is [18]elliptical curve cryptography (ECC). Most companies now have mobile devices that use ECC whenever processing power is an issue. ECC is based on a complex mathematical problem, making it difficult to break the protection it provides for a set of data. The popularity rests on the fact that it requires fewer bits for strong protection. Fewer bits imply that the algorithm can be processed more quickly and with reduced requirements for computational speed. In addition, the bandwidth required is reduced because fewer bits need to be passed back and forth between sender and recipient.

Form Factor

Due to the small size of mobile devices, screen space is very limited. As a result, different methods of data entry and data delivery must be applied to mobile devices versus wired devices. WAP is designed specifically to manage the display constraints on a mobile device. The use of microbrowser, as required for WAP, allows a user to see and enter only the essentials of an M-commerce transaction. In addition, in the design of a mobile device, creating a lighter smaller device means giving up some battery life and some key functionality, such as memory storage.

Bandwidth

One of the biggest topics for conversation in the mobile phone industry is how to improve bandwidth. 3G (3rd generation mobile phone networks) are slated as the next evolution of our current mobile phone network infrastructure with desktop-like internet speed. Among the unique aspects of mobile device communication are long round-trip times and periods where connections are broken. Short-range wireless devices such as cordless phones or radios, can manage this more effectively, however, for M-commerce applications,

[1] ***NOTE: Elliptic curve cryptography (ECC)*** *is an approach to public-key cryptography based on the algebraic structure of elliptic curves over finite fields.*

invariably the transactions must take place some distance away and over different types of networks, including wired networks. Again, standards such as WAP allow mobile devices to minimize bandwidth use.

Wired devices generally have more tolerance as they can accommodate better connection States and reconnect much more quickly if a connection is broken. One place where mobile device will outperform wired device is in the area of always-on connection. Mobile devices, in the next generation networks will have the capability to always be connected, or atleast to have the appearance. Security implications for always on devices are more complex than for other types of systems. Mobile devices, if they are always connected to the Internet, increase their exposure to being discovered and hacked.

Security Model

Having a background on the specific constraints and issues of mobile devices, we can now approach the security issues created by these unique features. It is important to keep in mind that every M-commerce implementation will require a link back to the wired world. Thus, security issues for the traditional wired world still affect M-commerce.

There are many aspects to security since there are so many components in a typical M-commerce transaction. This section will note any similarities between wired and mobile worlds and then focus on the M-commerce security specifics. We will break down the discussion into these components.

- Client (originates transaction)
- Client network (transaction starts transmission)
- Internet (transaction flows over the public network)
- .Merchant network (receives transaction)
- Server (receives and terminates transaction)

Client

A client is basically defined as a device or terminal that initiates a M-commerce transaction. For the mobile world, that could be a PDA or a mobile phone, for example. For the wired world, that could be a PC or laptop computer.

This first component poses the first set of security threats. Considering that the physical device may be stolen, compromised, or left unattended, the easiest way to penetrate a strong security system is to get physical access to an unprotected client. There are several methods mobile device manufacturers have devised to mitigate damage due to the physical loss of a mobile device:

- Encryption software Encodes information protected by a PIN code or password.
- Power lock codes PIN codes that are required as soon as power is turned on the device.
- Physical cables Some PDAs, such as Palm Pilots, have steel cable cradles that can secure the device.

In general, these mechanisms are fairly weak against determined, deliberate attacks. Generally, we can assume loss of the physical device will eventually lead to the compromise of all data on the device.

One interesting method Dutch police have used in the theft of mobile phones is the SMS message bomb. Through some basic research, police can determine the unique number identifying the stolen mobile phone and send SMS messages every few minutes with notification that the phone has been stolen. Such a method is a defense mechanism akin to automobile alarms that go off during or after a vehicle has been stolen. With such a message, it is much harder to resell the phone at this point.

Mobile and wired devices both have operating systems, that drive the applications they run. However, wired devices such as PCs are more vulnerable to attacks against their operating system than are mobile devices. Mobile devices generally tend to have smaller operating systems, and sometimes the OS is burned into a chip for faster access. More recent PDAs have read/write operating systems to allow easier upgrades for functionality. Wired devices generally tend to have software-based operating systems or at least some type of read/write chip access.

Attacks on the operating system of a device are common for wired devices. Generally, wired devices have full-featured operating systems and thus pose many security risks. For example, with desktop PCs, memory is heavily swapped to a disk medium to accommodate multiple application threads. In addition, many PCs create log files when the OS kernel crashes, leaving sensitive data from memory in readable disk format.

On the other hand, mobile devices generally do not suffer these problems because the OS does not get overwritten or replaced. In addition, mobile devices have stripped-down and very basic feature sets (to conserve space and increase speed).

Generally, most client applications in wired devices are based on Microsoft platforms (Windows 98, 2000, NT, XP). However, due to the complexity of such operating systems there are many weaknesses that can be used to compromise a security system. Some common examples include gaining access to administrator accounts, forcing buffer flows in computer memory, and reading operating system kernel dumps. Generally, Microsoft provides patches to fix security holes as they are noted; however, there is always a significant gap between the noting of a security issue and the resolution of that issue.

The other most common operating system is the UNIX operating system, implemented in various forms by many companies such as Sun Microsystems and Hewlett-Packard (HP). Considering that UNIX has been around for so long, a large number of security holes exist, with patches widely available. Typically, the setup of a UNIX system is complex and so are efforts to improve the security of the system.

In a process called hardening, the operating system in use is stripped of unneeded features, debugging tools, and anything else not essential for the direct purpose of that function. By this means, security threats are minimized.

Next we move to the application layer of the client. The application layer handles programs such as the browser (Microsoft Internet Explorer, for example). Applications pose the greatest risk to security compromise, whether on a wired or a mobile device. Because applications share resources with each other on a computer system, all sorts of security threats can be exploited at this level. Some common threats on wired devices include.

- Viruses: These come in many forms, but most replicate themselves and cause malicious data destruction or theft.
- Port attacks: Attacks that take advantage of certain parts of a program that are awaiting instructions from other programs.
- Memory attacks: Attacks that take advantage of information in memory or data temporarily written to disk.

Mitigation of application threats can be achieved through additional programs such as virus checkers, estriction of program scope, and reduced application functionality. A fundamental principal of computer security says that if you do not need something on a device, then disable it.

Although not widespread today, the security risks discussed for wired applications are slowly becoming problems for mobile device as well. Viruses on mobile phones started to appear in late 2000 and 2001. Hacks created through manipulation of applications can yield a hacker information such as the cell site, carrier, and diagnostic information, and possibly even the ability to read mobile traffic through a particular cell site.

Client Network

Network security is another crucial aspect of M-commerce. Security issues depend on the design of the network that hosts the client. This area is where the biggest difference lies in the security of wired and mobile devices. We will first address wired networks and then discuss mobile networks.

Wired Client Network Security Issues

If the client is hosted inside a corporate network, for example, then most likely the client receives some type of protection against threats from the Internet. Such devices may include firewalls, proxy servers, and routers. Most studies show that compromise in a corporate environment generally is due to insiders. Network security threats to be aware of include.

- Sniffing: The ability for a hacker to monitor traffic as it crosses the wires
- Port attacks: The ability to access an idle process on a hardware or software system
- Dos: Denial of service for the network by sending garbage across the network or otherwise keeping servers busy with dummy requests.

A particularly vulnerable setup includes a typical dial-up or remote-access user. In this scenario, a road warrior uses a regular modem or other means to connect to the corporate office. In the past, many companies maintained large banks of modems so that computers could dial into the network. Today most companies create a secure way in through their firewalls, such as the use of virtual private networks (VPNs). Attacks at this point, depending on the setup, could include.

- Sniffing: Same as defined previously except applied to dial-up lines
- IP spoofing: Going to a site believed to be the destination, but in fact ending up at an impostor's site

MOBILE NETWORK ISSUES

Generally, mobile security varies greatly among the types of mobile networks being used. For example, there are several standards for mobile phones, including GSM, I-mode, and CDMA..Wired devices are each assigned some type of IP address that identifies them; similarly, mobile devices are assigned some type of electronic serial number (ESN) that uniquely identifies that hardware device. In addition, a phone number (for mobile phones) may also be associated with the device (usually programmed at the time the service for the device is purchased).

In general, authentication (today) is very difficult to forge, especially for GSM. Initially, when analog phones were common, theft and cloning of phones was common. At that time, thieves would simply use a scanner and listen on the airwaves and pick up the broadcasted ESN of a phone. Then, they would get a production phone and replace the production chip with another programmed with the new ESN. Advanced techniques included tumbling in which a series of ESNs were used. In this manner, one ESN be could used for a phone and then another for the second call and so on, making it more difficult to identify stolen ESNs.

Today, with standards such as GSM, it is much more difficult to fake the authentication of a device. However, identity theft is on the rise. A thief steals personal data and uses that data to get real credentials, which can then be used to initiate a phone purchase or service setup. In this manner, a thief may use a phone for one or two months before detection.

In addition to using standards such as GSM, mobile carriers have also used profiling systems to detect fraudulent use of mobile phones. In this type of detection, the historical data of a caller is surveyed, and calls outside of this pattern are flagged as possible fraudulent calls. Automated profiling systems can immediately turn off access if a pattern of fraud is detected. The main drawback to this system is that it is based on historical data and must have sufficient data from which to draw.

Other systems of fraud detection, such as radio frequency (RF) fingerprinting, have been used extensively for military applications. In this method, the assumption is that most phones have a unique RF pattern and can be detected accordingly. The system relies on capturing an RF pattern and associating it with an EIN/MIN pair stored in a database. Subsequent use of that EIN/MIN pair would cause the system to verify the RF pattern against the version stored in the database. In addition, this technique does not work on all models of phones. Finally, the carrier is required to purchase and set up equipment to employ RF fingerprinting and not every carrier has done so (although the majority of the top 100 Metropolitan Service Areas (MSAs) do use RF fingerprinting today). In addition several variations are implemented in the market, thus making roaming more difficult as RF fingerprinting solutions are not necessarily compatible.

One mechanism for protection of mobile network communication is the use of VPNs for mobile networks. The concept is similar to that of VPNs for traditional wired networks. VPN clients for mobile devices, initially PDAs with sufficient memory and processing power, have been developed by companies such as Certicom. Initial releases of Certicom's VPN client in 2000 did not include major functionality such as digital certificates (a fundamental part of the IPSec standard to which most VPN vendors conform). Their later solutions, such as Movian VPN, did include some rudimentary key exchanges; however, the connection time to set up a VPN session took from 10 seconds to a minute or more. Other solutions, such as Carrier VPN solutions from Ericsson that came out in June 2001, include a service provisioning concept that does not require specialized VPN equipment at the customer's site. VPNs on large mobile devices, such as laptop PCs, are what are most common in the VPN business. Because there are no storage and processing constraints to prohibit full-featured VPN clients, the best VPN clients are available for laptop PCs. Finally, another solution that was announced in May 2001 is the SafeNet/Texas Instruments joint effort to create a specialized chip to handle PDA VPN functions to increase speed. Because VPNs can slow bandwidth speed, a hardware-based solution could alleviate performance problems that may appear in a client-based (software) solution.

Internet

The next step in the M-commerce security model addresses transmission flow over the Internet. Given that the Internet is a shared, public medium, the last guarantee that anyone can make is for security on the Internet. All M-commerce transactions flow over the Internet. Therefore, the same security issues are common to both M-commerce and E-commerce applications. Although most sites seem credible and it does not appear that data can be compromised, the likelihood of unprotected data being stolen or altered is high.

Recall from the previous chapter that for M-commerce, a gateway or PKI portal is required to convert from the use of WTLS certificates to a regular SSL connection. This is the only unique aspect of M-commerce versus wired E-commerce for the Internet component. After the transaction flows past the gateway, it is then carried over the Internet just like any other transaction, including E-commerce transactions. This "gap in WAP," as we described it in the previous chapter, is one of the main areas of vulnerability in an M-commerce infrastructure.

We have chosen two main areas of vulnerability to discuss in more detail (there are many more areas, but we will focus on the ones most relevant to M-commerce):

- Spoofing Setting up a fake site or set of data to look authentic
- Sniffing Ability to read data that passes over the Internet

Spoofing

Spoofing can take many forms. At the simplest level, fake information can be circulated on the Internet as has happened with several news articles. One particular case involved a technology company in which a press release, written to appear authentic, was sent out by a hacker. The press release found its way to legitimate news wires, and they in turn published the information as authentic. As a result, the word got to the financial community that this company was having severe financial difficulties. The stock of that company nose-dived minutes after the press release was issued. On the Internet, how can you know that data that you are reading is legitimate?

A more complicated and sophisticated spoof involves tricking people into thinking they are going to a particular web site when, in fact, they are being lured to a fake one. This has been done by publishing the IP address of a site instead of a URL. People go to the site and it appears to look like the site they have seen before, but in fact it is not the real site. Alternatively, a web server or network device may be compromised so that even when the correct URL is typed, the client will be routed to the impostor's site. Such an attack may be used to trick users into entering valuable information such as passwords, bank account numbers, social security numbers, and other confidential data the compromise of this data could allow an attacker to steal a person's identity and buy things on credit or take loans against the victim's assets. Direct compromise of credit card information can allow the attacker to buy goods on the Internet with the victim's line of credit.

Both types of spoofing just described can be mitigated through the use of a web server security technology called Secure Sockets Layer (SSL). By obtaining a digital certificate from vendors such as VeriSign, SSL certificates can validate the site you are accessing and create an encrypted tunnel from the client to the merchant's web server. The certificate will identify the merchant and provide the validity period of that certificate. In the most popular web browsers, the use of SSL is usually indicated by a lock symbol or a key symbol at the bottom of the screen. Other devices or browsers may use a different display to represent the use of SSL.

Spoofing in M-commerce can take a further spin through the use of new services offered by some companies. Due to the form-factor constraints of mobile phones, some companies have offered mapping services from a short address to a full, standard URL. This would allow, for example, someone to enter 411 and then connect to www.informationdirectorypages.com. Having to enter that URL on a mobile phone can take well over 5 minutes! Now we need to ensure that spoofing does not occur in this mapping process as well.

Sniffing

Sniffing, as previously described, is when a hacker intercepts data en route from the client and server and back. Sniffing on the Internet, however, is much easier than on a client network, due to the openness of the Internet. For some corporate networks, a hacker may need physical access to the network. For the Internet, there are myriad entry points to the data. Most sniffing can be done through simple software that grabs data over a particular machine or network segment and displays the data. For unencrypted data, a hacker can easily read data flowing over the Internet.

The only way to mitigate this risk of eavesdropping, or sniffing, is to encrypt data. There are many tools available to encrypt data. Microsoft Outlook, a popular mail package, allows for the use of digital certificates to encrypt mail in transit. SSL certificates, as described in the previous section, can protect data in transit during a web commerce session.

For mobile devices, the constraints of the devices do not allow encryption of all possible data. Therefore most sites from down what is necessary to conduct M-commerce. However, good security principles tell us to encrypt all data so that an eavesdropper will not know what important data is and what is useless. Consider this example from World War II, where cryptography was a major aspect of the war. Just before the Japanese bombing of Pearl Harbor, U.S. intelligence agencies noted a massive increase in coded traffic. This trapped the Aries off to a major a cavity; however they were unable to decipher the messages in time to halt the bombing of Pearl Harbor. If they had been able to decode the messages in time, the surprise attack on Pearl Harbor might have been averted. Likewise, when conducting M-commerce transactions, it is important that the commerce site take care in deciding what to encrypt if it cannot, as it ideally should, encrypt all traffic. Most hackers have an easier time when all they have to focus on is a few transactions and how to break them instead of having a continuous stream of encrypted data to sift through.

Other areas unique to mobile devices include launched sniffer attacks. It is common for hackers to break into an E-commerce server and then place a sniffer program on that server. From here, they arrange to get the sniffer data remotely. This technique allows them to capture data on networks they would not normally be able to access or break into. In the mobile world, with phones and PDAs being increasingly used to access corporate or private networks, it is possible to put a sniffer program onto a mobile device through some type of Trojan horse. From this, the sniffer program could capture account or personal information and perhaps even PIN codes used to access the device itself. The biggest risk of this is in the always-on mobile networks planned for the future.

Merchant Network

Although the client or initiator of a M-commerce transaction may have taken great lengths to ensure that security measures were taken, the receiver of that transaction, or the merchant, must also protect his or her network.

Risks similar to those posed for the client network face the merchant network. In addition, the merchant network faces additional risks. For example, the merchant most likely will be conducting some type of payment processing. This makes the merchant network a more likely target of an attack by hackers since the merchant is an aggregator of many transactions, as opposed to the client network, which may initiate only a few transactions. Risks include:

- Denial of service
- Payment processing compromise
- Credit fraud

Denial of Service

Many news stories during 2000 and 2001 described commerce sites that went down due to denial-of-service (DoS) attacks. These attacks consist of numerous dummy requests made to a site's servers every second to keep them so busy that legitimate transactions cannot get through. Eventually, the server becomes overloaded and crashes. The scenario is similar to what would occur if a million people called one company for a catalog with false addresses; legitimate customers wanting a catalog may not get through, and catalogs may run out. The nature of the Internet makes stopping denial-of-service attacks impossible. However, software and tools known as intrusion detection systems can observe traffic patterns and make guesses as to whether a denial-of-service attack is being performed; if it is, then the suspect data packets can be ignored.

Although DoS attacks have been well-documented for the wired Internet, the new mode of communication using mobile devices will feature a new breed of DoS. For example, a computer-generated set of SMS messages to GSM phones could fill up all memory and take up network traffic if done on a large scale. Distributed DoS attacks, in which multiple sites take part in a DoS attack against the same target, could easily cripple mobile traffic.

Payment Processing

Naturally, every M-commerce merchant wants to get paid. As a result, there is a need for payment processing. Payment processing may involve another network connection (private or public) to the payment processor.

Information that flows to the payment processor may include credit card information and personal data of the buyer. In addition, there are data services now that allow for real-time validation of a buyer's identity, age, and credit history.

Generally, secure communication through SSL can work some payment processors have private networks, making it more difficult for an outsider to get to the data in transit.

Credit Card Fraud

Most credit card companies consider a M-commerce transaction to be a person-not present transaction this means the physical identity of the buyer has not been confirmed, lacking a physical signature, as would be required when a person physically presents a credit card. In these cases, should the transaction be disputed, the merchant bears the loss. This means that in a security compromise of credit card numbers, for example, a merchant may inadvertently accept a stolen credit card and then have to bear the cost of loss of goods shipped or services performed.

Most goo payment processors provide some type of automatic fraud detection capability. Such detection consists of an automatic scoring system calculated based on the transactional and credit card holder buying pattern. Using this score as a basis, the merchant can then decide whether or not to proceed with the transaction.

One advantage M-commerce has in the area of payments is that mobile devices can easily be set up to handle micropayments. Because the device usually is physically with a person, micropayments (usually no more than US$50) can be an efficient means of paying for fuel, small amounts of goods, and tolls. Since micropayments usually work on either a debit or low-ceiling credit system, the damage from a compromise of a device with micropayment capability is very low. Although the wired world is also attempting to roll out micropayments, the main mode of payment, through credit cards, is not suited for this purpose because of credit cards high transactions fees (2 to 3 percent of the transaction value).

Server

To highlight the importance of server security, let's take a simple example. Say that you are using your PC or mobile device to buy some movie tickets for tonight. You use the best virus-scanning software, connect to trusted sites only, use SSL protection, and ensure that the network you are sending from is secure. However, if the network that the movie theater uses to receive your request is weak and is hacked, the hackers can take the credit card number you gave to buy those tickets. So despite your best efforts, the transaction is compromised.

Good network defense devices, such as intrusion detection systems (IDSs) and firewalls, can also help. IDSs are monitors that detect a pattern of data traffic that appears to signal a hack. When a pattern is found, logs are generated and system administrators are alerted. In addition, some advanced IDSs can dupe the hacker by redirecting him or her to a fake area (called a honey pot) until administrators can track down the hacker. In the end though we can simply make it difficult for a hacker to get through, but never impossible.

In addition, we also have to be aware of insider threats with servers. The majority of data compromise risks are from internal employees. With the recent downturn in the economy, there will likely be more disgruntled employees. This situation - the ability to access privileged resources and instable work environments - can lead some to insider theft or vandalism. Insider threats are security risks from an employee or administrator of the server company who steals or manipulates data on the server. Insider risks can be mitigated through separation of duties (keeping one administrator from having access to all parts of the server), encryption of data, and regular third-party auditing (keeping the auditor role separate from the administrator role).

Database Security Issues

Protection of the server encompasses protection of applications such as databases. In any M-commerce transaction, a database is an essential application component. Transactions must be displayed, logged, and resolved. Generally, databases provide mechanisms for error recovery and data rollbacks to compensate for dropped connections. In a mobile environment, data connections are dropped frequently. Such erratic connection behavior is due to signal loss, cell site handovers, and operator disconnection.

Some specific issues related to mobile database security include.

- Limiting transparency operations
- Proper state locking
- Separate mobile context
- Replay attacks

Limiting Transparency Operations

Most applications perform standard operations in the background, transparently, to improve user experience. Due to the lack of ability to manage stateful connections in the mobile world, when connections are dropped, it is unclear whether that same user has reconnected, or whether another user forging authentication datajacked the session. Datajacking can be defined as stealing data and control from a previously authenticated session. It is much easier to datajack a session than to forge authentication to initiate a session. Limiting transparency be keeping the user informed of disconnects, reconnects, and data operations can keep users aware of the state of their data security.

Proper State Lock

If data is being read or written to, then it may be worthwhile to ensure that the database is automatically locked from changes when a disconnect occurs. Keeping a lock open can allow a datajacker to continue that session as if he or she were the legitimate user.

Separate Mobile Context

Normally, good database security principles demand separation of duties and information. Separation of duties prevents a single person from abusing data privacy and prevents data manipulation by spreading a particular task over two or more people. Likewise, in a mobile database context, it is important to separate data access or simply avoid the use of individual data record keeping. Furthermore, because a user's physical location may be tracked, it is important, if that data must be kept, to protect the user's identity.

Replay Attacks

It is possible for unauthorized parties to pick up sessions that have been dropped in mid session. This pickup could take place after authentication has occurred, allowing the hacker easy access to that user's database and other privileges. Although certain standards, such as CSM and PKI make this sort of attack more difficult, depending on the implementation of the database, it is not impossible to implement for example, an attacker might intercept session or authentication keys and reuse them over and over. A good implementation will not allow session or any temporary data or keys to be reused, but the risk still remains.

Database Information Aggregation

A common technique for capturing data without tying the data back to an individual user is to aggregate the data points from many users and track statistics over multiple numbers of users. This abstraction allows data such as location to be tracked, but not necessarily tied to specific devices. Such methods are required when a mobile user leaves a home area and needs to roam. Roaming requires cooperation with cells not directly tied to the same privacy policies. In this case, data aggregation can be used to query the various cells and determine the pattern of movement and predict the future location of the roaming user. For example, if a person is using a mobile phone while driving, it would be easy to predict the person's location in the next minute based on his previous communications with mobile cell sites.

To sum up, Obstacles for M-business adoption are:

- One of the challenges is to discover just how consumers might be inclined to use wireless devices for shopping.
- Wireless service is not universally available or reliable and still relatively expensive.
- Limited bandwidth restricts the amount of data that can be sent over the wireless network.
- Wireless devices have significantly smaller memory capacity and less powerful processors than desktop computers.
- Application development and security standards still evolving.

Usability Problem

Commonly found usability problems are:

- Small size of mobile devices (screens, keyboards, etc).
- Limited storage capacity of devices.
- Hard to browse sites.

Technical Limitations

Technical limitations are as follows:

- Lack of a standardized security protocol.
- Insufficient bandwidth.
- 3G licenses.
- Transmission and power consumption limitations.
- Poor reception in tunnels and certain buildings.
- Multipath interference, weather, and terrain problems and distance-limited connections.

WAP Limitations

Wireless Application Protocol limitations are as follows:

- Speed.

- Cost.
- Accessibility.
- Heterogeneity of fragmented networks.
- Frequent disconnections.
- Limited communication bandwidth.
- Limitations imposed by mobility.
- Lack of mobility awareness by system/applications
- In the process of translating one protocol to another, information is decrypted and re-encrypted.

Potential Health Hazards

Mobile users are subjected to potential health hazards and they are as follows:

- Cellular radio frequencies = cancer?
- No conclusive evidence yet.
- Could allow for myriad of lawsuits.
- Mobile devices may interfere with sensitive medical devices such as pacemakers.

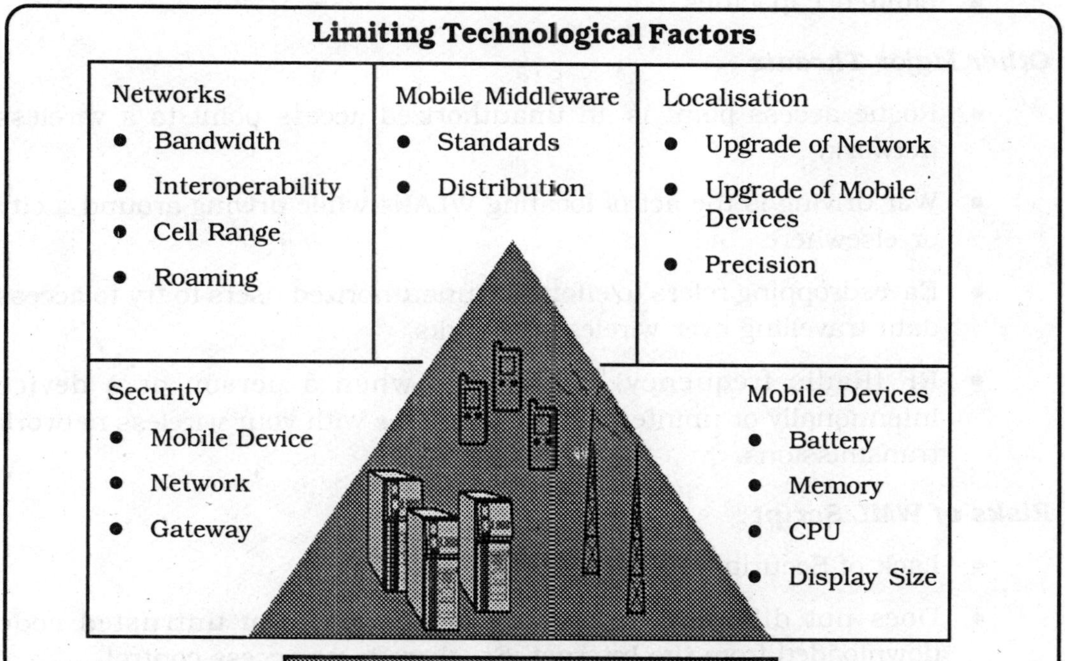

Fig. 9.1: LIMITING TECHNOLOGIES

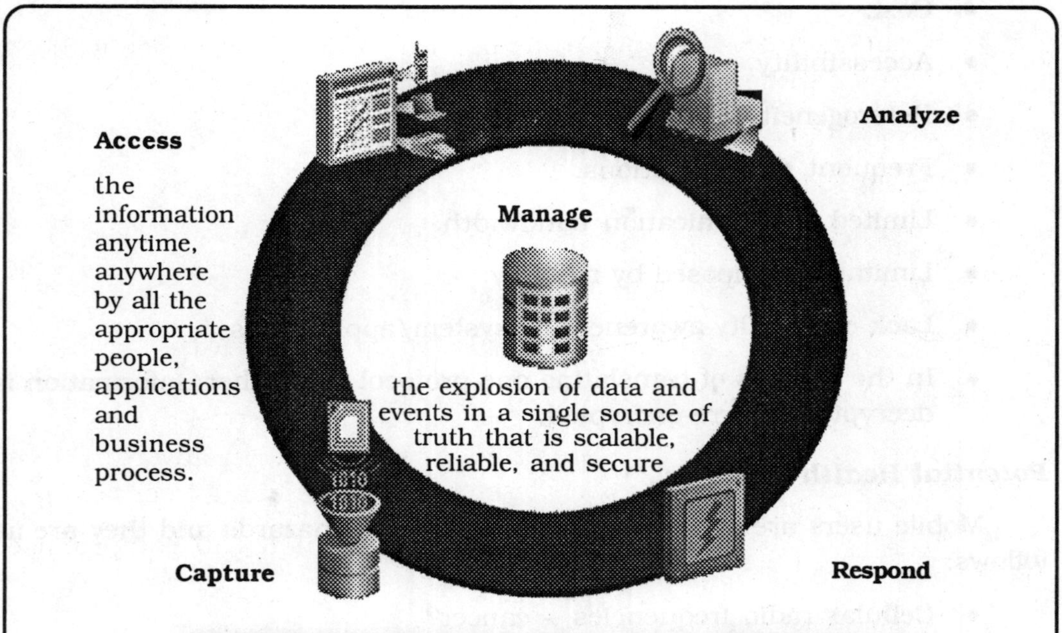

Fig. 9.2: LIMITATIONS OF MOBILE ENVIRONMENT

Limitations of the Mobile Computer

- Short battery lifetime
- Limited capacities

Other Major Threats

- Rogue access point is an unauthorized access point to a wireless network.
- War driving is the act of locating WLANs while driving around a city or elsewhere.
- Eavesdropping refers to efforts by unauthorized users to try to access data travelling over wireless networks.
- RF (Radio frequency) jamming is when a person or a device intentionally or unintentionally interferes with your wireless network transmissions.

Risks of WML Script

- Lack of Security Model.
- Does not differentiate trusted local code from untrusted code downloaded from the Internet. So, there is no access control.

- WML Script is not type-safe.
- Scripts can be scheduled to be pushed to the client device without the user's knowledge.
- Does not prevent access to persistent storage.
- Possible attacks:
  - Theft or damage of personal information.
  - Abusing user's authentication information.
  - Maliciously offloading money saved on smart cards.

New Security Risks In M-commerce

- Abuse of cooperative nature of adhoc networks. An adversary that compromises one node can disseminate false routing information.
- Malicious domains. A single malicious domain can compromise devices by downloading malicious code.
- Roaming. Users roam among non-trustworthy domains.
- Launching attacks from mobile devices. With mobility, it is difficult to identify attackers.
- Loss or theft of device.
- More private information than desktop computers.
- Security keys might have been saved on the device.
- Access to corporate systems.
- Bluetooth provides security at the lower layers only: a stolen device can still be trusted.
- New Privacy Risks
- Monitoring user's private information
- Offline telemarketing
- Who is going to read the "legal jargon"
- Value added services based on location awareness (Location-Based Services)
- M-commerce Challenges
- Slow data transfer speeds on second-generation cellular networks, resulting in higher costs to customer

- Limited memory and power supplies
- More Web sites need to be designed specifically for small wireless devices.
- Keyboards and screens on cell phones are still tiny and awkward to use.

Usability Challenges

- Hard Data Entry
- Poor Handwriting Recognition
- Numeric Keypads for text entry is error-prone
- Poor Voice Recognition
- Further complicates security (entering passwords/speaking pass-phrases is hard!)
- Small Screens
- i.e., can't show users everything in "shopping cart" at once!
- Voice Output time consuming

Heterogeneity Challenges

- Many link layer protocols (different security available in each)
- Many application layer standards
- Businesses need to write to one or more standards or hire a company to help them!
- Many device types:
- Many operating systems (Palm OS, Win CE, Symbian, Epoch, ...)
- Wide variation in capabilities

Challenges for Mobile Electronic Payment Systems

- Legal
- Technical
- Cooperation
- Higher risk
- Social

- Health
- Profit

SUMMARY

In this chapter, we have gone through the various threats and challenges M-commerce has to face in case of mass adoption.

- M-commerce weaknesses.
- Obstacles for M-business Adoption.
- Technical and WAP Limitations.
- Potential Health Hazards.
- Limitations of the Wireless Network.
- Limitations Imposed by Mobility.
- New Security Risks in M-commerce.

STUDY QUESTIONS

1. Discuss the various threats M-commerce has to face in case of mass adoption.
2. Explain the technological limitation in case of M-commerce.
3. Describe the WML challenges in M-commerce.
4. Mention the bluetooth security.
5. What are the different security risk in M-commerce?

CHAPTER – 10

M-COMMERCE: COMING OF AGE

LEARNING OBJECTIVE

This chapter gives a generic view of M-commerce usage by giving day to examples of:

- Mobile Ticketing
- Mobile Vouchers, Coupons and Loyalty Cards
- Content Purchase and Delivery
- Location-based Services
- Information Services
- Mobile Banking
- Mobile Brokerage
- Auctions

Mobile commerce was born in 1997 when the first two mobile phone enabled Coca Cola vending machines were installed in the Helsinki area in Finland. They used SMS text messages to send the payment to the vending machines. In 1997 also the first mobile phone based banking service was launched by Merita bank of Finland also using SMS. In 1998, the first digital content sales were made possible as downloads to mobile phones when the first commercial downloadable ringing tones were launched in Finland by Radionlinja (now part of Elisa). In 1999, two major national commercial platforms for M-commerce were launched with the introduction of a national m-payments system by Smart as Smart Money in the Philippines and the launch of the first mobile internet platform by NTT DoCoMo in Japan, called i-mode. I-mode was revolutionary also in offering a revenue-sharing deal where NTT DoCoMo only kept 9% of the content payment and returned 91% to the content owner. Mobile commerce related services spread rapidly in early 2000 from Norway launching mobile parking, Austria offering mobile tickets to trains, and Japan offering mobile purchases of airline tickets. The first conference dedicated to mobile commerce was held in London in July 2001 and the first book to cover M-commerce was Tomi Ahonen's M-profits in 2002. The first university short course to discuss M-commerce was held at the University of Oxford in 2003 with Tomi Ahonen Steve Jones lecturing. UCL Computer Science and Peter Bentley now run dedicated courses in mobile commerce as of 2008.

PDAs and cellular phones have become so popular that many businesses are beginning to use M-commerce as a more efficient method of reaching and communicating with their customers. Although technological trends and advances are concentrated in Asia and in Europe, Canada and the United States are also beginning to experiment with early-stage M-commerce. The less price sensitive early adopters from the 13-25 age group could drive the initial growth. Growth in mobile products such as ringtones, games, and graphics may displace spending on many traditional youth products such as music, clothing, and movies. This would radically change the dynamics of all visual entertainment and product-service distribution worldwide so marketers could target end-users with diverse youth mind sets. The youth market has historically shown rapid viral growth which later gains acceptance in the mass market. While emerging markets are proving to be the ideal solution for sustaining revenues in the face of falling ARPU average price per unit, analysts say the rapid commercialization of 3G services is likely to open up new opportunities in developed markets.

In order to exploit the M-commerce market potential, handset manufacturers such as Nokia, Ericsson, Motorola, and Qualcomm are working with carriers such as AT&T Wireless and Sprint to develop WAP-enabled smart phones and ways to reach them. Using Bluetooth technology, smart phones offer fax, e-mail, and phone capabilities. Since the launch of the iPhone M-commerce based systems like FanGo, a popular M-commerce platform mainly for the iPhone and Blackberry, have increasingly moved away from SMS systems and into actual applications. SMS has proved to have significant vulnerabilities with security and congestion even though it is widely available and accessible. In addition improvements in the capabilities of modern mobile devices make it more prudent to carry more of the resource burden on the actual device. As phones like the iPhone become more prevalent we will see an increasing exodus from E-commerce platforms to applications and systems that will readily integrate mobile interface with the existing E-commerce back end.

Most Availed Services By The Users

Mobile Ticketing

Tickets can be sent to mobile phones using a variety of technologies. Users are then able to use their tickets immediately by presenting their phones at the venue. Tickets can be booked and cancelled on the mobile with the help of simple application downloads or by accessing WAP portals of various Travel agents or direct service providers. Mobile ticketing for airports, ballparks, and train stations, for example, will not only streamline unexpected metropolitan traffic surges, but also help users remotely secure parking spots (even while in their vehicles) and greatly facilitates mass surveillance at transport hubs.

Mobile Vouchers, Coupons and Loyalty Cards

Mobile ticketing technology can also be used for the distribution of vouchers, coupons and loyalty cards. The voucher, coupon, or loyalty card is represented by a virtual token that is sent to the mobile phone. Presenting a mobile phone with one of these tokens at the point of sale allows the customer to receive the same benefits as another customer who has a loyalty card or other paper coupon/voucher. Coupons may be sent to a customer utilizing location based services when he is in a certain physical proximity.

Content Purchase and Delivery

Currently, mobile content purchase and delivery mainly consists of the sale of ring-tones, wallpapers, and games for mobile phones. The convergence of mobile phones, mp3 players and video players into a single device will result in an increase in the purchase and delivery of full-length music tracks and video. Download speeds, if increased to 4G levels, make it possible to buy a movie on a mobile device in a couple of seconds, while on the go.

Location-based Services

Unlike a home PC, the location of the mobile phone user is an important piece of information used during mobile commerce transactions. Knowing the location of the user allows for location based services such

- local offers
- local weather
- people tracking and monitoring

Information Services

A wide variety of information services can be delivered to mobile phone users in much the same way as it is delivered to PCs. These services include:

- news services
- stock data
- sports results
- financial records
- traffic data and information

Particularly, more customized traffic information, based on users' travel patterns, will be multicast on a differentiated basis, instead of broadcasting the same news and data to all Users. This type of multicasting will be suited for more bandwidth-intensive mobile equipment.

Mobile Banking

Banks and other financial institutions are exploring the use of mobile commerce to allow their customers to not only access account information, but also make transactions, e.g. purchasing stocks, remitting money, via mobile phones and other mobile equipment. This service is often referred to as Mobile Banking or M-Banking.

Mobile Brokerage

Stock market services offered via mobile devices have also become more popular and are known as Mobile Brokerage. They allow the subscriber to react to market developments in a timely fashion and irrespective of their physical location.

Auctions

Over the past three years mobile reverse auction solutions have grown in popularity. Unlike traditional auctions, the reverse auction (or low-bid auction) bills the consumer's phone each time they place a bid. Many mobile PSMS commerce solutions rely on a one-time purchase or one-time subscription; however, reverse auctions are high return applications as they allow the consumer to transact over a long period of time.

Mobile Browsing

Mobile browsing allows customers to shop online at any time in any location. Just like a pc, you have a choice of browser.

Mobile Purchase

Instead of using paper catalogues, retailers can send customers a list of products that the customer would be interested in, directly to their mobile device or consumers can visit a mobile version of a retailer's E-commerce site. Additionally, retailers will also be able to track customers at all times and notify them of discounts at local stores that the customer would be interested in.

Mobile Marketing and Advertising

Mobile marketing is an emerging concept, but the speed with which it's growing its roots is remarkable. Mobile marketing is highly responsive sort of marketing campaign, especially from brands' experience point of view. And almost all brands are getting higher campaign response rates. Corporations are now using M-commerce to expand everything from services to marketing and advertisement. Although there are currently very few regulations on the use and abuses of mobile commerce, this will change in the next few years. With the increased use of M-commerce comes increased security. Cell phone companies are now spending more money to protect their customers and their information from online intrusions and hackers.

Options are available, but there's still a long way to go before M-commerce finally becomes a craze. Mobile phones may become a way for customers to make purchases, receive coupons, and interact with retailers, but there are several hurdles. Creating the ecosystem of service providers, merchants, banks, and users coming on to the mobile platform is the first challenge against quick arrival. Creating standard platforms, which can interact with all systems, is another challenge that needs to be addressed for M-commerce to become a big money spinner for the stakeholders.

Big in India?

India has a substantial addressable market, with over 45 mn credit/debit cards, 440 mn bank accounts, and 177 mn mobile subscribers. In M-commerce, two types of transactions take place-low-value and high-value transactions. Low-value transactions usually imply music downloads, logo downloads, picture downloads, ring tone downloads, etc. There can be some banking and value-added services like news and stock alerts. Then there are services like m-coupons and wallets. High-value transactions involve credit and debit card transactions, point-of-sale terminals, going to the merchant location, and paying through the handset. Presently, only low-value M-commerce transactions are happening in India; the concept of m-coupons and wallets has not yet picked up. There is no major development in terms of high-value transactions. However, service providers are gradually waking up to the opportunity, and we are seeing a lot of activities on this front.

Another M-commerce based segment is mobile ticketing, which is already available to users. Vodafone subscribers can book Jet airways ticket, and Airtel subscribers can book cinema tickets for PVR multiplexes in Delhi. Train tickets are also already available on the mobile. There is a lot of enthusiasm in the market, and we have seen many new services this year. Mobile ticketing is emerging in a big way. Mobile coupon is another emerging segment. Using this service, discount coupons can be delivered on mobile and redeemed at counters by producing your mobile at counters. Active Media Technology is pioneering this in India. It has already done a show with Spice in Chandigarh where passes were distributed using M-commerce technology. It is in talks with retail chains to provide this service. PayMate is targeting offline merchant sign-ups, which include large chains to stand-alone retail establishments. SMS has been the platform of choice for online and remote payments so far, but the company has now introduced a voice-based module keeping in mind unique requirements of the retail industry. To begin with, this solution will be implemented by Future Bazaar, CRS Health, Gold Cabs, and Planet M. Another M-commerce company, C-SAM provides the technology for integration of credit card into the mobile phone. It has tied up with IRCTC, VISA, ICICI, and Hutch to provide services. It has also sold the technology to Motorola for its m-Wallet service in the US.

Speed and Power

Wireless application protocol (WAP) is the current mobile Internet platform. It works currently on the GSM network. But, in the future, there will be GPRS, and UMTS, (Universal Mobile Telecommunications System). They can be divided into fast, faster, and really speedy. The worry for the mobile companies now is how to make a profit from all of this.

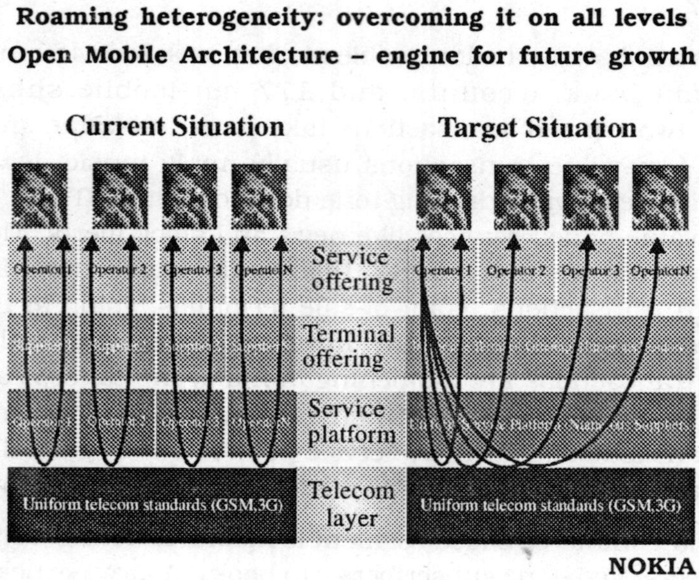

Fig. 10.1: OPEN MOBILE ARCHITECTURE

Pricing Issues

To give the reader an idea of how the revenue sharing model actually works, here is an insight into the Indian Idol revenue model. During the voting period from November 2004 to March 2005, Indian Idol got more than 55 million votes via SMS. At ₹ 3 per SMS, that is ₹ 16.5 crore. The telecom companies made ₹ 11.5 crore, and Sony about ₹ 5 crore. So as one can see, the creators of the content as of now do not demand as much of the revenue margin as the distributors (i.e. the mobile phone operators). The sole reason behind this is that even though content is supposedly king, the distribution has access and without access there would be no content. In short, the supply of mobile phone operators is relatively inelastic, i.e., they are fewer in number and not growing that fast. The supply of content makers however is relatively elastic - there are loads of people trying to produce exclusive content and there is a certain level of quality that is being made due to the proliferation of so called 'exclusive' content creation tools. So obviously the distribution takes a higher premium because there are scores of people lining up with content for distribution while everything cannot really be distributed. One may even see a scenario where distributors may create or buy over content and handle its exclusive rights to gain a better control over revenues. As of now a lot of the football content that ESPN Star Sports produces is centered around the South East Asian fans which is where all the monies lie with respect to football, especially EPL content frankly. Of course a market exists in India as well but the scope and magnitude of it will be much more in the countries that have the numbers in terms of football fanatics.

The 3 main 'stakeholders' when it comes to mobile distribution of content more clearly are:

- Mobile Phone Operators (the distributors).
- The Media companies: They have exclusive content to share that viewers like to watch.
- The aggregators: They are the people who modify content exclusively to suit it for viewing on the mobile screen.

In the past, the impression was that content over the mobile will be paid for, and the revenues will be much bigger on the Mobile phones than on the Internet. This was primarily because of the mindset that exists in the consumer's mind who thinks that everything on the Internet is (or should be) free, while everything on mobile phones is, or can be paid for. The other is to do with logistics. Mobile phone companies can charge premium content directly to a person's bill or even cut money from his/her prepaid balance. This is something your cable operator cannot do because he does not OWN the content you are viewing. And that's the key so far, mobile phone operators have OWNED content. That will change once users start to generate exclusive content through the Internet which then will not be owned by the mobile phone operators.

Once users start accessing exclusive content from the Internet, it may then be supported by advertising. So if mobile phone companies want to maintain their VAS revenues over the Internet in the future, they must start building strong brands from now so that they can leverage on the brand equity that such services may accumulate when the phenomenon of accessing VAS and TV from the Internet really takes off. If they do not do so, they will be reduced to mere service providers which quite clearly is where they do not want to be. There is probably another insight with respect to TV and other Value Added Services (VAS) over mobile.

Even handset providers are joining in the fray especially Nokia who currently has about 70% of the market share with respect to GSM Handsets. Nokia is spending a lot of time, money, and resources to ensure that dealers are educated with respect to the usability of high end applications and services. Estimates from various sources project the value of the Mobile Data Market to touch $10 billion by 2010. A lot of the reasons have already been outlined – another aspect to add is that the mobile can fill a real hole with respect to the rural entertainment space in India. The number of Cable connections in India are currently at only 70 million. The potential for handset penetration in numbers is 500 million plus. Apart from having access to entertainment, rural consumers would also be willing to spend a little more on the mobile space primarily because it is a device that places a lot of 'power' in their hands. The ability to know the weather or book railway tickets without moving from your room is something that will boost both the ego as well as morale of the rural consumer. The stage is set for a lot of momentum in the mobile space expect a lot of changes, a lot of forecasts and a lot of new players. There are essentially 3 phases that a mobile market can go through:

Phase 1: Voice and SMS.

Phase 2: Ringtones, Wallpapers, Information, Entertainment.

Phase 3: Rich Media, Open Internet, Convergence.

Today, the Internet is PC Centric. In the future internet access from mobiles will overtake the PC. One will see that 3 years down the line in India as well primarily because of the volume of mobile penetration. Mobile in the future will not only be mobile 'phones'. Mobile will extend to cameras, DVD players, books maybe – a ubiquitous Internet. Another thing that one finds becoming popular in the Mobile Internet market is mobile widgets. One has already seen that on the PC's with Apple's OS. Now we will see widgets for mobiles as well. This makes the touch and feels experience better and users can have a more 'graphic experience'. This will also lead to users bookmarking favorites as widgets. One also sees mobiles becoming advanced communication devices with high end cameras, voice recorders, etc. Thus mobiles automatically need to be tapped as avenues that can crowd the space of user generated content.

But in the period since IBM Corp. introduced the world to the idea of M-commerce in the late 1990s with its commercials depicting the vending-machine scenario, M-commerce has struggled to live up to its initial hype. This is especially true in the United States, where mobile-phone technology has historically lagged behind developments in trend-setting countries in Asia, such as South Korea and Japan, and even Europe.

CASE STUDIES

CASE - 1

ICERON's M-COMMERCE APPLICATIONS

ICERON's software development services include development for Internet-based information services for wireless devices such as mobile phones and Internet-enabled PDAs and Java-enabled mobile phones. Their software compatibility spans a wide range of devices and networks, and they have cultivated strategic partnerships with major players in this field especially in the ASIA-Pacific Rim. Besides WAP, they are working on other Mobile technologies like I-mode and J-Phone to cater Asia-Pacific region where these technologies are more dominant in the mobile computing domain. ICERON is now preparing to expand to new horizons to address Europe, America and rest of world and as well as on the technical front to address the upcoming Java-enabled devices market.

The backbone of these applications is the J2EE based framework. ICERON has developed core competency in addressing the wireless applications market with a combination of J2EE and J2ME. ICERON provides wireless solutions for a variety of applications. Following are the niche areas they have expertise in:

1. *Mobile Enabling your Business*

It is clear from the studies done by Gartner by 2005, people would be accessing information more on handheld devices as compared to conventional access on PC. For such a scenario, if you do not have presence in the mobile Internet market, you can yourself judge what that means to your business. ICERON helps businesses to mobile enable their core services. With the ICERON's expertise, one can reach their customers at anytime as well as anywhere. Services like travel facilities, hotels and airlines are the most sought after by the people on move. Giving your customers to contact you while they are on move would make it very convenient for them while at the same time it means more business for you.

2. Messaging Solutions — SMS Reach out to the World

Communication has made the world a global village. You can reach anybody, anywhere in the world from the comfort of your home by using a phone. But this, of course, involves human interaction. For your business, there should be a mechanism which keeps your customers informed about your new services and that too irrespective of their location as well as their availability on a particular place at anytime. For this, ICERON provides with integration of SMS (Short Message Service) with your business. Using this service one can send SMS to his customers for promotion of new services that keeps rolling out. Also since SMS is the most reliable way of communication as of now, it is assured that he has communicated what he wants to the world. There are a number of ways by which you can enable SMS messaging on your applications. Following diagrams depict the various scenarios.

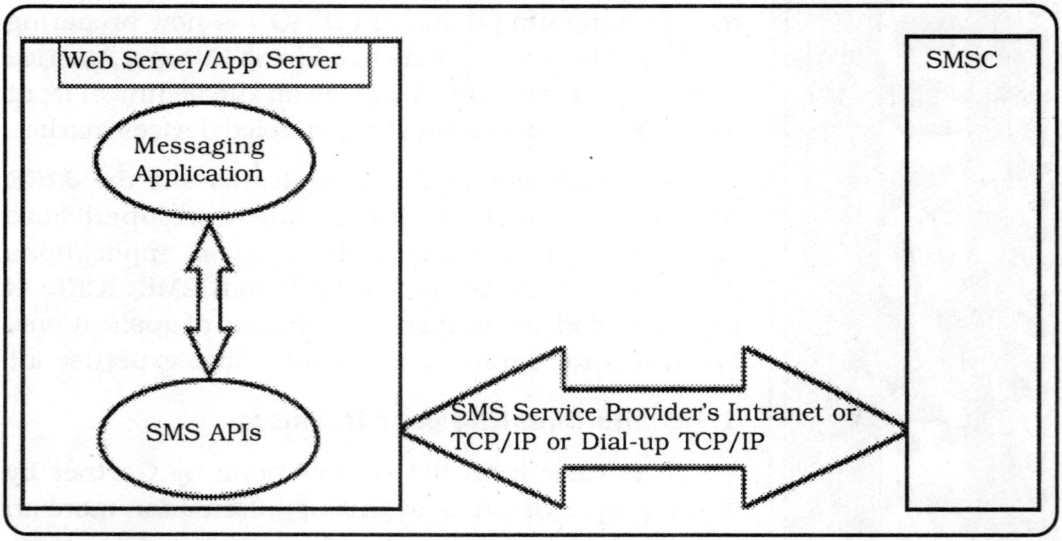

From the diagram it can be seen that the messaging solution can be implemented in three ways i.e.

- By deploying the complete solution within the service provider's intranet. This is the most robust solution as it provides the best connectivity for the application with the SMSC.
- The same solution can be implemented over TCP/IP over X25.
- A solution in which the SMSC and the application hosting services are provided by different vendors then we can opt for Dial-up TCP/IP.

3. M-commerce solutions

With the expansion of B2B and B2C market, a large amount of online transactions are being conducted over internet using secure connections. As the use of mobile devices would increase to access internet, this demand would also be there to provide secure financial transactions over the internet using mobile devices. This market is still evolving and the standards are being laid out. ICERON has taken an early initiative on this front too. It provides M-commerce solutions by providing secure transaction over mobile devices by clubbing the transactional services provided by other industry majors by implementing micro payment solutions.

4. Mobile Entertainment – Games

This industry is already going very fast as this the area, which is attracting more and more users towards use of mobile devices of course apart from the utility factor. ICREON has already developed gaming software for its Japanese client. ICERON provides online games, online lottery systems coupled with secure payment channel integration from industry majors. These games could be developed in a completely online mode and also as a J2ME based application, which runs on a Java-enabled device.

QUESTIONS

1. Describe the company profile of ICERON 's software development services. Also mention its significance in service.
2. Explain the area of applications of ICERON 's software development services.
3. Write a note on the communication media of ICERON 's software development services.
4. How ICERON 's software development services is helping in area of business.

CASE-2

SYNTEL BUILDS M-COMMERCE APPLICATION THAT HELPS INSURANCE AGENTS SERVE THEIR CUSTOMERS BETTER AND FASTER

About Syntel

Syntel (NASDAQ: SYNT) is a leading global provider of integrated information technology and Knowledge Process Outsourcing (KPO) solutions spanning the entire lifecycle of business and information systems and processes. The Company is driven by its mission to create new opportunities for clients by harnessing the passion, talent and innovation of Syntel employees worldwide. Syntel leverages dedicated Centers of Excellence, a flexible Global Delivery Model, and a strong track record of building collaborative client partnerships to create sustainable business advantage for Global 2000 organizations. Recently named one of the "50 Best Managed Global Outsourcing Vendors" by The Black Book of Outsourcing, Syntel is assessed at SEI CMMi Level 5, and is ISO 27001 and ISO 9001:2000 certified. As of March 31, 2009, Syntel employed more than 11,700 people worldwide. Syntel, Inc. (NASDAQ:SYNT), a leading e-Business and applications outsourcing firm, announced, it has completed work on a Wireless Application Protocol (WAP)-based application that enables insurance agents to use WAP-enabled personal digital assistants (PDAs) and mobile phones to complete insurance transactions in real time, in the field."Our teams were able to blend Syntel's deep expertise in the financial services industry sector with our growing body of knowledge in developing innovative wireless solutions," said Rajiv Tandon, Syntel Vice President of Global Delivery. "The result is an innovative wireless application that can dramatically impact how insurance professionals serve their customers more effectively." The development project was completed in approximately two months in collaboration with nekema.com, a New Jersey-based financial services aggregator. Nekema plays the role of a modern day matchmaker, arranging the successful marriage of electronic commerce technology with the business requirements of insurance and financial companies and their intermediaries. The application has a specially built wireless client services layer that interfaces with the business rules engine powering the nekema.com web site. After accepting information from a series of easy-to-navigate screens, inquiries are made to the appropriate business logic components. A quote is displayed and if accepted, the policy is bound instantaneously. The quote and bind confirmation letters are automatically produced and faxed or e-mailed to the agent and customer. The application has built-in intelligence to automatically adapt to the needs of the wireless device used by selecting suitable style sheet(s). Challenging segments of the project included creating 100 percent reuse of business rules and components in the existing insurance product, generating specially customized WML (Wireless Mark-up Language) pages for the type of client and serving them intelligently to WAP clients. The Syntel development team successfully managed all of these challenges. According to the U.S. Department of Commerce, there will be more than 1 billion wireless subscribers worldwide by 2004 and that level of activity is expected to create a $12 billion global market for wireless professional services by that time.

About nekema.com

Nekema.com is an E-commerce provider based in Jersey City, NJ, formed as a joint venture between Kemper Insurance Companies and Madison Consulting Group. Nekema develops E-commerce platforms, which permit financial institutions to communicate with their distributors and customers using web technology.

QUESTION

1. Make a SWOT analysis of this case and explain how M-commerce application is going to bring change in customer service of Syntel.

Case-3

MAKEMYTRIP.COM TARGETS MOBILE SUBSCRIBERS, LAUNCHES HOLISTIC M-COMMERCE PLATFORM.

TT Bureau 07 Apr 2008

The online medium seems to be finally waking up to the mobile medium potential as the latter is increasingly assuming importance in new business plans of established portals. One such established travel portal, makemytrip.com is now all set to target the huge mobile subscriber base in India as it announced the launch of what it claims is a holistic M-commerce platform for mobile consumers. Among a range of new applications the portal will now enable mobile subscribers to search, book, pay and even receive their ticket on their mobile phones at no additional cost. The portal has tied-up with multiple players for its aggressive foray in the mobile space. The company's one such tie-up with mChek branded as 'MakeMyTrip Anymobile' requires the customer to send only an SMS 'MakeMyTrip' to 543219 following which an instructional menu appears on the screen of the mobile subscriber. The customer needs to have an account with mChek and the tie-up claims that such mobile subscribers will not be charged for sending SMS to book tickets.

MakeMyTrip has also aligned with Airtel to launch a dedicated WAP site for Airtel subscribers. The service allows Airtel subscribers with GPRS connection to have a one-click access to MakeMyTrip services on their mobile handsets. Additionally the company has also tied-up with Nokia wherein Nokia NSeries range of mobile phones have a pre-built MakeMyTrip JAVA application that allows easy access of the portal on the mobile phones. Sachin Bhatia, CMO and Co-Founder, MakeMyTrip.com, said, "This launch positions MakeMyTrip as the first travel Company to offer a true M-commerce platform for travelers in India. It is our biggest mobile initiative so far and strengthens the existing channels of access that we offer. Our mobile booking facility is now accessible to the user-base of 60 million Airtel subscribers. This development is also a triumph for our R&D division since the WAP application has been designed indigenously."

QUESTION

1. How M-commerce is going to help MakeMyTrip to increase its market share and to sustain in highly competitive market?

CASE-4

ABACUS, AMADEUS FORAY INTO M-COMMERCE ARENA

(Source — Krupa Vora | Mumbai)

Mobile Commerce or M-commerce technology which permits consumers to carry out transactions on their mobile device, will now be pushed in a big way through Global Distribution companies like Amadeus and Abacus International. While Abacus has announced the launch of the mobile version of Abacus Virtually. There, Amadeus will soon launch their mobile technology. Both companies plan to roll out these mobile solutions in the international market and India will be included at a later stage. Amadeus is currently working on developing the mobile technology which can be compatible on the Apple i-phone along with regular handsets which work on GSM and CDMA networks. The company has heavily invested in technology including technology for M-commerce so that it can cater to different segments of users. "We are currently working with a few airlines to launch the services, however it is very premature to disclose the airline names and the nature of the technology offered," said Damian Hickey, Vice President, Airline Business Group Asia Pacific, Amadeus. Further more, Abacus recently launched 'Abacus Virtually'. This is for traveller's to access flight information from their mobile device. The technology is equipped to feed destination information to the traveller upon arrival. They have enabled agents to send updates and assist their clients round the clock, even when they are travelling. The efficiency is such that agencies using the solution can offer clients round-the-clock access to their travel schedules, instant notification of flight delays and changes in gate information, confirmation and details of ground reservation and information about entertainment options regardless of the model of mobile phone a client uses. As per a survey conducted by Euromonitor, the top five countries for mobile subscribers include China, India, Japan, Indonesia and Pakistan; accounting for 1.2 billion or 80 per cent of mobile subscribers in Asia Pacific. All these point to the fact that China has the largest number of mobile phone subscribers amounting to 540 million as of March 2008, while India has overtaken the United States to become the second largest mobile market.

QUESTIONS

1. Make an analysis how the new launch of Abacus is going to help it in the long run.
2. How M-commerce is going to benefit the clientele of Abacus?

CASE-5

CELLNEXT-VALUE ADDED SERVICES

Mid 2007, Delhi-based Cellnext, a wireless solutions provider and that belong to the Escorts group, felt that it was at a cross roads. While the company had been able to build up Value Added Services (VAS) business that delivered services to Telco's and other enterprises, the company needed a scaling strategy to take it to the next level. Margins were under pressure due to skewed revenue sharing with Telco's, a major source of revenue, and the company was looking to identify new growth drivers for its next 5 year strategic growth plan. It was at this juncture that Cellnext applied for was accepted for the NASSCOM mentorship programme.

One of the first things that the three member panel did was to carry out a detailed analysis of the strategic plan, questioning all key assumptions along the way. "They kept asking us – why are you doing this, and not that?" recalls Cellnext CEO AD Mehta. 'They took their job very seriously, and added a lot of value," he says.

So what was the single largest contribution of the mentor panel to the business plan? According to Mehta, a key input was that the panel urged Cellnext to go deeper into domains. "While we were servicing enterprises, we were only touching these areas," he says. For instance, instead of just offering an SMS media channel (calls-to-action involving SMS short codes/push marketing to handsets), Cellnext is now looking at deeper engagements, to see how mobile technology could be harnessed for customer information management, sales force automation, digital advertising and product campaigns. So, has the strategy paid off? "Well we are now beginning to do this for a few accounts," says Mehta.

Another key input that came from discussions with the panel was a decision to better leverage revenue streams from existing customers. "We had reduced our thrust, and only showed incremental growth. The panel felt that the experience and customer knowledge gathered in the past was not being reaped/ leveraged to its full potential for the future. The discussions helped us understand that reduction in the area of services would have been counter productive, due to the loss of ready ongoing revenue streams that did not have many associated costs," details Mehta.

But clearly, as a detailed discussion with Mehta showed, the biggest take-away from the mentorship process for Cellnext was that it provided a framework and a structure to fine-tune strategy. According to the CEO, "It really helped us internalize our thought process. We asked ourselves – what is the killer game plan? Doing that helped remove any chaff from the business plan and we were able to define our goals more sharply." From these discussions came two important recognitions for Cellnext: A decision to focus on B2B services rather than B2C and to create strong offerings in the M-commerce space that would leverage its technology capabilities. So, did the mentorship panel work in a manner similar to a business consulting exercise? Mehta doesn't think so: "While they looked at business strategy, this was within the framework and context offered up by the company. You must remember that this was a group of CEOs and what they were bringing in were elements of validation, by challenging our business strategy and by rigorously discussing the business plan". The company also benefited form tactical advice proffered by the panel members.

What changes would Cellnext like to see in the way the mentor programme is run? "Well, what we would now like to do is to focus on individual areas where a specific member of the panel has expertise," says Mehta. By way of suggestions, Mehta says that it would help if the programme were more structured by defining goals and objectives early on say, after the first or second meeting. "It would also be interesting if the panel could present to us, focusing on specific areas/expertise areas, he says. Another suggestion is to build in a mechanism for interaction – through meetings or even an online forum or blog – between mentee companies. "In the first round, each company leveraged the panel differently. It would add value and we could learn from each other if the companies were able to share experiences all through," he says.Clearly there was much to share – a testimonial to the success of the programme itself!

QUESTIONS

1. Make a report on the existing business scenario of Cellnext.
2. What strategic change the company should bring in order to improve its market?

CASE-6

I COLLABORATOR CASE STUDY

I-Collaborator has been structured upon the T2 real time platform. Unlike other real time communication systems, I-Collaborator has been designed from ground-up to ensure superior security, compliance and rules-based access for its users. It is an application designed to allow organizations worldwide, secure, real time communications and voice/data exchange capability. The future enhancements will include bridges to public messengers thereby, so to speak, "*taming of the shrew*" for businesses.

The Given

In its previous iteration, I-Collaborator (then known as Tandem) was dependent on DirectX technology for exchange of messages and voice. The customers' wished to base their technology upon something more sturdy, something which was less proprietary. The old Tandem had bloated with functionality, threading for multiple tasks was poor. While very functional, the platform was architecturally weak due to use of disparate components and technologies.

The Needs

The company researched the domain, the competing technologies, direction of the industry. Its engineers studied the intricacies of the technology and the exacting demands for security and compliance, need for speedy exchanges plus the need to plug-in applications for the future. The customer also needed to discrete design so as to be able to license components to developers.

Re-engineering I-Collaborator

They wrote the core communication layer in C# sockets. This was done to ensure superior performance based on the need to *futurize* and the ability to compile the core platform for minimized platform dependency in deployment. The re-engineering is an ongoing exercise and the project was broken down into the following parts:

Need Analysis

Due diligence of existing technology

Industry and domain study

Technology study

Proof-of-concept

Finalization of technology

Finalization of architecture

Commencement of coding

Release of Phase I

QUESTIONS

1. How the latest technology introduced by i-Collaborator has helped to re-engineer their business activity.
2. Enlist the various steps under process implementation of the technology at i-Collaborator.

CASE-7

BANKER'S TRAINING COLLEGE CASE STUDY

The BTC conducts operations and compliance related training and courses to bankers worldwide. These are typically two to five days training courses with specialized faculty, speakers, etc. The operational challenges included:

- Planning and scheduling of courses
- Planning and scheduling of facilities
- Planning and scheduling of trainers and specialists
- Transport and accommodation management

The Given

Banks wishing to send their representatives needed to send e-mail or written application for courses. These applications were processed manually as was the scheduling of trainers, guests, classrooms and facilities. Thereafter multi-lingual confirmations (based on the preference of the applicants) were sent out.

Due to gaps in the system, there were confusing scenarios of fees. Some banking institutions were paying for bulk in advance, whereas other were paying for the number of participants yet others were paying after the end of the course. Maintenance of fee records, per-diem allowances for trainers and honorarium for guest speakers was a labor intensive task.

Evolving over the years, there was a basic system designed in FoxPro for record keeping, and this required manual input of data.

The Needs

The need was to automate the processes starting with a web interface where the courses were outlined. Applications were acceptable via the web interface only (with the capability of registering bulk applicants in one step). Once the required number of participants was achieved, automated, language specific confirmations were sent out, the dates reflected on faculty calenders and notification sent to the trainers and to guest speakers via e-mail.

Facility management was crucial, with senior bankers given preference for premium accommodations and others to juniors. Program and participant details were sent out F&B department for provisioning of appropriate snack and foods, and to the transportation department for provisioning local transportation and sight-seeing.

Building the BTC software

The system was planned with web services concepts so as to ultimately integrate with the ERP system in place. Our solution was to accommodate for MS SQL database with easy migration to Oracle 9i at some time in the future. Customer and Management Reports were generated using the preferred Crystal Reports:

- Need Analysis
- Process study
- Multiple interviews with users - administrators & faculty
- Proof-of-concept
- Approval of flow
- Commencement of coding

Highlights

The customer has achieved full ROI within 100 days of the rollout!

QUESTION

1. Analyze how implementation of m-course will simplify this banker's training programme.

CASE-8

M-COMMERCE SOLUTIONS CASE STUDY

The Customer

Company is a leading global consulting and IT services company in India. The application under discussion is being used by various clients across the globe.

The Challenge

Entering business critical data using a mobile phone.

The Solution

Most of the users of the application were travelling most of the time from one region to another across the globe. They were having the need to enter critical data of their business at the end of ever day/week/month/year. These data then will be used by the application for further processing. The application is a web-based system for making existing system WAP enabled. User can create business rules of his interest in order to receive periodic alerts about the data entry. Whenever a user receives such email alerts through the cellular phone, users can log on to the site for entering data using a cellular phone. This particular feature is very useful for mobile users for entering critical data any time and from anywhere.

Benefits

- A user can enter business critical data from anywhere and any time without waiting for a PC.
- E-mail alerts based on the business rule of the user.
- Flexibility for the creation of business rules of interest in order to get the periodic alerts.

CASE-9

MOBILE WALLETS: CASE STUDY OF M-COMMERCE FROM JAPAN

(source::www.mobillcash.com)

A few years ago Mobile Commerce was touted as the killer application of mobile technology. With the overall lukewarm interest in 3G(3RD Generation), mobile commerce has also been slow to take off. Industry analysts often point to Japan and Korea for signs of early mobile technology adoption. The recent effort to introduce the so-called "mobile wallets" in Japan has been interesting. Here I'll share a news report from CARD TECHNOLOGY which ran a story with a subtitle "Japan's Mobile Wallets Fail To Inspire – Yet".

As the report argues, Japan's mobile telcos and payment card players haven't yet convinced subscribers to think of their handsets as mobile wallets. As you read the story note how the usability of the whole process has created hurdles for the users and technology adoption. Also note how preloading applications on the phone helped in increased usage.

Here are Excerpts from the News Report

Carried by 19 million commuters in what is reputed as the world's busiest mass transit system, East Japan Railway's *Suica contactless card* is used more than 200 million times per month. So it seemed like a natural for Suica to move to the contactless mobile wallet phones Telco NTT DoCoMo has been selling for more than two years, later joined by Japan's other mobile network operators. With Mobile Suica, commuters could download train tickets and recharge their Suica e-cash purse over the air to their phones, which they could tap to pass through transit gates or make purchases at more than 10,000 merchant locations in Tokyo.

But 13 months after its much-anticipated launch in January 2006, only 350,000 customers had signed up for the mobile service. That's only about a third of what the commuter rail operator had expected. It declines to release transaction numbers.

The registration process has been difficult for many prospective users, Akio Shiibashi, director of the Suica Systems Department at JR East, tells Card Technology. "Membership is a little complicated, so we need to make it simpler," he says. "The digital ticketing function has not materialized."

Nor was 2006 a breakthrough year for any of Japan's other contactless payment schemes that have launched service on wallet phones, known as "Osaifu-Keitai" in Japan. While a reported 2.6 million subscribers had signed up to tap their wallet phones to make credit payments in convenience stores, supermarkets, restaurants and vending machines as of January, it's obvious the number of transactions are less than what backers had hoped for. The 2.6 million doesn't include users of e-cash on the wallet phones.

Interestingly even in Japan consumer awareness remains an issue and there aren't enough places for consumers to tap.

"The most important thing is the number of acceptance points," says consultant Masayuki Yamamoto, a former executive with Visa International in Japan. "The number of merchants is not very great. (And) because the startup is slow, people are not aware they can use mobile payment."

Wallet-phone backers say it's only a matter of time before their investment pays off. But the teething pains in Japan,the most advanced mobile payment and ticketing market in the world, have implications for mobile operators, banks, transit operators and others in Europe and North America, which are planning to launch services in coming years using phones supporting similar contactless technology, NFC.

Among the issues facing the mobile-commerce players in Japan of interest to the outside world is how to solve difficulties in personalizing phones over the air with applications. After all, this is a major advantage contactless phones hold over cards. Transit operators could reduce the number of their ticketing agents by allowing customers to download monthly passes or e-cash for single rides. Banks could avoid card-issuing costs. And the handset could serve as the multi application platform cards never managed to become.

Pre-loaded Applications

This study shows that makes a big difference if the application comes pre-loaded on the handset and is ready for the end-user. Excerpts from the above story:

For most of the registered users of contactless mobile payment in Japan, applications are pre-loaded on the handsets. Every new wallet phone the Telco sells comes with iD pre-installed, ready to be registered by the subscriber-a much easier process than downloading the application itself. Japan's largest credit card company, JCB, says its registered users jumped by three times after DoCoMo chief rival, Telco KDDI, began pre-loading JCB's QUICPay service on to its phones.

"It's kind of difficult for average users to download the Java application," says Shusaku Maruko, general manager in the planning department for FeliCa Networks, the DoCoMo, Sony joint venture handling the secure downloads.

Japan's mobile-payment players face other challenges that those in the NFC world are unlikely to see. Foremost among them is the fact, there is no standard application for contactless payment in Japan, in part because contactless phones and cards use a nonstandard technology called FeliCa, from Sony. It means when consumers find a contactless point-of-sale terminal, it may not accept the brand of contactless credit or e-cash they are carrying.

There are 5 contactless schemes rolling out in Japan. Efforts to make the point-of-sale terminals and readers interoperable rely not on international standards bodies, but bilateral agreements between the schemes. And progress has been slow. There are perhaps 100,000 terminals and readers deployed by the various contactless schemes at merchant locations in Japan, not counting multiple brands accepted at the same shop or restaurant. But that is still a small number in Japan's vast retail market, says Yamamoto.

A Turning Point?

Still, wallet-phone backers are confident. DoCoMo's Hiromiki Moriyama, a director in the Telco's multimedia services department, tells Card Technology 100 Yen shops (Japan's counterpart to the U.S. dollar store) are among the latest retailers to accept iD. About 90 stores owned by the Aeon Group, one of Japan's largest retailers, have already installed iD terminals. And Aeon also is among the first merchants to deploy readers supporting more than one brand of contactless payment.

Such high-profile merchants as Seven-Eleven Japan, with nearly 12,000 convenience stores, and McDonald's restaurants are also planning to deploy contactless payment terminals. Seven-Eleven is launching its own contactless service, nanaco, this spring.

While the relative scarcity of acceptance points is a problem, the number of wallet phones is not. DoCoMo and its competitors have together sold nearly 30 million contactless phones since 2004, with 40 million projected by March 2008.

And service providers are also moving to ease the burden of signing up for the mobile services. For example, JR East had limited its mobile service only to holders of its own credit card, "View." But the rail operator realized its mistake and 10 months after Mobile Suica's launch, opened up the scheme to holders of all major credit card brands in Japan and three large banks. Subscribers can use these accounts to pay for the tickets and e-cash value they download. It is also making it easier to download the service, a task that took 30 minutes to 1 hour before. JR, like the other promoters of contactless payment, believe it can tap in on the estimated 60 trillion yen (US$514 billion) Japanese consumers spend every year on low-value purchases, nearly all of it with cash. But Japan's wallet-phone backers know changing the behavior of tens of millions of subscribers will not happen overnight.

Case-10

ISHOP MOBILE CASE STUDIES

LEUKAEMIA RESEARCH CHOOSE MPP TO PROVIDE SMS DONATION PLATFORM

Leukemia Research has chosen MPP to supply them with the txt2donate platform to allow its supporters to donate funds in conjunction with various Sponsored Walks. Celebrity runners include Sir Ian Botham and Tony Audenshaw (Bob Hope from Emmerdale), who will be walking with the text call-to-action on their clothing. All supporters have to do is simply text "BEEFY" to 82540 and they will have helped by donating £3.00 through Reverse-Bill SMS. The donation process is straightforward, fast and memorable so that users can tell their friends and family to also donate in this way. The charity has full access to MPP's Management Console which allows them to view all the details of the service including SMS reports, monthly statements and much more.

CASE-11

EMAP SIGN-UP TO MPP'S TXT-A-SONG TO SELL MUSIC DOWNLOADS FROM TV

EMAP Performance Television has signed up with MPP Global Solutions to be the first TV Company to sell digital music downloads off-screen to its viewers. From its seven music TV channels, txt-a-song, which uses text messaging to engage viewers, will enable EMAP to complement their music productions with the sale of digital music downloads and drive new revenue streams. Txt-a-song *'seizes the moment'* when music fans first see a video or hear a single, making impulse purchasing possible when fans are most likely to respond. Ordering couldn't be simpler, with the consumer simply texting a keyword to a mobile short code. Fulfillment is immediate, with consumers receiving a real-time text response enabling them to download the song immediately to their mobile phone, or providing instructions on how to receive and download the music from the channel's websites.

CASE-12

MPP POWER TXT2INSURE TRAVEL INSURANCE SERVICES

Text2Insure, part of the Hastings Insurance Services Group, has selected MPP to power its mobile SMS text messaging travel insurance service. The traveler is prompted to text the word "*Insure*" to the mobile short code 61066 from in-situ and press advertising and immediately receives a reply message, which provides simple instructions to obtain a quote. A real-time quotation is returned along with instructions on how to purchase the policy using MPP's secure M-commerce platform. All this can be done whilst waiting to check-in.

CASE-13

CHRYSALIS RADIO AND MPP LINK TO OFFER MUSIC DOWNLOADS TO MOBILE

In the first commercial radio activity of its kind, Chrysalis Radio announced the successful launch of a Motorola sponsored full-song-download promotion using MPP's Music Download service. The promotion launched across the Galaxy Network over the May bank holiday weekend as the culmination of 3 weeks' voting by Galaxy listeners for their 'Top Galaxy Anthems'. Five top tracks were then made available to download using MPP's txt-a-song service, with files provided in a variety of DRM-protected formats to ensure maximum device compatibility. The txt-a-song service encourages impulse purchasing when fans first hear a track and are most likely to respond. Ordering couldn't be simpler with the consumer texting a keyword to a mobile shortcode and fulfillment is immediate with consumers receiving a real-time text response allowing them to download the song immediately to their mobile phone, or instructing them how to download music to their PC.

CASE-14

NEW PUBLIC TRANSPORT FIRM NEXUS ARE FIRST TO GO LIVE WITH MPP'S MOBILE TICKETING SYSTEM

MPP Global has been contracted to develop a mobile ticketing system for public transport by Ticket Mobility, an initiative partly funded by the European Commission and spearheaded in the UK by NEXUS (Tyne & Wear Passenger Transport Executive based in Newcastle). The mTicket system offers a major step forward and is designed to reduce the costs involved with issuing and verifying traditional tickets. It gives users instant access to real-time, location-specific information and ticketing facilities. Users simply text a keyword in order to buy a ticket and by recognizing the mobile phone number the system will automatically purchase the ticket and send an mTicket by SMS. Payment is made using credit and debit cards, which are stored using MPP eWallet technology. If users are buying a ticket for the first time, a WAP page is automatically loaded on to their mobile phone and, like a mini-web page, enables users to securely add credit card information in order to activate their eWallet. The mTicket, delivered by SMS, cannot be forwarded by users and is easily verified by ticket inspectors on trains, trams and buses. Timetable, route and fare information is delivered to their email account for future use using MPP's txt2mail technology.

CASE-15

FOURFOURTWO PIONEER THE SALE OF MAGAZINES VIA MOBILE

FourFourTwo magazine has enlisted MPP to enable the sale of future editions of the magazine via SMS. Readers of the December 2006 issue were offered the chance to reserve/purchase a copy of the next edition by sending a simple text. Automatic payment is made via the user's mobile phone account and the reader is prompted to enter their delivery address via a link to a FourFourTwo branded WAP site. The service also provided the opportunity for readers to subscribe to 6 or 12 further issues of the magazine by entering credit or debit card information into the WAP screen. This was an exciting trial, the results of which was certainly interesting. Hopefully the project proved beneficial, leading to new ways of doing business by making Haymarket accessible to customers via an increasingly important and ubiquitous medium: the mobile telephone.

CASE-16

EMAP UTILISE MPP'S TXT2BUY FOR LAUNCH OF NEW RELEASES.

EMAP Music, the music division of the radio, TV and magazine giant, is launching 8 new releases over the coming weeks and is complementing its marketing campaign with text calls-to-action. With both physical and digital products to choose from, consumers simply text a mobile shortcode and are taken to a mobile WAP site where they can choose the format of their choice and securely enter their credit card details to purchase the product. An e-mail receipt is generated with download instructions or confirmation of purchase of the physical CD. In conjunction with New Woman magazine, the first to go live was the digital album "*The Very Best Of New Woman*". With extensive TV and radio promotion, consumers simply text NWC to 82540 to initiate the purchase process. Current campaigns include Kerrang! New Breed, which unleashes the finest new talent from the hottest new rock acts, to the prime of the underground and Max Power Booty Bass, which brings together some of the freshest sounds of today, with a few modern classics thrown in, the compilation spans all the genres that matter; Hip Hop, Drum and Bass, Dub Step, Grime and Breaks. Another imminent campaign is Kiss Does...Funky House which bring you the sexiest sounds and the funkiest beats.

CASE-17

SHOPPING CHANNEL TO OFFER WAP SHOPPING

MPP has been chosen to work with the world-leading TV shopping retailer Thane Direct, the first ever shopping channel to offer WAP purchasing. Using MPP's iShop Mobile product, Thane Direct 'seize the moment' when viewers first see a product on screen. Consumers use their mobile phone as an additional way of buying products by directly interacting with Thane Direct using text. The viewer texts the keyword SHOP to the mobile shortcode 82540 to initiate the transaction process.

CASE-18

McFly OFFICIAL WAP SITE LAUNCHED BY UNIVERSAL AND MPP

Universal Music and MPP Global Solutions, has launched the UK's first Official artist WAP site for Island Records Group artists McFly. The WAP site is an extension of the Official McFly website which is currently the most popular artist website for UK users (Source: Hitwise). McFly fans can access the Official WAP site anytime, anywhere to find out all the latest exclusive McFly news, tour dates and release information, use WAP Chat to talk to other fans and purchase the latest official ringtones and wallpapers all from their mobile phones. Registration to the services couldn't be simpler, fans simply text WAP MCFLY to 82540. The service will respond with a personalized welcome text message which automatically loads the McFly WAP site on their handset. The fan is also assigned a personalized PIN, enabling them to purchase products on the site without breaking their WAP session. All Billing is through their phone by Premium Rate SMS so there is no need to use a credit card or costly IVR lines.

The service is built on MPP's mobile content management system which removes the headaches associated with publishing mobile content to a plethora of mobile devices. The service automatically optimizes the display of pictures and text on the site for any handset. All hosting, delivery and content management is carried out by MPP. The service also manages billing of all services, including ringtones, wallpapers and access to the WAP Chat service on a subscription basis, using its micropayment product MicroFusion.

CASE-19

The Client

Wicaksana Overseas International deals in candies, snacks, beverages, milk powder, instant noodle, jelly, drinks, personal care, home care and health care and disposable cigarette lighters. The Company is listed on the Jakarta Stock Exchange (JSE). It is the biggest independent distributor in Indonesia.

The Challenge

Wicaksana Overseas International has a Sales Force of over 2000 sales representatives who take orders from outlets all over Indonesia. The system, as it existed, had a high level of manual interface. The salesforce would spend a substantial amount of time to collect orders from the customers, collate them at the end of the day, provide information to head office and arrange deliveries. Time which could have been spent making that extra call was instead being spent in managing the back end requirements of the customers. Wicaksana was looking for a solution to speed up this process accurately.

The Soltius Differential

With the M-Force technology being provided by Soltius Infotech, the sales activity has become real time. The Sales representatives now use a Personal Digital Assistant (PDA) to take the orders. The software resides in the device. The latest stock data and the daily schedule is uploaded in the device before the representatives leave for their daily work. The Sales representatives then enter the Order entry data in the device. The order is confirmed by the customer by Signature verification.

The order is uploaded to the database of Wicaksana Overseas International by connecting the PDA to the normal telephone line or cellular phone and dialing to the RAS (Remote Access Service) numbers provided by Wicaksana. This connects the PDA device to the database server and synchronizes the device data with the existing in-house built system. The sales representatives upload the data whenever they want just by connecting to the available telephone line (normal or cellular).

The Delivery personnel take the PDA while delivering goods to the customers. The Delivery Schedule is downloaded on the PDA before the delivery personnel go to deliver the goods. They see the schedule and go to the customers as per the delivery schedule. Once the goods are delivered, the customers confirm the delivery by Signature verification.

This system has enabled Wicaksana to make the data of Sales Force real-time.

The Benefits to the Client

Wicaksana has benefited immensely by the application of M-Force. The benefits have been manifold:

- Improvement in the sales conversion rate.
- Increase in cross-selling.
- Customer Satisfaction has shown tremendous increase.
- It has eliminated paperwork to a large extent as information is handled at single point of contact.
- Information is now more accurate as information flow is controlled by one location.
- Information availability has increased.
- Sales force turnover has reduced.
- Seamless integration with enterprise applications and corporate database.

These changes have been seen in the first phase itself. In the second phase, Soltius also plans to interface the system with the mobile payment gateway to facilitate mobile transactions through WAP or SMS.

CASE-20

TELECOMMUNICATION AND INTERNETWORKING

Mobile commerce framework helps in reducing time to build new solutions.

The Client

Our Client is a world leader in telecom solution provider with complete portfolio, which includes solution starting from setting Telecommunication infrastructure, Billing and Customer Solution and Operation Support System.

The Business Need

Our client needed a partner who could design, develop and test full-fledged scalable and secure Mobile Commerce Framework that supports various handheld devices and can interface with external accounts namely, Credit Card, Debit Card, PrePaid Systems.

How Wipro Helped?

Wipro developed a generic framework which could be used to build a complete M-commerce Solution. The framework was developed in JAVA and C++ using state of the art middlewares. The salient features of this solution were:

Charging Server

A highly scalable charging server which enables the consumer to make atomic, session and subscription based purchases using external accounts viz. Credit Cards, Debit Cards, PrePaid System.

Administration Server

Administration server for Consumer, Content merchants, and the Service Provider to administer information related to them.

Provisioning Server

Consumers and Content Merchants can register with the Service Provider.

Mobile Authentication Server

An Authentication server which authenticates mobile consumers at different security levels and using various security methods.

External Account Adapters

External Account (Payment Gateways) adapters for transacting with different Payment Gateways that can be seamlessly plugged in the framework without restarting the servers.

SMS Gateway Adapters

Adapters for communicating with different SMS Gateway adapters that can be seamlessly plugged in the framework without restarting the servers.

Reports

Generate various reports, invoices and billing information.

Simulators and Test Tools

Development and Testing done using simulators for WAP and SMS Devices. Test tools to perform functional and performance tests.

Security

A robust security framework using Public Key Infrastructure (PKI) and Secure Socket Layer – (SSL)

Framework

Highly Scalable framework for JAVA and C++. This framework was used to develop a content application where one can view his horoscope by different signs and categories namely, General, Romance, Business etc. The content application supported WEB and Mobile users. This framework was also used to develop a ticketing application where one could buy tickets for movies, sports matches, theatre, operas etc. This framework has been re-used for many other applications.

Superior Framework Design

Complete M-commerce solutions were built up in a very short time due to the re-usable framework. Flexible architecture which supported multiple terminal types with minimum effort because of the template based architecture. Support of charging through multiple payment instruments.

CASE-21

CELLEBRUM

Transferring the India Experience to Global Emerging Markets

Bharti Telesoft was established in 1999 and focused on delivering software services to customers in the US and Europe. The downturn in the telecom and IT world in 2000 necessitated a strategic review and the outcome was a complete reversal of the previous geographical and service approach. Bharti Telesoft became a product company, providing VAS for telecom operators in emerging markets.

With a new focus on emerging markets Bharti Telesoft was able to grow experience in the Indian home market, and translate this experience and success to other markets, which were experiencing similar challenges, and which offered similar growth opportunities. Bharti Telesoft has now deployed products and solutions for over 50 customers in over 35 countries across Asia Pacific, Africa, Middle East, Europe and Latin America. Bharti Telesoft now delivers a range of content, M-commerce, business support solutions and VAS products, enabling operators to deliver innovative services and achieve greater operational efficiencies.

PAPER – 1

RESEARCH PAPERS

1. (Paper presented by the author at the International Conference-09 organized by IES INSTITUTE OF MANAGEMENT, MUMBAI.)

FULL PAPER

M-COMMERCE — AN EMERGING MEDIA IN ADVERTISING

Mobile Commerce refers to wireless electronic commerce used for conducting commerce or business through a handy device like cellular phone or Personal Digital Assistant (PDAs). It is also said that it is the next generation wireless E-commerce that needs no wire and plug-in devices. Mobile commerce is usually called as 'M-commerce' in which user can do any sort of transaction including buying and selling of the goods, asking any services, transferring the ownership or rights, transacting and transferring the money by accessing wireless internet service on the mobile handset itself.

The next generation of commerce would most probably be mobile commerce or M-commerce. Presuming its wide potential reach all major mobile handset manufacturing companies are making WAP (Wireless Application Protocol) enabled smart phones and providing the maximum wireless internet and web facilities covering personal, official and commerce requirement to pave the way of M-commerce that would later be very fruitful for them.

Mobile Commerce (also known as M-commerce, M-commerce or U-commerce, owing to the ubiquitous nature of its services) is the ability to conduct commerce, using a mobile device e.g. a mobile phone (or cell phone), a PDA, a Smartphone while on the move, and other emerging mobile equipment, like dash top mobile devices. In an academic definition it is characterized in the following terms:

"Mobile Commerce is any transaction, involving the transfer of ownership or rights to use goods and services, which is initiated and/or completed by using mobile access to computer-mediated networks with the help of an electronic device." This definition provides for a differentiation of Mobile Commerce from other related fields such as Electronic Commerce, Electronic Business and Mobile Business.

Mobile Commerce is explained from the Customer's Point of View as Follows:

- The customer wants to access information, goods and services any time and in any place on his mobile device.
- He can use his mobile device to purchase tickets for events or public transport, pay for parking, download content and even order books and CDs.
- He should be offered appropriate payment methods. They can range from secure mobile micropayment to service subscriptions.

Mobile Commerce is explained from the Provider's Point of View as Follows:

- The future development of the mobile telecommunication sector is heading more and more towards value-added services. Analysts forecast that soon half of mobile operators' revenue will be earned through mobile commerce.
- Consequently operators as well as third party providers will focus on value-added-services. To enable mobile services, providers with expertise on different sectors will have to cooperate.
- Innovative service scenarios will be needed that meet the customer's expectations and business models that satisfy all partners involved.

"The core of mobile E-commerce is the use of a terminal (telephone, PDA, PC device, or custom terminal) and public mobile network (necessary but not sufficient) to access information and conduct transactions that result in the transfer of value in exchange for information, services or goods." (Ovum)

Typical examples of M-commerce are:

- Purchasing airline tickets
- Purchasing movie tickets
- Restaurant booking and reservation
- Hotel booking and reservation

M-commerce has several major advantages over its fixed counterparts because of its specific inbuilt characteristics such as ubiquity, personalization, flexibility, and distribution. Mobile commerce promises exceptional business market potential, greater efficiency and higher fruitfulness. Thus it is not surprising that mobile commerce is emerging much faster than its fixed counterpart. M-commerce is more personalized than E-commerce and thus needs a gentle approach to appraise M-commerce applications.

The difference between E-commerce and M-commerce is that E-commerce is limited to PC users with an Internet Connection. With M-commerce moving to an SMS platform among other things, M-commerce is open to almost the entire mobile population.

An important barrier to M-commerce is the state of mobile networks today because there is a risk of transactions not maturing due to poor networks. For M-commerce an eco system between application developers, financial institutions, and mobile phone networks is required, for its effective utility. Simplicity is the key to proliferation of M-commerce coupled with the idea of developing trust with audiences.

Nowadays the cell phone - on its own or in conjunction with an organizer is used for much more than simply making phone calls. It also acts as a flexible terminal for a huge range of applications. So the availability of information (weather forecasts, economic data, news), e-shopping, e-ticketing, e-banking and e-brokerage is greater than ever before, regardless of time or place. The WAP (Wireless Application Protocol) and WML (Wireless Markup Language) open standards mean the Internet's innovative solution strategies can now be applied to mobile telephony too.

The different areas that come under M-commerce

Travel and Ticketing

Movie Ticketing

Bill payments

Merchant Transactions & Retail Transactions

Money Transfer

The benefits from mobile commerce includes:

- Internet offerings are easier and more convenient to access
- It offers Considerable flexibility when conducting business
- It offers Intense customer orientation and high customer loyalty, and this is due to innovative service strategies

- It offers Lower transaction and personnel costs, which is due to the widespread automation
- M-commerce versus E-commerce

Frequently M-commerce is represented as a "subset of all E-commerce" thus implying that any E-commerce site could and should be made available from a wireless device. We believe that such conclusions are miss leading. M-commerce should be recognized as a unique business opportunity with its own unique characteristics and functions, not just an extension of an organization's Internet-based E-commerce channel. Of course there are similarities between E-commerce and M-commerce from being able to purchase a product or service in a "virtual" *vs.* a build and mortar environment.

M-commerce an Emerging Media in Advertising

Indian mobile subscriber base has crossed the 113 mn mark. And every month approximately 5 mn plus subscribers are added to this huge user base. Another interesting aspect is that though volumes in the Indian telecom segment are high but the margins are low, so the key for success here is innovation. The mobile market is maturing and competition between service providers is intensifying.

Mobile commerce (M-commerce) is an emerging discipline involving applications, mobile devices, middleware, and wireless networks. While most of existing E-commerce applications can be modified to run in a wireless environment, M-commerce also involves many more new applications that become possible only due to the wireless infrastructure. These applications include mobile financial services, user and location specific mobile advertising, mobile inventory management, wireless business re-engineering, and mobile interactive games. In addition to device and wireless constraints, mobile commerce would also be impacted by the dependability of wireless infrastructure.

Mobile advertising is one of the most popular applications of mobile commerce, particularly in the form of SMS advertising. However, little is known regarding the effectiveness of such campaigns and the factors contributing to their success. M-advertising addresses consumers with individualized advertising messages via mobile devices. In this paper I tried to identify, whether companies are using this media and whether they got the expected result. Even I have interviewed few Ad Agencies, to know whether, they advice their clients to adopt this media.

Objective of Study : To study about M-commerce as an emerging media in Advertising.

Hypothesis : M-commerce is becoming very popular as a media in Advertising.

Universe Study : Nagpur

Sample Size : 100 (quota sample)

Data Collection : Survey Method

DATA ANALYSIS

1. Respondent Profile

Table 1.1		
Sr. No.	**Type of Business**	**Number**
1	Super Shop	09
2	Computer Centre	17
3	Boutique	23
4	Service Station	11
5	Web World	13
6	Cell Companies	05
7	Coaching Centers	06
8	Bill Collection Centers	09
9	Restaurants	07
	Total	**100**

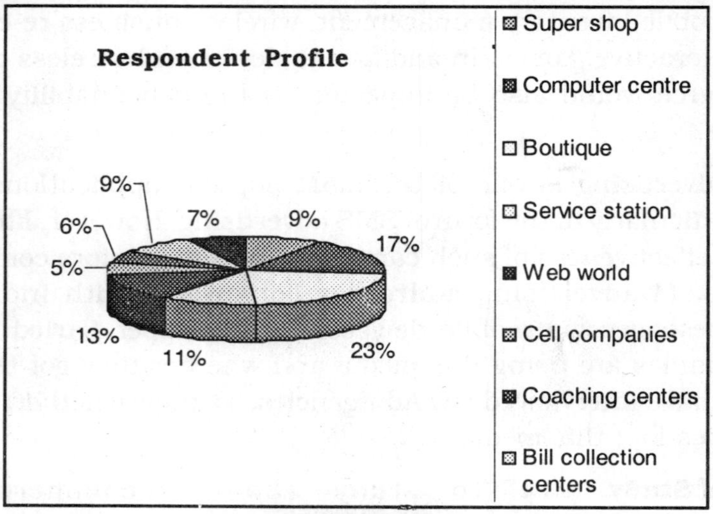

Fig. 1.1

Out of the stratified sample, the percentage of boutique is the maximum and the least percentage is of cell companies.

2. Response Regarding Advertisement

Table 1.2

Sr. No.	Response	Numbers
1	Yes	73
2	No	27
	Total	100

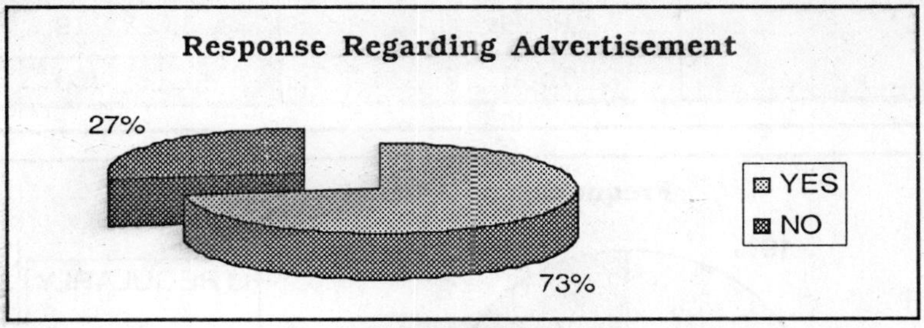

Fig. 1.2

Study shows that maximum firms, do advertise and they choose different media according to their business.

3. Special Budget for Advertising

Table 1.3

Sr. No.	Response	Numbers
1	YES	56
2	NO	44
	Total	100

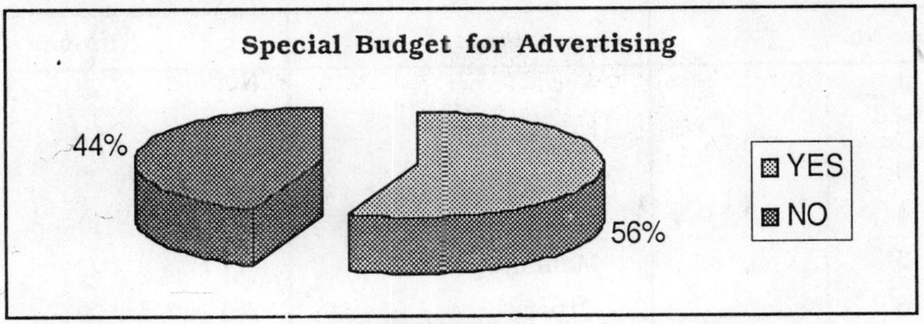

Fig. 1.3

56 % have special provision in their budget for advertisement, rest of the percentage have not reserved any budget for advertisement. They advertise when they feel there is a need.

4. Frequency of Advertisement

Table 1.4

Sr. No.	Response	Numbers
1	Regularly	23
2	During Festivals	42
	Sometimes	16
	Rarely	19
	Total	100

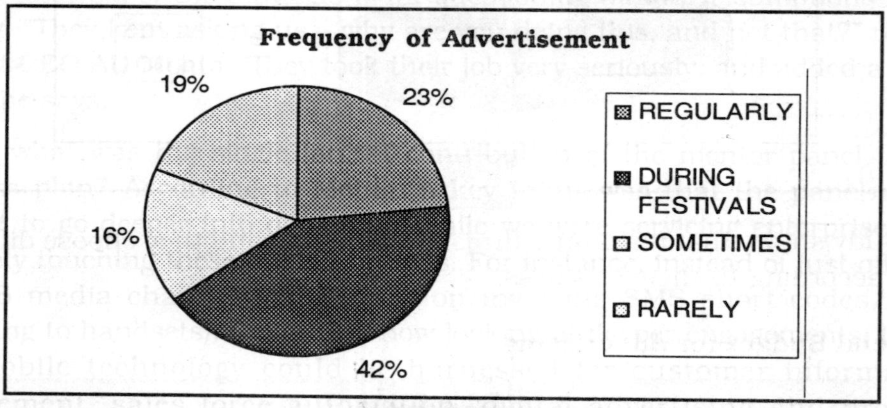

Fig. 1.4

Study shows that 42 % of firms mainly advertise during the festival season.

5. Media Preference

Table 1.5

Sr. No.	Media	Number
1	News Paper	27
2	Hoarding	08
3	Cable Tv	23
4	Transient Media	11
5	Mobile Phone	22
6	Others	09
	Total	100

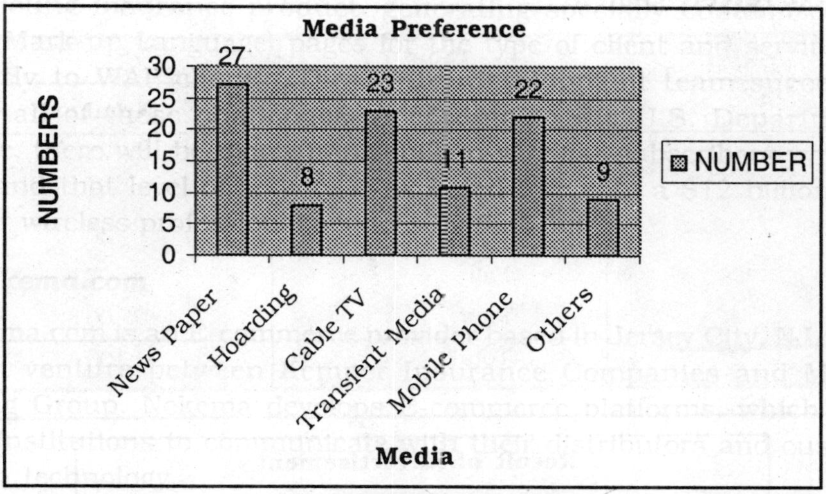

Fig. 1.5

Survey shows that firms generally prefer, Newspaper as their advertising media.

6. Tried M-commerce as a Media

Table 1.6		
Sr. No.	**Response**	**Numbers**
1	Yes	53
2	No	47
	Total	100

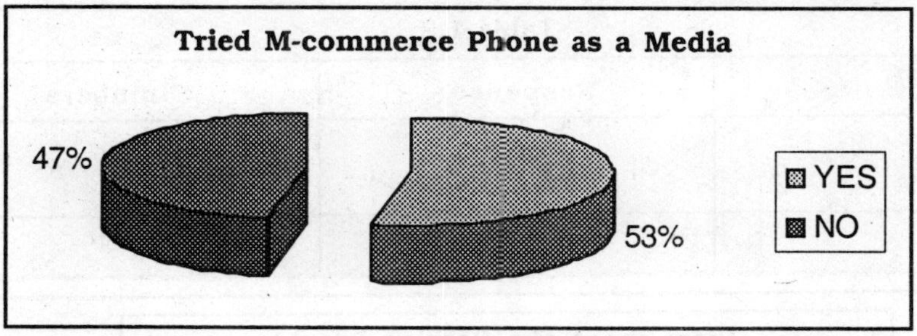

Fig. 1.6

Around 53% have tried this media at least once.

7. Result of Advertisement

Table 1.7		
Sr. No.	**Response**	**Numbers**
1	Excellent	23
2	Very Good	34
3	Good	36
4	Fair	07
5	Poor	00
	Total	100

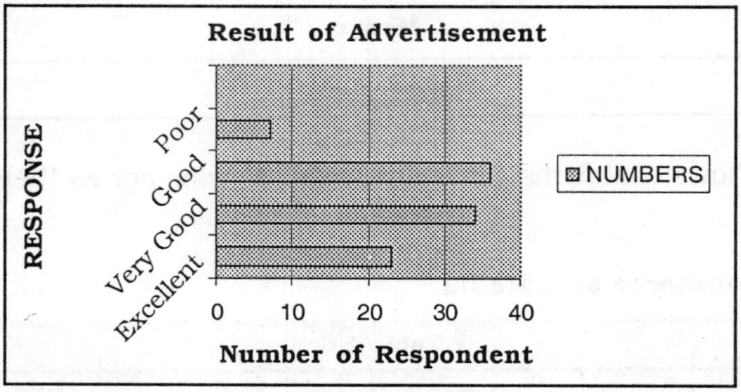

Fig. 1.7

Generally firms are satisfied with the results and out come of the advertisement through mobile phones.

8. View About The Service Provider

Table 1.8		
Sr.No.	**Response**	**Numbers**
1	Yes	52
2	No	48
	Total	100

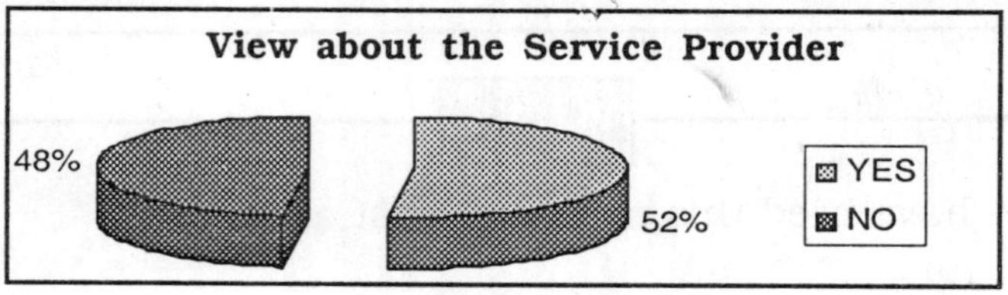

Fig. 1.8

Around 52% of respondents are satisfied with the service provided by the service provider.

9. Response Regarding this Media

Table 1.9

Sr. No.	Response	Numbers
1	Always	32
2	Sometimes	48
3	Rarely	20
	Total	100

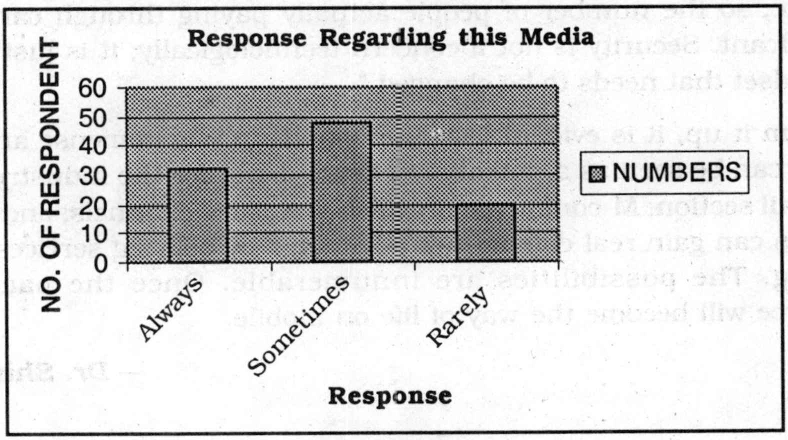

Fig. 1.9

Here the respondents have a mix view. They generally get the required response and effect of this media. In some cases they are not happy with the outcome.

Interpretation and Conclusion

- Study shows, that mobile media for advertisement is gaining momentum day by day.
- People generally prefer this media, as it is easy to use, information remains for long time, cost saving etc.
- People prefer this media, as it reaches to masses.
- Compare to E-commerce, M-commerce has more effect.
- Due to the continuous increase in the mobile subscription, more people are very keen to opt this media to advertise their product.

- Still it will take another 5 years, in non-metro city, like Nagpur to catch-up the expected momentum, as far as this media is concerned.
- Field of M-commerce promises a bright future in the field of advertisement.

Conclusion

Another area which needs to be dealt with is the issue of security and reliability. The Indian user is still not comfortable with the idea of giving away his debit or credit card number over the phone. Also, security is a major concern for M-commerce to flourish. But as Balachandran Unni says, "There are a number of payment options for people such as cheque pick up, cash on delivery etc, so the number of people actually paying through cards is not very significant. Security is not a concern technologically; it is just a matter of the mindset that needs to be changed."

To sum it up, it is evident that the opportunity is immense and mobile commerce can be seen as a potential revenue driver for the industry players. On the retail section, M-commerce provides new sales channels; and financial institutions can gain real competitive advantage by offering services such as m-banking. The possibilities are innumerable. Once the pace is set, M-commerce will become the way of life on mobile.

— Dr. Shiney Chib

(The article of the author published in the daily 'THE HITAVADA' on 16th September 2008.)

M-commerce-a New Panorama in Business

Mobile Commerce refers to wireless electronic commerce used for conducting commerce or business through a handy device like cellular phone or Personal Digital Assistant (PDAs). It is also said that it is the next generation wireless E-commerce that needs no wire and plug-in devices. Mobile commerce is usually called as 'M-commerce' in which user can do any sort of transaction including buying and selling of the goods, asking any services, transferring the ownership or rights, transacting and transferring the money by accessing wireless internet service on the mobile handset itself.

The next generation of commerce would most probably be mobile commerce or M-commerce. Presuming its wide potential reach all major mobile handset manufacturing companies are making WAP (Wireless Application Protocol) enabled smart phones and providing the maximum wireless internet and web facilities covering personal, official and commerce requirement to pave the way of M-commerce that would later be very fruitful for them.

Mobile Commerce (also known as M-commerce, M-commerce or U-commerce, owing to the ubiquitous nature of its services) is the ability to conduct commerce, using a mobile device e.g. a mobile phone (or cell phone), a PDA, a Smartphone while on the move, and other emerging mobile equipment, like dash top mobile devices. In an academic definition it is characterized in the following terms:

"Mobile Commerce is any transaction, involving the transfer of ownership or rights to use goods and services, which is initiated and/or completed by using mobile access to computer-mediated networks with the help of an electronic device." This definition provides for a differentiation of Mobile Commerce from other related fields such as Electronic Commerce, Electronic Business and Mobile Business.

Mobile Commerce is explained from the Customer's Point of View as Follows:

- The customer wants to access information, goods and services any time and in any place on his mobile device.
- He can use his mobile device to purchase tickets for events or public transport, pay for parking, download content and even order books and CDs.

- He should be offered appropriate payment methods. They can range from secure mobile micropayment to service subscriptions.

Mobile Commerce is explained from the Provider's Point of View as Follows:

- The future development of the mobile telecommunication sector is heading more and more towards value-added services. Analysts forecast that soon half of mobile operators' revenue will be earned through mobile commerce.
- Consequently operators as well as third party providers will focus on value-added-services. To enable mobile services, providers with expertise on different sectors will have to cooperate.
- Innovative service scenarios will be needed that meet the customer's expectations and business models that satisfy all partners involved.
- The core of mobile E-commerce is the use of a terminal (telephone, PDA, PC device, or custom terminal) and public mobile network (necessary but not sufficient) to access information and conduct transactions that result in the transfer of value in exchange for information, services or goods." (Ovum)

Typical examples of M-commerce are:

- Purchasing airline tickets
- Purchasing movie tickets
- Restaurant booking and reservation
- Hotel booking and reservation

M-commerce has several major advantages over its fixed counterparts because of its specific inbuilt characteristics such as ubiquity, personalization, flexibility, and distribution. Mobile commerce promises exceptional business market potential, greater efficiency and higher fruitfulness. Thus it is not surprising that mobile commerce is emerging much faster than its fixed counterpart. M-commerce is more personalized than E-commerce and thus needs a gentle approach to appraise M-commerce applications.

The difference between E-commerce and M-commerce is that E-commerce is limited to PC users with an Internet Connection. With M-commerce moving to an SMS platform among other things, M-commerce is open to almost the entire mobile population.

An important barrier to M-commerce is the state of mobile networks today because there is a risk of transactions not maturing due to poor networks. For

M-commerce an eco system between application developers, financial institutions, and mobile phone networks is required, for its effective utility. Simplicity is the key to proliferation of M-commerce coupled with the idea of developing trust with audiences.

Nowadays the cell phone - on its own or in conjunction with an organizer is used for much more than simply making phone calls. It also acts as a flexible terminal for a huge range of applications. So the availability of information (weather forecasts, economic data, news), e-shopping, e-ticketing, e-banking and e-brokerage is greater than ever before, regardless of time or place. The WAP (Wireless Application Protocol) and WML (Wireless Markup Language) open standards mean the Internet's innovative solution strategies can now be applied to mobile telephony too.

The different areas that come under M-commerce

Travel and Ticketing

Movie Ticketing

Bill payments

Merchant Transactions & Retail Transactions

Money Transfer

The benefits from mobile commerce includes:

- Internet offerings are easier and more convenient to access
- It offers Considerable flexibility when conducting business
- It offers Intense customer orientation and high customer loyalty, and this is due to innovative service strategies
- It offers Lower transaction and personnel costs, which is due to the widespread automation

M-commerce Versus E-commerce

Frequently M-commerce is represented as a "subset of all E-commerce" thus implying that any E-commerce site could and should be made available from a wireless device. We believe that such conclusions are miss leading. M-commerce should be recognized as a unique business opportunity with its own unique characteristics and functions, not just an extension of an organization's Internet-based E-commerce channel. Of course there are similarities between E-commerce and M-commerce from being able to purchase a product or service in a "virtual" *vs.* a build and mortar environment.

The Indian mobile subscriber base has crossed the 113 mn mark. And every month approximately 5 mn plus subscribers are added to this huge user base. Another interesting aspect is that though volumes in the Indian telecom segment are high but the margins are low, so the key for success here is innovation. The mobile market is maturing and competition between service providers is intensifying.

Another area which needs to be dealt with is the issue of security and reliability. The Indian user is still not comfortable with the idea of giving away his debit or credit card number over the phone. Also, security is a major concern for M-commerce to flourish. But as Balachandran Unni says, "There are a number of payment options for people such as cheque pick up, cash on delivery etc, so the number of people actually paying through cards is not very significant. Security is not a concern technologically; it is just a matter of the mindset that needs to be changed."

To sum it up, it is evident that the opportunity is immense and mobile commerce can be seen as a potential revenue driver for the industry players. On the retail section, M-commerce provides new sales channels; and financial institutions can gain real competitive advantage by offering services such as m-banking. The possibilities are innumerable. Once the pace is set, M-commerce will become the way of life on mobile.

— Dr. Shiney Chib

GLOSSARY

Access Control	The purpose of this is to ensure that only authorized users have access to a particular system and/or specific resources. That access and modification of a particular portion of data is limited to authorized individuals and programs.
Access Provider	A company that provides connectivity to the Internet. Customers of access providers pay a fee and are then granted access to the Internet through an electronic account defined and managed by the providers.
Automatic Crash Notification (ACN)	Automatic Crash Notification (ACN) is the next major advancement in consumer auto safety. Telecommunications, automotive and location definition technologies are now converging to make instant and automatic notification of serious vehicle collisions to emergency call centers possible. ACN systems employ wireless telecommunication technologies to immediately alert an emergency call center when a crash victim presses the car's Mayday button or the car's air bag deploys. In an emergency, the dispatcher at the call center quickly informs the appropriate emergency responder of the vehicle's location so care can be sent. Reducing emergency response times saves lives and reduces the impact of injuries.
Address	Every host on the Internet has a unique host address called an 'IP number'. these are the keys to the Internet's ability to link its millions of host together in a universal system of 'host addresses'. If a host wants to send a message (called an IP diagram) to another host, it merely puts the target host's IP number in the destination field of the diagram and sends this diagram to a router.
ADCCP	In telecommunication, Advanced Data Communication Control Procedures (or Protocol) (ADCCP) is a bit-oriented data link layer protocol

	used to provide point-to-point and point-to-multipoint transmission of data frames that contain error control information. It places data on a network and ensures proper delivery to a destination. ADCCP is based on the IBM's SDLC protocol.
Application Service Providers (ASPs)	Application service providers are hosting services that will support, manage and maintain your application with staff for a fee. Hosting services means a company that hosts your website at their facilities, offering high reliability and bandwidth along with redundancy, security and other services.
Augmented reality (AR)	Augmented reality (AR) is a term for a live direct or indirect view of a physical real-world environment whose elements are augmented by virtual computer-generated imagery. It is related to a more general concept called mediated reality in which a view of reality is modified (possibly even diminished rather than augmented) by a computer.
ARPANET (Advanced Research Projects Agency Network)	The first Internet developed in the 1960s as a way for US authorities to communicate with each other in the aftermath of a nuclear attack. This formed the basis that has subsequently evolved in today's Internet.
Automated Teller Machine (ATM)	A special purpose transaction terminal used to provide remote banking services.
Adaptive Modulation and Coding (AMC)	The principle of AMC is to change the modulation and coding format (transport format) in accordance with instantaneous variations in the channel conditions, subject to system restrictions. AMC extends the system's ability to adapt to good channel conditions.
ARPU	ARPU is the average amount of revenue a company collects from each user per month. Companies often try to boost this number by selling extra services to users such as data plans, messaging, and downloadable content.

Automobile navigation	Many PDAs are used in car kits and are fitted with differential Global Positioning System (GPS) receivers to provide realtime automobile navigation. PDAs are increasingly being fitted as standard on new cars. Many systems can also display traffic conditions, dynamic routing and roadside mobile radar guns. Popular software in Europe and in America for this functionality are TomTom, Garmin, iGO etc. showing road conditions and 2D or 3D environments.
BlackBerry	BlackBerry is a line of mobile e-mail and smartphone devices developed by Canadian company Research In Motion (RIM). While including typical smartphone applications (address book, calendar, to-do lists, etc, as well as telephone capabilities on newer models), the BlackBerry is primarily known for its ability to send and receive Internet e-mail wherever it can access a mobile network of certain cellular phone carriers.
bCODE	A bCODE is an identifier that can be sent to a mobile phone/device and used as a ticket/voucher/identification or other type of token. The bCODE is an SMS message that can be read electronically from the screen of a mobile device. Bcodes can be sent by text message, and as they are just a standard SMS they can be received on over 99% of all devices.Bcodes have many uses such as advertising, loyalty programs, promotions, ticketing and more.
Band width	The capacity of an electronic transmission medium, such as a cable, to carry electronic signals.
Banner advertising	Banner advertising is a long thin ad usually located at the top and bottom of web pages.
Bluetooth	Bluetooth is a computing, networking and telecommunications industry specification that enables mobile phones, computers and other WIDs to 'talk' to each other using radio waves.

Business to Business	Business to business is the portion of the Internet market that effects transactions between business operations and their partners in marketing, sales, development, manufacturing and support.
Bar Codes	Vertical marks or bars placed on merchandise tags or packaging that can be sensed and read by optical character reading devices. The width and combination of vertical lines are used to represent data.
Business to Consumer/Customer	Customers have access to the Internet. They operate from the homes or work places and wish to purchase items sold by the shops. For convenience sake, one can shop at any time from the house and items will be delivered to the house.
Buzz	Buzz is a term used to describe conversations and discussions about a particular company or technology.
CD	A Compact Disc (also known as a CD) is an optical disc used to store digital data. It was originally developed to store sound recordings exclusively, but later it also allowed the preservation of other types of data. Standard CDs have a diameter of 120 mm and can hold up to 80 minutes of uncompressed audio (700 MB of data). The Mini CD has various diameters ranging from 60 to 80 mm; they are sometimes used for CD singles or device drivers, storing up to 24 minutes of audio.
Contactless payment	Contactless payment systems (also known as "touch and go") are credit cards, key fobs, smartcards or other devices which use RFID for making secure payments. The embedded chip and antenna enable consumers to wave their card or fob over a reader at the point of sale. Some suppliers claim that transactions can be almost twice as fast as a conventional cash, credit, or debit card purchase.
Chat Room	An online place for people to post and read electronic messages.

CRL	Certificate Revocation List (CRL) is one of two common methods when using a public key infrastructure for maintaining access to servers in a network. The other, newer method, which has superseded CRL in some cases, is Online Certificate Status Protocol (OCSP). The CRL is exactly what its name implies: a list of subscribers paired with digital certificate status. The list enumerates revoked certificates along with the reason(s) for revocation. The dates of certificate issue, and the entities that issued them, are also included. In addition, each list contains a proposed date for the next release. When a potential user attempts to access a server, the server allows or denies access based on the CRL entry for that particular user.
CDPD	Cellular Digital Packet Data (CDPD) was a wide-area mobile data service which used unused bandwidth normally used by AMPS mobile phones between 800 and 900 MHz to transfer data. Developed in the early 1990s, CDPD was large on the horizon as a future technology. However, it had difficulty competing against existing slower but less expensive Mobitex and DataTac systems, and never quite gained widespread acceptance before newer, faster standards such as GPRS became dominant.
Channel	A website designed to deliver content from the Internet to your computer, similar to subscrising to a favourite website. Typically, it is not necessary to subscribe the web, but by connecting to the 'channel' suggested content can be delivered to your desktop browser.
Computer Virus or Worm	Program code that copies its destructive program routines into the computer systems of anyone who accesses computer systems that have used the program, or anyone who users copies of data or programs taken from such computers. This spreads the destructions of data and programs among many computer users. Technically a virus will not run unaided, but must be inserted into another

	program, while a worm is a distinct program that can run unaided.
Cryptography	Cryptography is the science of disguising messages to only the writer and the intended receivers are able to read them.
Cyber Squatting	It is the act of trying to divert customers from a Website by using a similar name and identical look as another site or the act of obtaining and holding domain names for resale.
Cookie	It stores personal preferences for Internet information and communication tools in files in a browser's folder. Cookie is a text file that contains the information of user's preferences in created and is stored in memory while the browser is running. It can also save information such as the data that the website was visited, what purchases were made, what ad banners were clicked on, what files were downloaded, and the information varied.
Convergence	Convergence broadly defined is the melding of consumer electronics, television, publishing, tele-communications and computers for the purpose of facilitating new forms of information based commerce.
Client	A computer that is connected to a network that is not a server or router.
Computer Crime	Computer crime is the use of computer resources to engage in unauthorized or illegal acts.
Channels of Distribution	A distribution channel is a method of providing you product/service to the target user of the system. This could be an online mail, portal, your own brand site or distribution supply chain.
Community	Electronic forum where individuals and groups gather to find relevant and pertinent information. They are often squinted by internet or geography.

Computer Security	Security is the protection of any computer device, communication device or network from unauthorized access to data, viruses etc.
Chat	Chat systems are used to allow users of networks and the Internet to communicate in real time. Messages today are typically posted via a desktop window with other members of the group. The message will then appear in the open chat windows of others in that particular group for review and further comment.
Click-through	The term that describes when a visitor to a website uses a link to access another website.
CD-ROM	CD-ROM (an acronym of "compact disc read-only memory") is a pre-pressed compact disc that contains data accessible to, but not writable by, a computer for data storage and music playback, the 1985 "Yellow Book" standard developed by Sony and Philips adapted the format to hold any form of binary data. CD-ROMs are popularly used to distribute computer software, including games and multimedia applications, though any data can be stored (up to the capacity limit of a disc). Some CDs hold both computer data and audio with the latter capable of being played on a CD player, while data (such as software or digital video) is only usable on a computer (such as ISO 9660 format PC CD-ROMs). These are called enhanced CDs.
CDMA	Code division multiple access (CDMA) is a channel access method utilized by various radio communication technologies. One of the basic concepts in data communication is the idea of allowing several transmitters to send information simultaneously over a single communication channel. This allows several users to share a bandwidth of different frequencies. This concept is called multiplexing. CDMA employs spread-spectrum technology and a special coding scheme (where each transmitter is assigned a code) to allow

	multiple users to be multiplexed over the same physical channel.
Cipher	In cryptography, a cipher (or cypher) is an algorithm for performing encryption or decryption - a series of well-defined steps that can be followed as a procedure. In non-technical usage, a "cipher" is the same thing as a "code"; however, the concepts are distinct in cryptography.
DTMF	Dual-tone multi-frequency signaling (DTMF) is used for telecommunication signaling over analog telephone lines in the voice-frequency band between telephone handsets and other communications devices and the switching center. The version of DTMF that is used in push-button telephones for tone dialing is known as Touch-Tone, first used by AT&T in commerce as a registered trademark.
Data Marts	A data mart is a body of DSS data for a department that has an architectural foundation of a data warehouse. The data that resides in the data warehouse is at a very granular level and the data in the data mart is at a refined level.
Dashtop mobile	Dashtop mobile equipment collectively refers to wireless mobile devices mounted on the vehicle dashboards. Indications are that there is a huge growth potential in dashtop mobile equipment (DME), associated applications and services. These wireless devices include satellite radios, GPS navigation, OnStar, mobile TV, HD radio, vehicle tracking system, MVEDR and BWA devices. Currently, the dashtop mobile devices are mostly satellite-based wireless technology.
e Choupal	e Choupal is an initiative of ITC Limited (a large multi business conglomerate in India) to link directly with rural farmers for procurement of agricultural/aquaculture produce like soybeans, wheat, coffee, and prawns. eChoupal was conceived to tackle the challenges posed by the unique features of Indian agriculture, characterized by

	fragmented farms, weak infrastructure and the involvement of numerous intermediaries.
Enhanced Messaging Service (EMS)	EMS is an intermediate technology, between SMS and MMS, providing some of the features of MMS. EMS is a technology that is designed to work with existing networks, but may ultimately be made obsolete by MMS. An EMS enabled mobile phone can send and receive messages that have special text formatting (such as bold or italic), animations, pictures, icons, sound effects and special ring tones.
1xRTT	1xRTT, often abbreviated as 1x, is a designation referring to an operating mode of CDMA2000, a wireless technology used in CDMA cellular networks. The 1x in 1xRTT stands for one times the number of 1.25MHz channels, while RTT stands for radio transmission technology. CDMA2000 1xRTT is also called 3G1X, IMT-CDMA Multi-Carrier, or IS-2000.
Data Link Layer	The Data Link Layer is the protocol layer which transfers data between adjacent network nodes in a wide area network or between nodes on the same local area network segment. The Data Link Layer provides the functional and procedural means to transfer data between network entities and might provide the means to detect and possibly correct errors that may occur in the Physical Layer. Examples of data link protocols are Ethernet for local area networks (multi-node), the Point-to-Point Protocol (PPP), HDLC and ADCCP for point-to-point (dual-node) connections.
DoCoMo	The term DoCoMo stands for do communication over mobile. • NTT docomo (Japan) • Tata DoCoMo (India)
Data Mining	As the name itself indicates, it refers lightly to finding relevant information or discovering knowledge from a large volume of data. It attempts to discover statistical rules and patterns

	automatically from data, in a similar way as knowledge discovery found in Artificial Intelligence (AI).
Data Visualization	Data visualization is the graphical representation of data collection, often in an interactive form. Modern data visualization tools present data to users as charts, graphs or maps and let users sort, sub-divide and combine groups of data in graphical form to help discover patterns and illustrate what they have discovered.
Data Warehouse	A data warehouse is a database that collects business information from many sources in the enterprise, covering all aspects of the company's processes, products and customers. The warehouse provides business users with a multi-dimensional view of the data they need to analyze business conditions.
Denial of Service	Shopping portals are more vulnerable to attacks by hackers unless special precautions are taken. One such nuisance called 'denial of service' is there in which a large number of frivolous enquiries are posted onto a portal, making it inaccessible to legitimate customers.
Desktop Publishing	Organizations can use and develop publishing systems to produce their own printed materials. They can design and print their own newsletters, manuals, brochures and books with several type styles and graphics and colours on each page.
Digital Signature	A digital signature is a cryptographic mechanism that performs a similar function like a written signature, used to verify the origin and contents of the message.
Domain Name	It is a unique name that is used to identify a website and contains two or more parts separated by a dot. The existing domain names fit into one of seven categories like educational institutions, commercial organizations, military, government,

	non-profit organizations, networking organizations and international organizations.
Domain Name Server (DNS)	DNS is the server connected to the Internet that translates the URL/domain name into the IP address to direct you to the correct location on the Internet.
Dotcom Companies	Many new Internet-Savvy Companies, known as 'dotcoms' have proliferated in the markets everywhere and has grown like mushrooms both in India and world over. Most of these companies try to compile information needed by a large number of people. It serves the popular world with music, sports, news, etc.
EDGE	EDGE (also known as Enhanced GPRS or EGPRS) is a data system used on top of GSM networks. It provides nearly three times faster speeds than the outdated GPRS system. The theoretical maximum speed is 473 kbps for 8 timeslots but it is typically limited to 135 kbps in order to conserve spectrum resources. Both phone and network must support EDGE, otherwise the phone will revert automatically to GPRS.
E-Bay	Consider the list of functions e-Bay has developed to its users. The company does not decide what product areas it should be in because the user defines these with their offers. E-Bay does'nt have to describe the goods being exchanged. It certainly does'nt set their prices because value setting is the prime users benefit of the service. And not only does e-bay have zero stock, it does'nt undertake fulfillment. E-Bay users organize their own shipments.
E-Tailing	e-tailing is online sales of retail style goods. Many consumer and specialist goods are now available via these online e-tailers.
Early Adopters	Groups of users and individual that will typically adopt technology and new work processes early in their introduction to the market place.

Electronic Business	Electronic business is a term now used broadly for the act of doing business using the Internet and other electronic means to conduct business.
Electronic Cheque	A type of electronic funds transfer that can be given to an online company for deposit at an online financial institution.
Electronic Commerce	E-commerce can best be described as buying and selling of goods and services over the Internet.
Electronic Data Interchange (EDI)	Is the direct computer to computer exchange between two organizations.
Electronic Serial Numbers (ESNs)	Electronic Serial Numbers (ESNs) were created by the U.S> Federal Communications Commission (FCC) to uniquely identify mobile devices from the days of AMPS in the United States from the early 1980s. The administrative role was taken over by the Telecommunications Industry Association in 1997. ESNs are mainly used with AMPS, TDMA and CDMA phones in the United States, compared to International Mobile Equipment Identity (IMEI) numbers used by all GSM phones.
Electronic Document Management	An image processing technology in which an electronic document may consist of digitized voice notes and electronic graphics images, as well as digitized images of traditional documents.
Electronic Funds Transfer (EFT)	An electronic transfer of information that equates moving funds from one financial institution to another.
Electronic Data Processing	The use of electronic computers to process data automatically.
Electronic Mail	Sending and receiving text messages between networked PCs over telecommunication networks. E-mail can also include data files, software, and multimedia messages and documents as attachments.
Electronic Payment Systems	Electronic payment systems are alternative cash or credit payment methods using various electronic

	technologies to pay for products and services in electronic commerce.
Elliptic curve cryptography (ECC)	Elliptic curve cryptography (ECC) is an approach to public-key cryptography based on the algebraic structure of elliptic curves over finite fields.
Encryption	Encryption is a process that conceals meaning by changing messages into unintelligible messages.
Enterprise Information Portal (EIP)	From a conceptual view, it is important to understand that EIPs represent the integration of business intelligence and knowledge management techniques. The technologies that integrate the various pieces are the Internet, corporate intranets and extranets.
Enterprise Resource Planning (ERP)	A model for building software in which all the operation processes that impact resource management use integrated software.
Extranets	Private wide area networks that run on public protocols with the goal of fostering collaboration and information sharing between organizations. A feature of extranets is that companies can allow certain guests to have access to internal data on a controlled basis.
File Transfer Protocol	File transfer protocol is a protocol web on the Internet to transfer many different types of information in the form of files and data. These files and data may contain software, text documents, sound or images.
Filter	Filter is nothing but a computer program or a piece of hardware associated with software for monitoring the message packets which either enter or leave an organization's network, based on the information contained in the header of the packet or on the contents of the packet.
Firewall	It is a piece of software that regulates who can access. It is a software/hardware combination that separates an internal local area network from the external Internet.

Frequently Asked Questions (FAQ)	A listing of questions that have already been asked along with the answers to those questions.
3GPP	The 3rd Generation Partnership Project (3GPP) is a collaboration between groups of telecommunications associations, to make a globally applicable third generation (3G) mobile phone system specification within the scope of the International Mobile Telecommunications-2000 project of the International Telecommunication Union (ITU). 3GPP specifications are based on evolved Global System for Mobile Communications (GSM) specifications. 3GPP standardization encompasses Radio, Core Network and Service architecture.
Gateway	Gateway is a hardware or software component that links two otherwise incompatible applications or networks.
Global Positioning System (GPS)	A series of low level satellites that transmit a signal used by devices on the ground to indicate the longitude and latitude of the device.
GPRS	General packet radio service (GPRS) is a packet oriented mobile data service available to users of the 2G cellular communication systems global system for mobile communications (GSM), as well as in the 3G systems. In 2G systems, GPRS provides data rates of 56-114 kbit/s. GPRS data transfer is typically charged per megabyte of traffic transferred, while data communication via traditional circuit switching is billed per minute of connection time, independent of whether the user actually is using the capacity or is in an idle state. GPRS is a best-effort packet switched service, as opposed to circuit switching, where a certain quality of service (QoS) is guaranteed during the connection for non-mobile users.
GSM	GSM (Global System for Mobile Communications: originally from Group Special Mobile) is the most popular standard for mobile telephony systems in the world. The GSM Association, its promoting

	industry trade organization of mobile phone carriers and manufacturers, estimates that 80% of the global mobile market uses the standard. GSM is used by over 2 billion people across more than 212 countries and territories. Its ubiquity enables international roaming arrangements between mobile phone operators, providing subscribers the use of their phones in many parts of the world. GSM differs from its predecessor technologies in that both signaling and speech channels are digital, and thus GSM is considered a second generation (2G) mobile phone system.
HDML	The Handheld Device Markup Language (HDML) is a markup language intended for display on handheld computers, information appliances, smartphones, etc.. It is similar to HTML, but for wireless and handheld devices with small displays, like PDA, mobile phones and so on.
High-Level Data Link Control (HDLC)	High-Level Data Link Control (HDLC) is a bit oriented synchronous data link layer protocol developed by the International Organization for Standardization (ISO). The original ISO standards for HDLC are: • ISO 3309 - Frame Structure • ISO 4335 - Elements of Procedure • ISO 6159 - Unbalanced Classes of Procedure • ISO 6256 - Balanced Classes of Procedure The current standard for HDLC is ISO 13239, which replaces all of those standards.HDLC provides both connection-oriented and connectionless service. HDLC can be used for point to multipoint connections, but is now used almost exclusively to connect one device to another, using what is known as Asynchronous Balanced Mode (ABM).
Home Page	Using HTML, Internet developers are able to create a homepage, which is the first page that a user sees after entering a URL for a website. Also called 'Index page'.

Hacking	Hacking is a computer crime in which the criminal breaks into a computer system just for the challenge of doing so.
Hyper Media	Documents containing multiple forms of media, including text, graphics, video and sound, that can be interactively searched like Hypertext.
HTML (Hyper Text Markup Language)	A standard markup language created by a worldwide consortium and used to format web documents.
Hyper Link	Electronic link that can be programmed so that it is possible to make a jump from one document or web page to another. There are three primary tools for navigating the Internet.
Hyper Text	Text in electronic form that has been indexed and linked (hyper links) by software in a variety of ways, so that it can be randomly and interactively searched by a user.
Hyper Text Transfer Protocol (HTTP)	It is an advanced file retrieving application program which can be used for accessing distributed and linked documents on the worldwide web.
IBM WebSphere	In computing, IBM WebSphere refers to a brand of software products, although the term also refers in popular usage to one specific product: IBM WebSphere Application Server (WAS). WebSphere is designed to set up, operate and integrate electronic business applications across multiple computing platforms, using Java-based Web technologies. It includes both the run-time components and the tools to develop applications that will run on WAS.
i-mode	NTT DoCoMo's i-mode is a mobile internet(as opposed to wireless internet) service popular in Japan. Unlike Wireless Application Protocol or WAP, i-mode encompasses a wider variety of internet standards, including web access, e-mail and the packet-switched network that delivers the data. i-mode users have access to various services such as e-mail, sports results, weather forecast, games,

	financial services and ticket booking. Content is provided by specialized services, typically from the mobile carrier, which allows them to have tighter control over billing.
Internet service provider (ISP)	An Internet service provider (ISP), also sometimes referred to as an Internet access provider (IAP), is a company that offers its customers access to the Internet. The ISP connects to its customers using a data transmission technology appropriate for delivering Internet Protocol datagrams, such as dial-up, DSL, cable modem, wireless or dedicated high-speed interconnects. ISPs may provide Internet e-mail accounts to users which allow them to communicate with one another by sending and receiving electronic messages through their ISP's servers. ISPs may provide services such as remotely storing data files on behalf of their customers, as well as other services unique to each particular ISP.
IRDA	Infrared Data Association, in information and communications technology, a standard for communication between devices (such as computers, PDAs and mobile phones) over short distances using infrared signals.
Image Processing	A computer based technology that allows end users to electronically capture, store, process and retrieve images that may include numeric data, text handwriting, graphics, documents and photographs (uses optical scanning and optical disk technologies.
Internic	Governing body controlling the issue and control of Internet domains and addresses. Currently a partnership between the US government and network solutions, Inc.
Internet Relay Chat (IRC)	Allows individuals to chat on the Internet.
Internet Work	A connection of networks usually connected through routers.

Intranet	Internet based computing networks that are private and secure. Typically used by corporations, government and other organizations, these are based upon Internet standards and provide the means for an organization to make resources more readily available to its employees online.
Internet Protocol (IP)	Software that divides information into packets. It then transmits this information in its divided form. This is required for all computers on the Internet to communicate.
Internet	Internet is a network for the elite, but it is very egalitarian. It has valuable information but works at no extra charge.
Information Super Highway (i-way)	An advanced high-speed Internet-like network that connects individuals, households, businesses, government agencies, libraries, schools, universities, and other institutions with interactive voice, video, data and multimedia communications.
Interactive Marketing	It is a dynamic collaborative process of creating, purchasing and improving products and services that build close relationship between a business and its customers, using a variety of services on the Internet, intranets and extranets.
IP Address	Internet protocol address is the numeric address used to locate physical or virtual computers or sites on the Internet.
IPO (Initial Public Offering)	The first public offering of a stock.
ISDN (Integrated Services Digital Network)	Telephone service that has become a popular cost effective solution to traditional dial-up speeds over the Internet . ISDN allows ordinary telephone lines to transmit digital instead of analogue signals, thereby permitting much faster dialup and transmission speeds.
ISP (Internet Service Provider)	A company that has a connection to the Internet and charges the public a fee to use part of that connection.

IEEE	The Institute of Electrical and Electronics Engineers or IEEE is an international non-profit, professional organization for the advancement of technology related to electricity. It has the most members of any technical professional organization in the world, with more than 395,000 members in around 150 countries.
IEEE 802.11	IEEE 802.11 is a set of standards carrying out wireless local area network (WLAN) computer communication in the 2.4, 3.6 and 5 GHz frequency bands. They are created and maintained by the IEEE LAN/MAN Standards Committee (IEEE 802).
IEEE 802.15	IEEE 802.15 is the 15th working group of the IEEE 802 and specializes in Wireless PAN (Personal Area Network) standards.
IEEE 802.16	IEEE 802.16 is a series of Wireless Broadband standards authored by the IEEE. The current version is IEEE 802.16-2009 amended by IEEE 802.16j-2009. IEEE 802.16 is written by a working group established by IEEE Standards Board in 1999 to develop standards for the global deployment of broadband Wireless Metropolitan Area Networks. The Workgroup is a unit of the IEEE 802 LAN/MAN Standards Committee. Although the 802.16 family of standards is officially called WirelessMAN in IEEE, it has been commercialized under the name "WiMAX" (from "Worldwide Interoperability for Microwave Access") by the industry alliance called the WiMAX Forum. The mission of the Forum is to promote and certify compatibility and interoperability of broadband wireless products based on the IEEE 802.16 standards.
IEEE 802.20	IEEE 802.20 or Mobile Broadband Wireless Access (MBWA) is an IEEE Standard to enable worldwide deployment of multi-vendor interoperable mobile broadband wireless access networks.
IMS	The IP Multimedia Subsystem (IMS) is an architectural framework for delivering Internet

	Protocol (IP) multimedia services. It was originally designed by the wireless standards body 3rd Generation Partnership Project (3GPP), as a part of the vision for evolving mobile networks beyond GSM. Its original formulation (3GPP R5) represented an approach to delivering "Internet services" over GPRS. This vision was later updated by 3GPP, 3GPP2 and TISPAN by requiring support of networks other than GPRS, such as Wireless LAN, CDMA2000 and fixed line.
Internet Over Satellite System	Internets may employ a variety of electronic transport media, such as telephone lines, optical fiber, satellite systems, local area networks, etc. The most common method of sending and receiving computer information today is a land line service (i.e., a switched service, a dedicated line, and/or an analog modem, each using telephone wire lines). Entry into the Internet is furnished by Internet service providers (ISPs). ISPs operate networks that connect with each other at network access points (NAPs). Information is transmitted between NAPs in the form of individual data packets. Each packet contains an embedded source and destination address to which the packet is routed across the networks.
Infrared	Infrared technology allows computing devices to communicate via short-range wireless signals. With infrared, computers can transfer files and other digital data bidirectionally. The infrared transmission technology used in computers is similar to that used in consumer product remote control units.
Just-in-time (JIT)	Just-in-time (JIT) is an inventory strategy that strives to improve a business's return on investment by reducing in-process inventory and associated carrying costs.
Interactive Voice Response (IVR)	Interactive Voice Response (IVR) is a technology that allows a computer to detect voice and dual-

	tone multi-frequency signaling (DTMF) keypad inputs. IVR technology is used extensively in telecommunication, but is also being introduced into automobile systems for hands-free operation.. In telecommunications, IVR allows customers to access a company's database via a telephone keypad or by speech recognition, after which they can service their own inquiries by following the instructions.
Java	Programming language that was created in 1995 Developed by Sun Microsystems. It is an object oriented programming language that allows content and software to be distributed through the Internet. Applications that are written in Java must be run by a Java enabled web browser.
KASUMI	KASUMI is a block cipher used in UMTS, GSM, and GPRS mobile communications systems. In UMTS KASUMI is used in the confidentiality (f8) and integrity algorithms (f9) with names UEA1 and UIA1, respectively. In GSM KASUMI is used in the A5/3 key stream generator and in GPRS in the GEA3 key stream generator. KASUMI was designed for 3GPP to be used in UMTS security system by the Security Algorithms Group of Experts (SAGE), a part of the European standards body ETSI. Because of schedule pressures in 3GPP standardization, instead of developing a new cipher, SAGE agreed with 3GPP technical specification group (TSG) for system aspects of 3G security (SA3) to base the development on an existing algorithm that had already undergone some evaluation.
Kiosks	Kiosks are displays used to provide merchandise information in a remote location, such as a retail store or shopping mall.
Knowledge Base	A computer accessible collection of knowledge about a subject in a variety of forms, such as facts and rules of inference, frames and objects.

Knowledge based Information System	An information system that adds a knowledge base to the database and other components found in other types of computer-based information systems.
Knowledge Management	Knowledge management (KM) is somewhat difficult do define precisely. Basically, it is a practice that blends document management and content-management technique. Typically content search, categorization, and content retrieval. for processing unstructured data (documents, Internet files, news feeds, e-mail and other text-based information).
Link	Also known as a hyperlink, a link is an address embedded in a web document. The browser transfers to that address when the link is clicked.
Local Area Networks (LAN)	Local Area Networks are a group of micro-computes or terminals located in the same general area and connected by a common cable (communication circuit) so that they can exchange information. LANs are typically used within the same building or a set of buildings situated close together.
Memory cards	Although many early PDAs did not have memory card slots now most have either an SD (Secure Digital) and/or a Compact Flash slot. Although originally designed for memory, SDIO and Compact Flash cards are available for such things as Wi-Fi and Webcams. Some PDAs also have a USB port, mainly for USB flash drives. Some PDAs are now compatible with micro SD cards, which are physically much smaller than standard SD cards.
M-commerce	M-commerce is a subset of E-commerce that deals with electronic transaction using mobile communication equipments for conducting businesses and transactions using wireless media.
Malicious Access	Hacking in computers is the obsessive use of computers or the unauthorized access and use of networked computer systems.
Mobile positioning	Mobile positioning refers to determining the position of the mobile device. Mobile location refers

	to the location estimate derived from the mobile positioning operation. There are various means of mobile positioning, which can be divided into two major categories - network based and handset based positioning. The purpose of positioning the mobile is to provide location-based services (LBS), including wireless emergency services.
Message Switching	Here, intermediate switching centers on a long communication path are used to store data items in a message format. It is different from packet switching. Here all message packets are received and stored by a centers router, which is connected to all the terminals. This central node then routes messages to their addresses but this method is used where message delays do not matter.
Metadata	Metadata is information that describes the contents of a database. Metadata tells users when a piece of data was last updated, its format intended uses. Metadata in its simpler form is a 'Data within data'.
Micropayment	A micropayment is a very small fee paid when a visitor is sent from another website to your site.
MP3	A digital file standard for recording sound. The files can be sent and played on the Internet.
Mobile browser	A mobile browser, also called a microbrowser, minibrowser or wireless internet browser (WIB), is a web browser designed for use on a mobile device such as a mobile phone or PDA. Mobile browsers are optimized so as to display Web content most effectively for small screens on portable devices. Mobile browser software must be small and efficient to accommodate the low memory capacity and low-bandwidth of wireless handheld devices.
MMS	Multimedia Messaging Service, or MMS, is a standard way to send messages that include multimedia content to and from mobile phones. It extends the core SMS (Short Message Service)

	capability which only allowed exchange of text messages up to 160 characters in length.
Mobile switching centre server (MSCS)	The mobile switching centre server is a soft-switch variant of the mobile switching centre, which provides circuit-switched calling, mobility management, and GSM services to the mobile phones roaming within the area that it serves. MSS functionality enables split between control (signalling) and user plane (bearer in network element called as media gateway/MG), which guarantees more optimal placement of network elements within the network.
Nokia Toolkit 4.1	Nokia Mobile Internet Toolkit facilitates the creation of different mobile media content via a comprehensive set of editors and wizards. These include Web page creation, MMS creation and Push message creation.
Net	Abbreviation of Internet.
Neural Network	The storage and retrieval of data by systems that have the capability of making changes to their methodologies through the use of statistical and mathematical algorithms.
Network Marketing	New approaches to marketing, like relationship marketing and network marketing - that are built upon buyer-seller relationship have been receiving increasing attention in recent years as more and more organizations focus their attention on retaining existing customers rather than attracting new ones.
Netscape Navigator	The browser created by Netscape Communications Corporation (earlier known as Mosaic Communications Corporation) first released in October 1994.
Network	A series of computers connected together in some way to allow for the sending of electronic information.

News Groups	Electronic discussion group, comprising collections of postings to particular topics. These topics are posted to the designated news server for this group. These can be an invaluable source of information and advice when trying to resolve problems and get advice.
Niche	A small subdivision of a large market demographic.
Niche Marketing	Niche marketing is the large market demographic.
Near Field Communication or (NFC)	Near Field Communication or NFC, is a short-range high frequency wireless communication technology which enables the exchange of data between devices over about a 10 centimetre (around 4 inches) distance. The technology is a simple extension of the ISO/IEC 14443 proximity-card standard (contactless card, RFID) that combines the interface of a smartcard and a reader into a single device. An NFC device can communicate with both existing ISO/IEC 14443 smartcards and readers, as well as with other NFC devices, and is thereby compatible with existing contactless infrastructure already in use for public transportation and payment. NFC is primarily aimed at usage in mobile phones.
OWA	Outlook Web Access (OWA) originally called Exchange Web Connect (EWC), is a webmail service of Microsoft Exchange Server 5.0 and later. The web interface of Outlook Web Access resembles the interface in Microsoft Outlook. OWA is used to access e-mail, calendars, contacts, tasks, and other mailbox content when access to the Microsoft Outlook desktop application is unavailable.
Office Automation Systems	Office automation systems are computer-based information system that collect, process, store and transmit electronic messages, documents and other forms of communications among individuals, work group and organizations.
Outsourcing	The contracting work to another company.

Open Systems Interconnection (OSI) Model	The OSI model is a model based on a proposal developed by the International Standards organization (ISO) in 1984. The model is called the ISO, OSI Reference Model because it deals with connecting open systems. An open system is one that is open to communicating with other systems using non-proprietary architecture.
Online Shopping	Whether you are looking for a hard-to-find item, need something to b delivered to a friend on the other side of the world, or are seeking the perfect birthday present, online shopping lets you find what you are looking for with the click of your mouse. No more travelling from store to store, looking for a parking spot and waiting online.
Online purchasing	Online purchasing is the technology infrastructure for the exchange of data and the purchase of a product over the Internet.
One-to-one marketing	One-to-one marketing is the customization and personalization of both product and prospect requirements to meet an individual set of established needs. Once matched, a one-to-one marketing program delivers an exact marketing message, with the appropriate product to meet the prospects' needs.
Packet	A term used to describe data being transferred over a network in a unit.
Palm OS	Palm OS (also known as Garnet OS) is a mobile operating system initially developed by Palm, Inc. for personal digital assistants (PDAs) in 1996. Palm OS is designed for ease of use with a touchscreen-based graphical user interface. It is provided with a suite of basic applications for personal information management. Later versions of the OS have been extended to support smartphones. Several other licensees have manufactured devices powered by Palm OS.
Push Technology	The delivery of content to users periodically as opposed to when the user requests it. Primarily

	used to deliver time-sensitive information like stock market quotes, news or sport scores.
Packet Switching	A communications paradigm used to minimize latency and optimize the use of bandwidth available in a network. It does this by individuals routing a packet between hosts using the most expedient route. Once the packets are sent, the destination computer reassembles the packets into their appropriate sequence.
Peer-to-Peer (P2P) Networking	The basic technology for peer-to-peer networking is already available — it is the same technology that Napster, Gnutella and other file-trading systems use. Participants in a peer-to-peer network, whether individuals or companies, exchange information directly with one another, bypassing central exchanges.
Permission Marketing	It is a concept that producers should be willing to pay consumers for certain behaviors that the merchants want to reinforce, which includes visiting a website, completing a survey or questionnaire or buying a product or service.
Personal Digital Assistants	Are used to provide relevant computer functions to the individual without the overhead of a laptop or local computer. These now include e-mail, contact information, paging, web browsing and access to remote corporate applications.
Personal Knowledge Management	This involves a range of relatively simple and inexperienced techniques and tools that anyone can use to acquire, create and share knowledge, extend personal networks and collaborate with colleagues without having to rely on the technical or financial resources of the employer.
Plug-ins	By extending the standard capabilities of a web browser, the plug-in permits the running of other programs and many multimedia applications through the web-browsers.
Personalization	Customization of web information to specifically meet the needs and desires of the individual user.

Premium Short Message Service (PSMS)	Premium Short Message Service (PSMS) is the most widely available payment channel that allows operators to charge subscribers for mobile products and services. Subscribers are charged either when they send a short code text message to request a product (known as Mobile Originated or MO billing) or when they receive a product on their phone (known as Mobile Terminated or MT billing). PSMS revenues are shared by the content provider, aggregator (Sybase 365) and the operator.
Point of Presence (POP)	An ISP's point of connection to the Internet in a specific city or community.
Portal	Portal is term, generally synonymous with gateway, for a world wide web site that is or proposes to be a major starting site for users when they are connected to the Web or an anchor site that users tend to visit.
Protocol	A standardized way to transfer data so that computers on a network can communicate with each other.
Point to point Protocol (APP)	Internet communication protocol for transferring/ network data over serial point to point links.
Pull Marketing	Pull marketing involves the marketing method which rely on the use of web browsers to end users to access marketing materials and resources at Internet, intranet and extranet web sites.
Public Key Encryption	Public key is used to encrypt messages whereas a private key is used to decrypt. The public encryption key is made available to whomever wants to use it, but the private key is kept secret by the key owner.
Public Key Infrastructure (PKI)	PKI is the engine that drives certificates. It is essentially a mechanism for the storage of public key along with a certificate that identifies the owner.
Paging	In computer operating systems there are various ways in which the operating system can store and

	retrieve data from secondary storage for use in main memory. One such memory management scheme is referred to as paging. In the paging memory-management scheme, the operating system retrieves data from secondary storage in same-size blocks called pages. The main advantage of paging is that it allows the physical address space of a process to be noncontiguous. Prior to paging, systems had to fit whole programs into storage contiguously which caused various storage and fragmentation problems.
Paging Systems	Paging Systems are wireless communication systems that are designed to send brief messages to a subscriber. It's a one-way messaging system in which Base Station send messages to all subscribers. The Paging System transmits the message also known as Page, along with Paging System access number, throughout the service area using Base Station, which broadcast the page on a radio link.
Pocket PC	A Pocket PC, abbreviated P/PC or PPC, is also known by Microsoft as a 'Windows Mobile Classic device'. It is a hardware specification for a handheld-sized computer (Personal digital assistant) that runs the Microsoft 'Windows Mobile Classic' operating system. It may have the capability to run an alternative operating system like NetBSD, Linux, Android or others. It has some of the capabilities of modern desktop PCs.
PDA	A personal digital assistant (PDA), also known as a palmtop computer, is a mobile device which functions as a Personal information manager and connects to the internet. The PDA has an electronic visual display enabling it to include a web browser,

	but some newer models also have audio capabilities, enabling them to be used as mobile phones or portable media players. Many PDAs can access the internet, intranets or extranets via Wi-Fi, or Wireless Wide Area Networks (WWANs). Many PDAs employ touchscreen technology.
POS	Point of sale (POS) or checkout is the location where a transaction occurs. A "checkout" refers to a POS terminal or more generally to the hardware and software used for checkouts, the equivalent of an electronic cash register. A POS terminal manages the selling process by a salesperson accessible interface. The same system allows the creation and printing of the voucher.
POS	A point-of-sale (PoS) terminal is an electronic device that is used for verifying and processing credit card transactions. Typically connected via highly reliable telephone wired connections, they require rapid dial up time, low power and reliable performance. Silicon Laboratories' embedded modems and silicon DAAs offer the most integrated solution available. When paired with our high-performance mixed-signal MCUs, Silicon Laboratories offers a cost effective bundle for PoS applications.
RFID	Radio-frequency identification (RFID) is the use of an object (typically referred to as an RFID tag) applied to or incorporated into a product, animal, or person for the purpose of identification and tracking using radio waves. Some tags can be read from several meters away and beyond the line of sight of the reader.
Real Video	Technology that allows users to see video as it is being down loaded.

Relationship Marketing	Relationship Marketing makes one to perform incredible feats on the Internet. He has to find opportunities to make up totally new ways of accessing consumers and prospect, while at the same time, fine tuning the message and product according to their needs.
Replication	Describes the process of controlled copying of certain elements of a website, database or other collection of information.
Real-time computing (RTC)	In computer science, real-time computing (RTC), or reactive computing, is the study of hardware and software systems that are subject to a "real-time constraint"-i.e., operational deadlines from event to system response. By contrast, a non-real-time system is one for which there is no deadline, even if fast response or high performance is desired or preferred. The needs of real-time software are often addressed in the context of real-time operating systems, and synchronous programming languages, which provide frameworks on which to build real-time application software.
Rich Media	Online advertising that has some form of functionality that allows the user to obtain objects, such as video or sound or interact with the ad by providing information, choosing information, etc.
Road Show	A series of presentations used to gather interest in a company or an application.
Robot	A program that is designed to automatically go out an explore the Internet for a specific purpose.
Robotics	The technology of building machines (robots) with computer intelligence and humanlike physical capabilities.
Routers	Routers are switches that were built to operate at the internet ting layer. They have a rich set of functionality that allows them to be used in even the largest internets.

Rule-based Knowledge	Knowledge represented in the form of rules and statements of fact.
Smartphone	A smartphone is a mobile phone offering advanced capabilities, often with PC-like functionality (PC-mobile handset convergence). There is no industry standard definition of a smartphone. For some, a smartphone is a phone that runs complete operating system software providing a standardized interface and platform for application developers. For others, a smartphone is simply a phone with features considered advanced at the time of its release - e.g., in the early 2000s this was features such as e-mail and Internet, but now these are commonplace on non-smartphones.
Scanner	A scanner is a radio receiver that can automatically tune, or scan, two or more discrete frequencies, stopping when it finds a signal on one of them and then continuing to scan other frequencies when the initial transmission ceases. The terms radio scanner or police scanner generally refer to a communications receiver that is primarily intended for monitoring VHF and UHF landmobile radio systems, as opposed to, say, a receiver used to monitor international shortwave transmissions.
SMS	Short Message Service (SMS) is a communication service component of the GSM mobile communication system, using standardized communications protocols that allow the exchange of short text messages between mobile phone devices. The term SMS is used as a synonym for all types of short text messaging, as well as the user activity itself, in many parts of the world. SMS as used on modern handsets was originally defined as part of the Global System for Mobile Communications (GSM) series of standards in 1985 as a means of sending messages of up to 160 characters, to and from GSM mobile handsets. Most SMS messages are mobile-to-mobile text messages, though the standard supports other types of broadcast messaging as well.

Subscriber identity module (SIM)	A subscriber identity module (SIM) on a removable SIM card securely stores the service-subscriber key (IMSI) used to identify a subscriber on mobile telephony devices (such as mobile phones and computers). The SIM card allows users to change phones by simply removing the SIM card from one mobile phone and inserting it into another mobile phone or broadband telephony device.
Symbian OS	Symbian OS is an operating system (OS) designed for mobile devices and smartphones, with associated libraries, user interface, frameworks and reference implementations of common tools, originally developed by Symbian Ltd. In 2008, the former Symbian Software Limited was acquired by Nokia and a new independent non-profit organisation called the Symbian Foundation was established.
S-HTTP	It is an encryption algorithms advanced by commerce Net. S-HTTP is a higher level protocol that only work with the HTTP protocol on the server site, S-HTTP is currently being implemented on the Open Marketplace Server (Market by open market) and on the secure HTTP Mosaic browser (Enterprise Integration Technologies) on the client's side.
Search Engine	A website that allows a visitor to enter a search phase and have the engine search all the shared files on a network. Search world wide website., usenet news groups and other Internet resources to match descriptor words.
Specialized Mobile Radio (SMR)	Specialized Mobile Radio (SMR) is any two-way radio system in which two or more mobile/portable wireless transceivers are linked by a single repeater. The repeater is elevated above average terrain; this maximizes the area of coverage. Operating frequencies are in the VHF (very-high-frequency) or UHF (ultra-high-frequency) range, that is, between approximately.
Secure Electronic Transaction (SET)	The industry is counting on SET to accelerate Internet electronic commerce. SET is becoming the defacto standard for security.

Secure Socket Layer (SSL)	SSL is a technology that encrypts or codes the packets of information sent over the Internet so that only the sending and receiving Computers can reassemble and read the information.
Security	'Security' may be defined as the protection of both physical and conceptual resources from natural and human hazards.
Security Threats	Information systems have many components, which are at several location . It is therefore, these are vulnerable., to many potential hazards. The hazards may be: Accidental - such as errors or natural disasters; Intentional - such as theft, viruses and malicious attacks on a computer centre.
Server	A server is a program on a computer that accepts and carries out requests to perform various function from that computer as well as others.
Shareware	Is a software that is made available by the developers to users at no cost. It is available on websites like www.jumbo.com, www.shareware.com and www.tucows.com.
Shopping bots	Shopping bots are like Santa's little search engines. Type in the name of a product and these binary buyers scour the Web, looking for bargains, In theory, these are wonderful tools. Finding the cheapest books, videos, computer games, sound cards or even cigars and home fitness equipment in cyberspace.
Shopping Cart	Shopping cart is a software that creates the interface between a company's website and its catalog database, allowing customers to choose products to buy, review items on their order, add to or delete items from their order and make their purchases.
Simple Mail Transfer Protocol (SMTP)	The protocol for Internet e-mail where the host name of the Internet provider's mail server must be designated in order to send mail.

Simple Network Management Protcol (SNMP)	SNMP was derived from an earlier management protocol known as simple gateway monitoring program. Which was again derived from one more protocol called the high level entry management system (HEMS).
Smart Card	It is a portable device that contains some non-volatile memory and a microprocessor. A smart card computers a password or encryption key and furnishes it directly to the computer for the log-on procedure.
Sniffing	Sniffing describes the act of reading unprotected packet information as it travels over a network.
Spam	Unsolicited e-mail usually sent to try to sell or market a product or service.
Spider	Spider is a tool to automate the indexing and registration of your site with popular search engines to ensure that your content is indexed.
Spoofing	Hackers can spoof or configure, a system to masquerade as another system, thus gaining unauthorized access to resources or information on systems that 'trust' the system being mimicked.
Standard Generalized Markup Language (SGML)	SGML means that any fully conformant SGML system will be able to read XML documents. However, using and understanding XML documents does not require a system that is capable of understanding the full generality of SGML.
Stickness	General time to describe the characteristics of a website to attract and keep users in the area. Also a measurement of how many users return to the site for more information or products.
Storage Area Network (SAN)	The storage of data in various storage server on the same network.
Secure Socket Layer (SSL)	Transport Layer Security (TLS) and its predecessor, Secure Socket Layer (SSL), are cryptographic protocols that provide security for communications over networks such as the Internet. TLS and SSL

	encrypt the segments of network connections at the Transport Layer end-to-end. Several versions of the protocols are in widespread use in applications like web browsing, electronic mail, Internet faxing, instant messaging and voice-over-IP (VoIP).TLS is an IETF standards track protocol, last updated in RFC 5246, that was based on the earlier SSL specifications developed by Netscape Corporation.
Supply Chain	The entire process of accepting a customer order through to the delivery of the product to the customer inclusive of supply procurement and production of the product.
Supply chain Execution	SCE is also a framework of execution oriented applications that enable the efficient procurement and supply of goods, services and information across enterprise boundaries to meet customer-specific demand.
Supply chain inventory visibility	Supply chain inventory visibility (SCIV) are the applications that allow enterprises to monitor and manage events across the supply chain to plan their activities more effectively and pre-empt problems.
Supply chain Management	Supply chain management pertains to integrating management practices and information technology to optimize information and production flow among the processes and business partners within a supply chain. SCM is a management concept that integrates the management of supply chain process.
Surfing	Using a browser to visit sites on the Internet.
Synchronous Communication	Simultaneous communication using applications such as Internet Relay chat, net phone and video conferencing where communication occurs at the same time.
Telesurgery	Telesurgery is a new approach to surgical care in which a surgeon performs operations using a surgical robot and advanced computer technology on a patient located miles away.

Transmission medium	A transmission medium (plural transmission media) is a material substance (solid, liquid or gas) which can propagate energy waves. For example, the transmission medium for sound received by the ears is usually air, but solids and liquids may also act as transmission media for sound.
TDMA	Time division multiple access (TDMA) is a channel access method for shared medium networks. It allows several users to share the same frequency channel by dividing the signal into different time slots. The users transmit in rapid succession, one after the other, each using his own time slot. This allows multiple stations to share the same transmission medium (e.g. radio frequency channel) while using only a part of its channel capacity. TDMA is used in the digital 2G cellular systems such as Global System for Mobile Communications (GSM), IS-136, Personal Digital Cellular (PDC) and iDEN, and in the Digital Enhanced Cordless Telecommunications (DECT) standard for portable phones. It is also used extensively in satellite systems, and combat-net radio systems.
Transport Layer Security (TLS)	Transport Layer Security (TLS) are cryptographic protocols that provide security for communications over networks such as the Internet. TLS and SSL encrypt the segments of network connections at the Transport Layer end-to-end. Several versions of the protocols are in widespread use in applications like web browsing, electronic mail, Internet faxing, instant messaging and voice-over-IP (VoIP).
Touch screen	Many of the original PDAs, such as the Apple Newton and Palm Pilot, featured touchscreen for user interaction, having only a few buttons usually reserved for shortcuts to often used programs. Touch screen PDAs, including Windows Mobile devices, usually have a detachable stylus that can be used on the touch screen. Interaction is then done by tapping the screen to activate buttons or

	menu choices, and dragging the stylus to, for example, highlight.
Targeted Marketing	Development of marketing programs by identifying segments in specific markets and designing the product or service to specifically meet these needs.
TCP/IP	TCP is a connection -oriented transport protocol that sends data as a stream of bytes. TCP establishes and maintains a connection between the requesting port and the port providing services. TCP can provide a sending node with delivery information about packets transmitted to a destination node.
Telnet	Telnet allows users to log onto different computers and run resident programs. Although this is not as lauded as the World wide Web and requires commands to navigate, it is essential for Internet travel. It is a TCP/IP protocol for remote login.
Templates	Pre-defined application components that allow rapid development and deployment of computer based systems.
Third Generation Mobile	This objective makes mobile internet access, multimedia services and the integration of different mobile networks, including Mobile Satellite systems (MSS) possible through universal coverage.
Trapdoor Routines	These are routines used in program development to allow developers access to various parts of the computer system in order to see that the program is performing correctly.
Trojan Horse Technique	The name Trojan horse in Greek mythology represents a large wooden horse left by the Greeks upon their pretended retreat of the siege of Troy.
Trust intermediary	Trust intermediary is an entity that creates trust between the buyer and the seller.
Universal Mobile Telecommunications System (UMTS)	Universal Mobile Telecommunications System (UMTS) is one of the third-generation (3G) mobile telecommunications technologies, which is also being developed into a 4G technology. The first

	deployment of the UMTS is the release99 (R99) architecture. It is specified by 3GPP and is part of the global ITU IMT-2000 standard. The most common form of UMTS uses W-CDMA (IMT Direct Spread) as the underlying air interface but the system also covers TD-CDMA and TD-SCDMA (both IMT CDMA TDD). Being a complete network system, UMTS also covers the radio access network (UMTS Terrestrial Radio Access Network, or UTRAN), the core network (Mobile Application Part, or MAP), as well as authentication of users via USIM cards (Subscriber Identity Module).
Unified Messaging	The ability to send and receive e-mail, voice mail and fax messages by the computer or by telephone improves response time and is effective for mobile users. It is important that users have easy access to all types of messages, whether sitting at the office computer or from any distant telephone. Fax messages cannot be got on the road. The user must access e-mail and phone messages separately. Half-a-day delay in receiving or noticing the arrival of a message is creating lot of problems. Unified messaging solutions can boost ease of use for end-users and facilitate rapid responses to critical messages.
Ubiquitous computing	Ubiquitous computing (ubicomp) is a post-desktop model of human-computer interaction in which information processing has been thoroughly integrated into everyday objects and activities. In the course of ordinary activities, someone "using" ubiquitous computing engages many computational devices and systems simultaneously, and may not necessarily even be aware that they are doing so. This model is usually considered an advancement from the desktop paradigm.
URL	A URL (uniform resource locator) is your full address on the Internet. Fax example, http//www.yourname.com includes the prefix http://www, and the TLD extension.com as well as the actual domain name. When you type a URL into your

	browser's location field, it takes you to a specific location/site on the Internet.
Usenet	Usenet (Users network) is a collection of thousands of ongoing topical discussion called news groups. Each newsgroup covers a specific topic such as alternative living or zoology. Also known as Bulletin boards or discussion groups, news groups are used by people to share common interests. Usenet is not a part of the Internet, or a network of any kind. It is a system for carrying on discussions that can be delivered in a number of ways, the Internet being just one of them.
User Interface	That part of an operating system or other program that allows users to communicate with it to load programs, access files and accomplish other computing tasks.
VAS	Mobile value-added services (VAS) are those services that offer differentiation and the ability for mobile operators to charge a premium price. Mobile VAS include non-voice advanced messaging services such as SMS, MMS etc.
Value Chain	The value chain is an analytical framework to disaggregate a firm into the different interdependent activities that add value to its raw materials and bring the firm's product or service to the customer.
Veronica	(Very easy rodent oriented network index to computerized archives) A network utility that lets individuals search all of more than 6,000 gopher servers in the world.
Virtual facility	The use of multisensory human/computer interfaces that enable human users to experience computer simulated objects, entities, spaces and 'worlds' as if they actually existed.
Virtual Mall	An online multimedia simulation of a shopping mall with many different interlinked retail websites.

Virtual Memory	The use of secondary storage devices as an extension of the primary storage of the computer; thus giving the appearance of a larger main memory than actually exists.
Virtual Private Network (VPN)	Virtual private network (VPN) is a computer network that is layered on top of an underlying computer network. The private nature of a VPN means that the data travelling over the VPN is not generally visible to, or is encapsulated from, the underlying network traffic. Similarly, the traffic within the VPN appears to the underlying network as just another traffic stream to be passed. A VPN connection can be envisioned as a "pipe within a pipe", with the outer pipe being the underlying network connection.
Virtual Team	A team whose members use the Internet, intranets, extranets and other networks to communicate, coordinate and collaborate with each other on tasks and projects, even though they may work in different geographic locations and for different organizations.
Virus	A program created to cause problems on the computer systems they invade virus protection has become a major component in maintaining the health of computer systems everywhere.
Virtual Private Network	A VPN is a secure network that uses the Internet as its main backbone network, but relies on the firewalls and other security features of its Internet and Intranet connections and those of participating organizations.
Virtual Terminals	The concept of VT makes a complex process (though not simple, atleast straight forward) ; It relieves one of the great potential impediments to true universal connectivity; that of connecting multiple incompatible terminals to a single remote server.
Voice Conferencing	Telephone conversations shared among several participants via speaker phones or networked PCs with Internet telephone software.

Voice Mail	Unanswered telephone messages are digitized, stored and played back to the recipient by a voice messaging computer.
Vortal	Vertical portal is a type of portal which showcases a single product category and provides information on multiple brands of that product as well as closely related product information. Only a subset of the audience is catered by this who are interested in that product alone either as a buyer, user or a seller and will seek out the portal to meet their needs.
WebLogic	WebLogic was a company (from 1995 to 1998) credited with creating the first J2EE application server, the WebLogic Application Server. Owned by Oracle Corporation, Oracle WebLogic consists of a Java EE platform product family that includes: • a Java EE application server, WebLogic Application Server • an enterprise portal, WebLogic Portal • an Enterprise Application Integration platform • a transaction server and infrastructure, WebLogic Tuxedo • a telecommunication platform, WebLogic Communication Platform
Wi-Fi	Wi-Fi is a trademark of the Wi-Fi Alliance that manufacturers may use to brand certified products that belong to a class of wireless local area network (WLAN) devices based on the IEEE 802.11 standards. Because of the close relationship with its underlying standard, the term Wi-Fi is often used as a synonym for IEEE 802.11 technology. The Wi-Fi Alliance, a global association of companies, promotes WLAN technology and certifies products if they conform to certain standards of interoperability.
WML	Wireless Markup Language, based on XML, is a markup language intended for devices that implement the Wireless Application Protocol (WAP) specification, such as mobile phones, and preceded

	the use of other markup languages now used with WAP, such as HTML/XHTML (which are gaining in popularity as processing power in mobile devices increases).
Windows CE	Windows CE (also known officially as Windows Embedded Compact or Windows Embedded CE post version 6.0, and sometimes abbreviated WinCE) is an operating system developed by Microsoft for minimalistic computers and embedded systems. Windows CE is a distinctly different operating system and kernel, rather than a trimmed-down version of desktop Windows. It is not to be confused with Windows XP Embedded which is NT-based. Windows CE is supported on Intel x86 and compatibles, MIPS, ARM, and Hitachi SuperH processors.
WAP	Wireless Application Protocol (WAP) is an open international standard for application-layer network communications in a wireless-communication environment. Most use of WAP involves accessing the mobile web from a mobile phone or from a PDA.A WAP browser provides all of the basic services of a computer-based web browser but simplified to operate within the restrictions of a mobile phone, such as its smaller view screen. Users can connect to WAP sites: websites written in, or dynamically converted to, WML (Wireless Markup Language) and accessed via the WAP browser
Wireless Application Environment (WAE)	The WAE space defines application-specific markup languages.For WAP version 1.X, the primary language of the WAE is WML, which has been designed from scratch for hand-held devices with phone-specific features. In WAP 2.0, the primary markup language is XHTML Mobile Profile.
WiMAX	WiMAX, an acronym for Worldwide Interoperability for Microwave Access, is a telecommunications technology that provides fixed and fully mobile internet access. The current WiMAX revision provides up to 40 Mbps in real world end-user

	throughput. WiMAX is based on the IEEE 802.16 standard (also called Broadband Wireless Access). The name "WiMAX" was created by the WiMAX Forum, which was formed in June 2001 to promote conformity and interoperability of the standard. The forum describes WiMAX as "a standards-based technology enabling the delivery of last mile wireless broadband access as an alternative to cable and DSL".
WEF	The World Economic Forum (WEF) is a Geneva-based non-profit foundation best known for its annual meeting in Davos, Switzerland, which brings together top business leaders, international political leaders, selected intellectuals and journalists to discuss the most pressing issues facing the world, including health and the environment. Beside meetings, the WEF produces a series of research reports and engages its members in sector specific initiatives.
W-CDMA (Wideband Code Division Multiple Access)	W-CDMA (Wideband Code Division Multiple Access), UMTS-FDD, UTRA-FDD, or IMT-2000 CDMA Direct Spread is an air interface standard found in 3G mobile telecommunications networks. It is the basis of Japan's NTT DoCoMo's FOMA service and the most-commonly used member of the UMTS family and sometimes used as a synonym for UMTS. It utilizes the DS-CDMA channel access method and the FDD duplexing method to achieve higher speeds and support more users compared to most time division multiple access (TDMA) schemes used today.
Wired connectivity	While many earlier PDAs connected via serial ports or other proprietary format, many today connect via USB cable. This served primarily to connect to a computer, and few, if any PDAs were able to connect to each other out of the box using cables, as USB requires one machine to act as a host - functionality which was not often planned. Some PDAs were able to connect to the internet, either by means of one

	of these cables, or by using an extension card with an ethernet port/RJ-45 adaptor.
Wireless connectivity	Most modern PDAs have Bluetooth wireless connectivity, an increasingly popular tool for mobile devices. It can be used to connect keyboards, headsets, GPS and many other accessories, as well as sending files between PDAs. Many mid-range and superior PDAs have Wi-Fi/WLAN/802.11-connectivity, used for connecting to Wi-Fi hotspots or wireless networks. Older PDAs predominantly have an IrDA (infrared) port; however fewer current models have the technology, as it is slowly being phased out due to support for Bluetooth and Wi-Fi. IrDA allows communication between two PDAs: a PDA and any device with an IrDA port or adapter. Most universal PDA keyboards use infrared technology because many older PDAs have it, and infrared technology is low-cost and has the advantage of being permitted aboard aircraft.
Wallets	It enable shoppers on the Internet to automatically debit their accounts using e-money. They wallet contains electronic money which is usually deposited in advance, and is replenished as the account needs it.
Wide Area Network (WAN)	Wide Area Network spans a large geographical area, often a country or continent. Its nodes (micro-computers) can span cities, states or even national boundaries. This network interconnects computers, LANs, BNs, MANs and other data transmission facilities on a countrywide or worldwide basis. It provides long distance transmission of data, voice, image and video information over large areas.
Wireless Application Protocol (WAP)	The Wireless Application Protocol is a set of specifications, developed by the WAP Forum that lets developers using Wireless Markup Language (WML) built networked applications designed for handheld wireless devices.
Wireless LANs	Using radio or infrared transmissions to link devices in a local area network.

World Wide Web (WWW)	World Wide Web is a repository of information spread all over the world and linked together.
XHTML	XHTML is one other form of XML. It can be called as transition path from HTML to XML. XHTML by its very name, is meant to be extensible. XHTML allows authors to retain the semantics present in HTML.
XML (Extensible Markup Language)	The next generation of standard Internet presentation language created by a worldwide consortiums
ZigBee	ZigBee is a specification for a suite of high level communication protocols using small, low-power digital radios based on the IEEE 802.15.4-2003 standard for wireless personal area networks (WPANs), such as wireless headphones connecting with cell phones via short-range radio. The technology defined by the ZigBee specification is intended to be simpler and less expensive than other WPANs, such as Bluetooth. ZigBee is targeted at radio-frequency (RF) applications that require a low data rate, long battery life, and secure networking.The ZigBee Alliance is a group of companies that maintain and publish the ZigBee standard.

Books

- Tiwari, R. and Buse, S. (2007): The Mobile Commerce Prospects: A Strategic Analysis of Opportunities in the Banking Sector, Hamburg: Hamburg University Press.
- Tiwari, R., Buse, S., and Herstatt, C. (2006): From Electronic to Mobile Commerce: Opportunities through Technology Convergence for Business Services, in: Asia Pacific Tech Monitor, Vol. 23, No. 5 (Issue: Sept-Oct. 2006), pp. 38-45, New Delhi
- Kapil Raina and Anurag Harsh (2006): M-commerce Security-A Beginner's Guide:Tata McGraw-Hill Publishing company, New Delhi.

Websites

- http://teledict.blogspot.com/2007/10/m-commerce.html
- http://www.mobillcash.com/

- http://en.wikipedia.org/wiki/Mobile_Commerce
- http:/www.forester.com
- http://www.nokia.com
- http://europa.eu.int
- http://www.itu.int
- http://www.oftel.gov.uk
- http://www.palmgear.com,
- http://www.palmpilot.com/enterprise/studies/study17.html
- http://nrpb.org.uk
- www.epso.jrc.es
- http://europa.eu.int/comm/internal_market/en/finances/payment/instrument/study.htm
- http://www.internetworld.co.uk/mcomm/index.cfm
- http://www.epaymentsnews.com/
- http://epso.jrc.es/newsletter/

Research Paper

e-pso forum - database of several payment methods and discussion papers:

- For "Study on the implementation of Recommendation 97/489/ECconcerning transactions carried out by electronic payment instruments ..."
- Electronic newsletters covering m-commerce:

ABBREVIATIONS

ABBREVIATIONS	FULL FORM
ARC	Air Craft Resource Center
APAC REGION	Asia Pacific Region
CD	Compact Disk
CEO	Chief Executive Officer
CRM	Customer Relationship Management
CDPD	Cellular Digital Packet Data
CDMA	Code Division Multiple Access
DVD	Digital Video Disc
EMS	Enhanced Messaging Service
GSM	Global System for Mobile Communication
GEO	Geostationary
GIS	Geographic Information System
GPRS	Genral Packet Radio Service
JIT	Just in Time
HTML	Hypertext Markup Language
HDFC	Housing Development Finance Corporation
HP	Hewelt Packard
IBM	International Business Machines Corporation
IEEE	Institute of Electrical and Electronics Engineers
IOS	Internet Over Satellite
LEO	Low-Earth-Orbit
LAN	Local Area Network
MAN	Metropolitan Area Network
MCSS	Mobile Communications Server Switch
MPC	Mobile Positioning Center
MMS	Multimedia Messaging Service
MEO	Medium-Earth-Orbit
NIC	Network Interface Card

NSP	Network Service Provider
OPA	Open Patent Alliance
OMA	Open Mobile Software Alliance
POS	Point of Sale
PDA	Personal Digital Assistant
PDE	Position Determining Equipment
PTAS	Personal Trust Agent
PAN	Personal Area Network
PC	Personal Computer
RBI	Reserve Bank of India
RFID	Radio Frequency Identification
RNA	Ribonucleic Acid
SIM	Subscriber Identification Module
SMS	Short Message System
TCP/IP	Transmission Control Protocol/Internet Protocol
TV	Television
TDMA	Time Division Multiple Access
UMTS	Universal Mobile Telecommunications System
VAS	Value Added Services
VCR	Video Cassette Recorder
VBB	Voice-Browser Based
W3C	World Wide Web Consortium
WTLS	Wireless Transport Layer Security.
WML	Wireless Markup Language
WAP	Wireless Application Protocol
WAN	Wide Area Network
WCNIA	Wireless Computer Networks and Internet Access
WLAN	Wireless Local Area Networks
WMAN	Wireless Metropolitan Area Networks
WWAN	Wireless Wide Area Networks